For many people—most people, really—change *is* possible, even necessary. Although we must recognize that the degree of potential change will vary from individual to individual, in a few cases, even seemingly miraculous transformations of the self may occur. We won't know unless we try. It is the continuing and enduring task of the brain and behavioral sciences to foster the understanding of people's behavior, their limits and potentialities, and the delicate fortunes of the human spirit.

By the deficits we may know the talents, by the exceptions we may discern the rules, by studying pathology we may construct a model of health. And—most important—from this model may evolve the insights and tools we need to affect our own lives, mold our own destinies, change ourselves and our society in ways that, as yet, we can only imagine.

INNER NATURES

Brain, Self & Personality

Laurence Miller, Ph.D.

BALLANTINE BOOKS • NEW YORK

Copyright © 1990 by Laurence Miller, Ph.D.

The publisher appreciates permission granted to reprint the following: "First Fig" by Edna St. Vincent Millay. From *Collected Poems*, Harper & Row. Copyright © 1922, 1950 by Edna St. Vincent Millay. Reprinted by permission of Elizabeth Barnett, Literary Executor.

Library of Congress Catalog Card Number: 89-77804

ISBN 0-345-37201-8

This edition published by arrangement with St. Martin's Press, Inc.

Manufactured in the United States of America

First Ballantine Books Edition: November 1991

Cover photo © The Stock Market/Howard Sochurek 1988

For Gilbert, Lillian, and Beatrice,
who would have appreciated this book,
each in their own way.

And for Halle Brianne,
who tried to eat it.

CONTENTS

PART III
BASIC NATURES

PART IV
ALTERNATIVE NATURES

PREFACE

"Is it organic?"

While I was working at a well-known psychiatric and sub-stance abuse facility in the Northeast, the most common type of referral for neuropsychological assessment consisted of a young male with a long history of heavy drinking and drug abuse involving virtually every substance a person can smoke, shoot, or swallow. Overdoses and blackouts were common, the patient might have had hepatitis, pneumonia, and other infections, and sustained multiple head injuries from bar fights and auto wrecks while intoxicated. Accom-panying diagnoses might have included depression, schizoid disorder, or—quite commonly—one or more of the "per-sonality disorders."

Now the hospital unit staff was finding that this patient refused to respond as expected to the best notions of what proper psychotherapeutic, group milieu, and medication treatment should be. A reason had to be found, and so they would ask me: "Is it organic?" That is, if there's something the matter with this patient's *brain*, then we really shouldn't be wasting our time treating him as a psych patient, since "organic" patients don't need psychotherapy, they need . . . well, something else.

In doing neuropsychological evaluations on many of these patients, I began to observe that a fair number of them did indeed show test performance patterns similar to what I was taught to expect from working with neurologically impaired patients with focal brain lesions. The impaired performance patterns of these "personality disorder" patients were often seen even when no prior complicating neurological factors (for example, a head injury or drug coma) could be identified.

Yet despite the sometimes severe deficits seen on testing, these patients didn't *look* "organic"—overall, they certainly didn't behave like the stroke or head trauma or dementia patients I had seen on neurology wards. So why were the test findings often so similar?

That's when I began to realize that the tests we neuropsychologists use in clinical practice aren't measuring the brain directly. Rather, they're assessing how the person uses his individual pattern of thinking abilities—his cognitive style—to solve the problems posed by the test items. And if someone was using his particular God-given, brain-based cognitive style to deal with my little bag of tests and measures, why not for the larger problems of everyday life? Could the way people conceptualize and interact with their world and themselves be so intimately tied in with what we call their personalities? And not just for "patients" with personality "disorders," but for the rest of us as well—we all have personalities, don't we?

This book is an attempt to answer these questions. It owes its existence partly to the efforts and influences of a number of people who here deserve acknowledgment. Dr. Jon Winson of Rockefeller University put the original bug in my ear of doing a book on the brain and personality. Wray Herbert, former editor of *Psychology Today*, supported the development of many of this book's ideas in the form of my columns, articles, and reviews that have appeared in that magazine over the years. Wray also introduced me to my agent John Ware who, along with St. Martin's editor Bob Weil, guided this manuscript along the path to publication. Other colleagues and friends, numerous and here anonymous, have served as challenging interlocutors during the time that the main ideas of this book were being conceived and developed. Finally, my wife Joan deserves whatever medals of forbearance and understanding are awarded to the spouses of authors for enduring their partner's self-enforced troglodytic sequestration while completing projects of this type. She knows me well: Out of the office I'll pop for a breath, and then it's back to work.

Because of our frequent preoccupation with patterns of hemispheric laterality, neuropsychologists often get obsessive about two things: handedness and gender. That's because women frequently show different patterns of lateralization than men, and the brains of many left-handers seem to be organized differently from that of right-handers. Further, as the following chapters make clear, gender and handedness patterns are related to the way the brain encodes the different cognitive processing styles that contribute to different personality types.

Accordingly, in this volume, problems involving potentially sexist language will be dealt with as follows. In general, unless otherwise specified, "he" should be taken to mean "he or she." Although one can certainly argue about the sexism inherent in the original diagnoses described in the psychiatric and psychological literatures (see Chapter 8 for more on this), some of the different personality types have been found to have a higher proportion of either male or female members. In those chapters, the pronoun "he" will be used generically where males predominate (as in the impulsive personality or type-A personality), and "she" will be used generically where females predominate (as in the hysterical personality). Otherwise, ''he'' will mean ''he or she'' as usual. I hope this solves the problem of gender—as for handedness, you're on your own.

PART I

BRAIN AND NATURE,
SELF AND PERSON

CHAPTER 1

NEUROPSYCHOLOGY AND PERSONALITY

Why the Self Is Important

The test of a civilized person is first self-awareness, and then depth after depth of sincerity in self-confrontation.

—CLARENCE DAY

It is not enough to understand what we ought to be, unless we know what we are; and we do not understand what we are, unless we know what we ought to be.

—T.S. ELIOT

You have a reason for wanting to read this book, don't you? In fact, you probably have *reasons* for just about everything you do, even if you're not always fully aware of what those reasons might be. Most of us understand that there's a personal domain that's accessible to our self-reflection, our consciousness, and also a domain that remains hidden from our mind's eye, revealing bits and snatches of itself only under unusual or extreme circumstances.

Yet people have always sought new avenues into their selves—tried to hew through the lush denials, defenses, and self-delusions we all cultivate, attempted to discern the rules or principles or systematic laws of human behavior that might lead to a better understanding of our own thoughts, feelings, and actions. In our present day, the culture has been dominated by the quest to "find oneself," the desire to "be oneself." "I gotta be me . . ." we even sing.

But who is this "me" and what is this "self"? These are

not trite or simple questions. In psychology, the search for guiding principles of selfhood has evolved into the formal discipline of *personality theory*. Indeed, so academically well defined has this discipline become that we now have textbooks of personality, graduate psychology programs in personality, even a whole division of the American Psychological Association devoted to personality.

But as psychologists have looked back on their own hypotheses and conclusions about human nature,[1] they've encountered a problem: Even the experts don't always appreciate the sheer range and complexity of individual personality functioning. Nowhere is this more true than when it comes to trying to understand the relationship between affective (emotional) and cognitive (thinking) dimensions of personality—the relationship between how people *feel* about themselves, their fellows, and the world around them, and how they *think* about these things, conceptualize them, represent them in their own minds in ways that make personal sense.

Thus, a growing area of interest within psychology has to do with the concept of *self-knowledge* or *self-regulation*, on the idea that your behavior is tied to how you view yourself in relation to the rest of the world. And how you determine and control your own actions depends on your particular understanding of the reasons for doing so. That's what we'll be exploring in this book by looking at how the brain encodes and shapes the delicate nuances of our thoughts, feelings, and actions.

Where Did the Self Come From?

This modern preoccupation with the self is something relatively new. Indeed, the very concept of selfhood would have seemed alien to most people in the Western world only a few hundred years ago.[2] It wasn't until the late medieval period, from about the eleventh through the fifteenth centuries, that people even began to accept the concept of a single, individualized human life, existing apart from the highly stratified social-religious framework. Later, from about the 1500s to the 1800s, a distinction began to develop between the outer self—the persona exhibited in social discourse—and an ''inner self,'' a domain of more private self-consciousness, a valid world of experience not tied automatically to one's overt actions.

During that era, partly because of the Puritan philosophy of self-examination and the interdependence of right conduct and right thinking, people's self-consciousness gradually increased. To be good, you had to know your own mind, your moral strengths and failings, and to recognize the possibility of self-deception. This led to an intriguing concept that even today is difficult for many of us to accept, namely, that one's own attributed motives for doing something might not in fact be the ''true'' ones—or at least not the only ones.

The stage was thus set for the introspective, and ultimately psychoanalytic, explorations of the self that dominated psychological thinking in the middle and late nineteenth century. The hardheadedly rational and infinitely self-perfectible juggernaut of the Enlightenment found itself mired in the fens of self-doubt fed by the coalescing streams of empirical inquiry and analytic thought. The rise of the modern physical and biological sciences, astronomy, Darwinism, Marxism, and ultimately Freudianism all quickly disabused modern Western man of his centrality in the universe and of the primacy of sweet reason in his thought processes. While savage territories in the New World could be tamed or conquered, man's own mind was still a terra incognita that held potential dangers unimaginable by even the most stalwart charters of seas and continents.

Self-examination and self-doubt led to the existential crisis of modern times. Early in the twentieth century, despite the transient distractions of a glittering technology, popular themes of alienation and the devaluation of selfhood betrayed a deep concern over the individual's helpless dependency on society. This century has also seen the rise of mass movements, in which the surrender of selfhood to group mindlessness has too often purchased temporary and empty security at the price of autonomy. The paradox is, of course, that the century which has seen the greatest rise in scientific knowledge about both the physical world and the human self also bears the greatest physical and spiritual threat to that self. No wonder people seek answers.

What the Self Is and What It Does

When psychologists talk about the *self*, they usually talk like psychologists. Thus, Hazel Markus[3] describes the self as "a cognitive structure that influences attention, organization or categorization of information, recall and judgments about others." The self, in other words, serves as an internal point of reference that helps us conceptualize our relationships to our fellow beings and determine our interactions with them. A crucial aspect of self-knowledge has to do with the strategies or plans we use to manage our own behavior. And developing these strategies involves an appreciation of our self as an independent, autonomous actor in the world. It also requires a belief in our ability to be effective in what we do and to bring our behavior in line with personal and social standards.

Albert Bandura[4] expresses this idea in his concept of *self-efficacy*. This refers to the feeling of being capable and competent to manage the course of our own lives and to bring about changes in the world that bear favorably on our own values and aspirations. People with high degrees of self-efficacy are generally healthier, happier, and more productive, and they suffer fewer psychological and physical maladies. Without some measure of self-perceived control over our own destinies, the mental and bodily constitutions fail, we grow cynical and depressed, and withdraw into numb existential capitulation.

The concepts of self-knowledge and self-efficacy are also bound up with what I like to call *personal integrity*. You can think of this as a certain coherence or integration of the personality, of knowing "who you are." It also includes the capacity to realistically appraise your own behavior and its goals—immediate and far-reaching—and to use this self-appraisal to effectively make your way in the world. Just as important, it includes the ability to evolve a *personal identity* based on how the world reacts to your behavior and on the perception of your self as an actor in that world. Thus, we know who we are by a gradual process of assimilating the various reasons for our thoughts, feelings, and actions, based on our understanding of the consequences these activities produce.

The Self and the Ego—Identity and Autonomy

The notion of selfhood, of personal integrity, was underscored by Heinz Hartmann,[5] one of the first of the so-called *ego psychologists* within the psychoanalytic school of psychology. Early Freudian theory focused on the various perturbations of hidden instinctual forces and their role in accounting for individual forms of personality structure and psychopathological disorders. The later-arriving ego psychologists, for their part, chose to emphasize the ego's role in dealing with outside reality. Rather than a mere messenger to do the bidding of the drive-laden and impulse-ridden id (as the early Freudians thought), the ego came to be seen as having important functions of its own, as being a psychological structure or process suited to bear the conceptual mantle of what we now speak of as the self.*

---

*Although psychoanalytic theoreticians continue to debate whether the ego actually *is* the self or merely one component of it, such Ni-

In his writings, Hartmann spoke often of *ego autonomy*. This he regarded as the relative freedom of the ego—or self—from blind obedience to emotional and motivational demands, as well as from a dependency on immediate environmental reinforcement for every little action and plan. As an autonomous person, you are—or at least strive to be—your own master. What you can control in your life you do to the best of your ability. But even in the face of immutable adversity, you can marshal adequate coping resources and adjustment strategies so that your fundamental psychological stability isn't wholly undone, except perhaps by the most catastrophic of blows.

We often marvel at people we know who can roll with the punches and make the best of a bad situation, who are able to face adversity without losing their perspective and dignity. These are often the same people who seem to possess a certain inner sense of themselves, who aren't beholden to any one job, any one relationship, any one accomplishment or string of successes to define their identities. They embody the very qualities of self-esteem, self-efficacy, self-knowledge, and personal integrity. And we envy them.

Note that the kind of being-in-control I'm talking about is the exact opposite of the rigid "control" that many overexerted, overextended people try to grasp as they bulldoze their way through life. For these struggling souls, every opportunity is a challenge, every challenge a threat, every threat an imperiling of the very core of their self-esteem. Others make a lifelong practice of prematurely giving up on themselves and the world, adopting a take-it-or-leave-it attitude, acting recklessly and impulsively and wondering why it always seems to be the other guy who gets the gravy.

cene distinctions find little place within the daily discourse of most practicing psychoanalysts and other psychodynamically minded clinicians. Thus, a general equation of the ego with the self, while doctrinally debatable among psychoanalytic purists, can serve us adequately for the present discussion.

You're probably familiar with many other personality "types," many other degrees of greater or lesser ego autonomy, personal integrity, identity coherence. Some people ceaselessly blame the world for their failings, others mercilessly castigate themselves. Some elevate petty meanness to a cynical pseudoethic of looking out for Number One, playing hardball in the real world, doing it to them before they do it to you. Still others feel a need to be perennial victims, martyrs, patients.

Of course, most of us tread our life's path somewhere in between these extremes of beatific equanimity and soul-sapping despair. Most of us have *some* sort of integrated identity, *some* ego autonomy, *some* personal integrity, and *some* capacity and desire to self-reflect. We have a reasonably stable sense of identity that serves as a foundation for our interactions with the world. We continually impose some kind of organization on our knowledge of ourselves, the different environments in which we operate and our impressions of other people. This knowledge both guides our behavior and provides a basis for judgments about its efficacy. The system's not perfect and there's certainly room for improvement, but it serves reasonably well for most of the situations we find ourselves in, even if we always seem to be wishing that we could be just a little bit more together, a little less rattled. Yet some people's self-systems are decidedly *less* than adequate, and this book will examine why.

This is what Markus means when she speaks of *self-schemas*, the knowledge structures about the self that derive from past experience and that organize and guide the processing of self-relevant information gleaned from the individual's social experiences. Self-schemas provide for a point of view, a personal anchor, a frame of reference. They guide you in choosing those aspects of your social behavior that you regard as most relevant to your self, and they function to organize and give meaning to your own reflective understanding of your thoughts, feelings, and actions. And, as this book will show, these processes involve—indeed, depend on—the activity of the brain.

The Brain and Its Self

The struggle for personality integration is as much a biological struggle as a psychological one, as Goldstein and Maslow[6] understood. Kurt Goldstein spent the 1930s and '40s studying the effects of brain damage on the personality. He concluded that what is observed in the brain-damaged person's overall behavior is not the effect of a particular *lesion* on this or that isolated psychological *function*, but rather the attempt of what remains of the neuropsychological apparatus to come to grips with that person's world.

For example, the aphasic stroke patient deprived of language tries to make himself understood by any other means possible. If his speech is incomprehensible to others, he tries to write; if he can't write, he gestures. The memory-impaired patient, unable to correctly recall people and events, confabulates—fills in the memory gaps with imaginary or interpolated material—anything to preserve *some* coherence of the self and the situation, *some* dockpost on which to anchor the residual vessel of his identity.

Applying these observations to the neurologically intact, Abraham Maslow in the 1950s and '60s turned Goldstein's idea around by suggesting that some exceptional individuals naturally possess an inexorable drive toward making the most of their own inner resources, are impelled toward what Maslow called *self-actualization*. While very few achieve this goal fully, Maslow said, the desire to develop one's potential to the fullest is what marks the truly psychologically healthy and integrated human being. And in a later chapter, we'll examine how certain patterns of brain organization might operate to facilitate the complete realization of our human potential.

For now, let's realize that the drive for personality integration is as much organic as psychological; ironically, we see this most clearly at the two extremes of psychological integrity: in brain-injured persons groping for coherence and stability in a shattered experiential world and in psychologically mature, integrated, "together" persons seeking to develop their innate talents and potentials in ways that transcend basic practical, acquisitive, and bottom-line considerations.

Cognition and Passion, Thought and Action

Freud[7] believed that the purpose of thought processes—of cognition—was to allow the ego to achieve a reflective delay of behavior, to permit you to look, as it were, before you leap. Thinking, Freud said, represents a kind of "experimental action" that lets you explore various behavioral alternatives internally, mentally, and with far less effort than would be required to test each of these possibilities in the real world. Similarly, Hartmann emphasized that evolution leads to increasing independence of the organism from its environment, so that reactions that originally occur in relation to the external world are progressively displaced into the interior of the organism, to a *mental* domain. In order to effectively adapt to the world around you, even achieve a certain mastery of it, you don't have to test every possible response and observe every possible reaction. You can *think* about consequences, anticipate outcomes and create contingency plans of alternative means-end possibilities—all of which Hartmann regarded as part of the process of *internalization*.

What we ordinarily call "intelligence," said Hartmann, really involves the ability to choose, differentiate, execute, and evaluate a greater variety of response possibilities to different situations. Not only can you consider alternative behavioral possibilities, but you can evaluate their potential effects in terms of your prior experience in such situations.

Where you lack direct experience, you can extrapolate from similar, more familiar areas that bear on the related problem. Such cognitive processes thus free you from having to test out each behavioral hypothesis individually.

In trying to decide on the right approach to a business decision, vacation plan, or romantic ploy, you needn't actually *try* each alternative. What a waste of time and energy that would be. Imagine having to actually invest money in each issue on the stock market or each investment plan at a bank to see which one makes a profit: Even if you started out with a fortune, you'd run out of money long before the bank or market ran out of opportunities. Or what about trying every possible line on each romantic prospect: "Hey, you come here often?" "What's a nice girl like you doing . . ." Not very effective.

Instead, you can *think* about what to do, evaluate the known and potential consequences of each provisional plan of action, and finally decide which one to actually carry out. Part of this depends on assimilating information from the environment: the financial reports say T-bills are a good bet this year; this person looks too classy to fall for a snappy line, let's try the casual approach. If the strategy "works"— you make money, get a date—then fine, this becomes part of your personal knowledge base for future situations of this type.

But even if things don't pan out the way you'd hoped, you can still use the feedback from the experience in a productive way; this is what we ordinarily mean by "learning from experience." *Next* time, when faced with similar circumstances, you don't have to go through the same ill-conceived actions. Instead, you can consider their effects from *last* time. Don't just read financial reports—ask your accountant or your friends what they think; forget about pickup lines altogether—just be natural.

In this respect, said Hartmann, even the much maligned and misunderstood process of *fantasy* has its productive uses, for isn't fantasy after all a kind of inner behavioral rehearsal, a consideration of alternative possibilities and alternative selves? But fantasy is useful only if tethered to a firm foundation in reality. Freed of this grounding, it wanders aimlessly, its prospective plans and goals unrelated to the world of the possible, its provisional solutions useless for the real-life purposes at hand. You can undertake for yourself a course of spiritual development and live a selfless, saintlike existence, but you can't actually *be* Mother Teresa or Jesus Christ. An aspirant can dream of being a famous actress, but without consideration of the intermediate steps in the process—working hard, practicing her craft, actively seeking out agents and auditions—it remains just a pipe dream. We recognize these cold facts of life when we say that talk is cheap, wishing won't make it so, and actions speak louder than words.

Many people, even nonneurotic "normal" people, characteristically fool themselves and engage in maladaptive or self-defeating behaviors. And it's virtually impossible to disguise a part of your self without also partly obscuring the domains of the external world with which that self interacts. If you refuse to acknowledge that your behavior ticks off those around you, you're probably already pretty well tuned out to the signals that other people send when you commit the offending deed—or when you interact with them generally. That's why every instance of self-deception, said Hartmann, is accompanied by a misjudgment of the external world as well. Internal and external blinders go together. Haven't you occasionally been astounded at how some otherwise "smart" people seem to be psychologically deaf, dumb, and blind when it comes to their own actions? Or how they twist and distort reality to make it fit their idiosyncratic view? Well, we're *all* guilty of this a *little* bit, *some* of the time, aren't we?

If you're into computers and like to think in terms of computer metaphors, you'll appreciate the following cybernetic, or information-processing model, developed by Charles Carver and Michael Scheier.[8] These theorists talk about *self-focus*, a process that uses self-directed attention to compare a person's present state with certain relevant reference values. These values are derived from analyzing the current situation, from past experience, and from a knowledge of the individual's own thoughts, feelings, and motives as gauged by an *internal comparator*. This process, in turn, fosters self-regulation: If the functioning of the internal comparator reveals a discrepancy between a perceived state and some reference value, the result is some behavioral output—some activity—aimed at countering the deviation. This is similar to the idea in Bandura's social learning theory that people's motivations operate through the intervening processes of goal setting and self-evaluation. This form of self-motivation also involves internal comparison processes and requires personal standards against which to evaluate performance.

Carver and Scheier propose that much of the behavioral disruption we call neurotic or maladaptive really derives from an inability to distill higher-order goals, wishes, and plans down to the actual sequences of behavior that would secure these goals in reality. And when such goals involve issues that are important to identity, autonomy, and self-esteem, personality integration suffers.

Thus, while many people want to be "fulfilled" or "likable" or "successful" or whatever, they have no idea what *sub*ordinate actions will move them in the direction of those *super*ordinate goals. Moreover, the discrepancy between what they want and their inability to achieve it becomes painfully obvious time and time again. This all too frequently leads to a progressive disengagement from serious future attempts to achieve the once cherished higher-order goals. "Why knock myself over the head for nothing?" they tell themselves, as their disappointment and bitterness grow with each new failure. "Screw it."

Worse, the continued failure causes the expectation of *future* failure to become an increasingly stable part of the self-image. This leads to an even lower likelihood of exerting sustained effort toward higher-order goals later on. "I can't seem to get anything right, so why try at all?" Thus, a personality structure burdened with a surfeit of self-schemas related to failure or inefficacy is likely also to suffer a lack of coherence. This in turn sets up a vicious cycle of maladaptive behaviors and self-reproach that is inimical to self-knowledge, self-control, personal integrity and, ultimately, happiness.

Autonomy and Flexibility— On the Beam, Not Lost in Space

But computer and information-systems metaphors can go only so far in serving as models for complex human psychological processes. Unfortunately, there's a tendency to regard "intelligent" thinking as consisting of some sort of ultralogical, hyperrational, Mr. Spock-like style of cognition, devoid of passion or sentiment. This has given rise to the misconception that if everybody just behaved "rationally," the world would fall right into shape, the trains would run on time, and life would be secure and predictable. Indeed, many psychology texts describe the ego as the "rational" part of the psyche, and leave it at that.

But rationality is only a *tool* of intelligence, not the same thing. Reason and logic bridge the behavioral and cognitive spaces between aims and goals, but the goals themselves are ultimately determined by the individual's wants and wishes.

A true Mr. Spock is, ironically, a logical absurdity. This is because a total reliance on logic as a mode of thinking considers only the instrumentation of behavior, not its purpose, only the means aspect of means-end relationships. *How* to do something is only meaningful if you have some sense of *why* you should do it. Otherwise, who cares how?

Logic divorced from motives is meaningless. The writers of the original *Star Trek* series must have at least implicitly realized this, since Spock always seems to mobilize his prodigious powers of logic in the service of some goal that is *important* to him or his crewmates—saving a planet from the Klingons, for instance. But *why* this should be important to Spock or anyone else is a matter of *values*, not logic.

Humans, no less than Vulcans, can use logic to guide the direction of thought and behavior, but this direction is always toward some goal that has meaning and value for the person concerned. Emotion and intuition are typically what imbue goals and objects with motivational meaning, and it's in this sense that the fictional Vulcans seem to suffer a fundamental deficit in human experience. Indeed, when faced with problems unresolvable by pure logic, Spock is forced to concede to human intuition and gut-reaction judgment.

I don't want to stretch this space-opera analogy too thin, but Mr. Spock, as a cinematic-literary metaphor, does seem to appeal to us precisely because he stands for some real people we've met and known, people whose ultracoolness we *think* we admire until we get to know the true inner limits of their selfhood. There walk among us perfectly human but very Spock-like personalities, people for whom we alternately feel irritation and sympathy. Later chapters will discuss some of the brain-behavioral dynamics that may account for this type of personality variation and the implications it has for ego autonomy and adaptation to life.

For now, however, let's understand that while a person may possess intelligence, and while this intelligence may serve to guide and evaluate thought and behavior, this doesn't mean that he sits around all day pondering over every little thought and deed. Quite the opposite: Ideally, a lot of important behavior is routinized, taken for granted, or, as Hartmann described it, shows *automatization*. You keep a goal in mind, but the less you have to think about all the component steps toward reaching that goal, the more flexible and fluid, the more free and spontaneous, your behavior becomes.

You must have noticed how differently you approach a task—say, learning to drive a car—when the task is new, than when you've already mastered it. When you first learned to drive, didn't it seem like every particle of your being had to be thrown into the challenge of assimilating what *then* appeared the impossible intricacies of operating a motor vehicle? Each turn required precise attention to the detailed manipulation of pedals and switches, every braking and acceleration depended on acute analysis of traffic signals and road conditions, and so on.

Now, of course, driving has become routinized, automatized. The automobile is literally a sensory-motor extension of your own body and you can drive familiar routes virtually "unconscious" of what you're actually doing with the car, as when you're absorbed in a radio program or conversation. In fact, *try* to concentrate on each individual detail of driving (or typing or piano playing), and your skill and proficiency go all to hell. Yet, when the situation calls for it—getting used to a new car, a new route, or new traffic regulations—you're able to mobilize just enough conscious attention to accommodate the new aspects of the task.

And so with other behavior, even social behavior. As you grow close to another person, you get to know each other's "moves," which allows both of you to be more spontaneous, less affected, with one another. As you gain skill at a particular intellectual or athletic endeavor, you discover that peak performance often demands an abandonment of conscious moment-to-moment direction; you learn to "trust your instincts."

But the pro can trust his instincts and excel, while the novice doing the same instinct-trusting is likely to end up in a ditch. That's because, for the expert, most of the component processes in a given task—whether that task is intellectual, physical, aesthetic, or interpersonal—have become automatized. The pro is free to utilize conscious attention to deal with the novel rather than with the routine, to handle any unforeseen contingencies that may threaten ongoing excellence of performance; the beginner still needs to concentrate on the basics. The virtuoso can improvise, the student must practice his scales.

Where problems pop up is when there's a breakdown in the behavioral flexibility normally afforded by the smooth operation of automatized behavior. Later chapters will describe the kinds of personality types and so-called personality disorders that can result from disruptions of the delicate balance between automatized and purposefully directed behavior. This is a balance that changes from moment to moment and from situation to situation, as the relative familiarity or novelty of the circumstances demand. For now, it's important to recognize that an overfocus on means can disrupt progress toward important ends; conversely, a total disregard of methodology can likewise derail progress toward a goal. Most of us take thoroughly for granted the ordinary adaptiveness of our psychological functioning simply because the brain's neurocognitive dynamics allow us this luxury of unselfconscious preoccupation.

Neuropsychology, Personality, and Cognitive Style

Actually, "luxury" may be the wrong word, since what could be more *essential* to survival in an ever-changing and sometimes perilous world than the ability to flexibly, automatically delegate attention and self-control to varying aspects of the environment? How much personal tragedy is the result of not knowing when to retain control and when to let go, when to keep the reins on irresponsible, maladaptive impulses and when to go with your feelings and take a reasonable chance, when to exert intense vigilance on every jot and tittle of a situation and when to let yourself lie back and relax?

Different strategies of adapting to life's challenges are handled by different people in different ways, partly because of early and later learning experiences. But as the following chapters will make clear, the raw material of individual personality inheres fundamentally in individual differences in brain organization and cognitive style. Hartmann came very close to this concept when he spoke of *ego constitution*, the set of mental traits that comprise the self-directing faculty of the personality. These include individual variations in memory, attention, imagery, language, intelligence, and behavioral control. Back in the 1930s, he urged that research be carried out to determine how much of individual psychological variation is due to innate biological factors, how much to universal features of human development, and how much to variations in experience.

The term *cognitive style* was introduced by George S. Klein[9] to describe the particular pattern of thinking that in part defines the personality of each individual. According to this view, Freudian psychodynamics—unconscious conflicts, repressed fears and wishes, and so on—are still important. But the direction these psychodynamic influences take, said Hartmann, is shaped by the particular cognitive style that the person has been endowed with.

For example, a highly verbal person might express his particular neurosis by endless talking and writing about key themes in his life—think of Kafka's tortured letter to his father or Hemingway's chronicles of his compulsively masculine exploits. Or the vituperative politician or social critic may speechify or write endlessly on his particular pet societal peeve, the content of which might be influenced by his unique unconscious pattern—he rails against government interference, for example, because of unresolved conflicts about parental authority. But his tendency to use words and language, as opposed to some other medium, is determined by his verbal-oriented cognitive style. Someone with a more emotional or imagistic bent might be drawn to theater or the arts—Isadora Duncan and Vincent van Gogh come to mind, as do the nameless graffiitists who use their folk art as a form of rebellion or identity assertion, or the punk heavy-metal rockers whose music often represents a form of stylized sexuality and aggression.

Although we tend not to think of psychodynamic theorists as doing experiments—these Freudian types seem more at home with a couch than in a lab—in the 1950s a research project was begun by a team of empirically minded ego psychologists headed by Riley Gardner and Philip Holzman.[10] They assessed the psychodynamic profiles of a group of patients by means of projective personality tests such as the Rorschach (so called because the subject "projects" his own psychodynamic wishes, fears, and conflicts into his interpretations of the relatively amorphous and ambiguous test stimuli). They then compared these profiles with the subjects' performance on a large battery of tests measuring different aspects of cognitive functioning—concentration, memory, integration, speed of mental processing, and so on. Many of these measures were, in fact, what we might today refer to as neuropsychological tests.

As a result of their study, the investigators delineated what they called the *cognitive control principles* that underlie certain personality types. For example, some people's style of thinking involves a leveling-out of memories and experiences, others a sharpening of focus on what they perceive and remember. Some people can pick out the relevant features of a task and perform with great accuracy, albeit at a relatively slow speed; others zip through the task, but make clumsy errors. Some tend to see the similarities among things, others are more sensitive to differences. Some can use the power of logical analysis flexibly to deal with unexpected changes in form or routine; others get stuck in a rut or try to force the situation into the Procrustean bed of their own preconceptions.

These types of cognitive style characteristics were found

to be associated with different patterns of psychodynamic defense. Mushing memories and perceptions together in an undifferentiated mélange sets the stage for repression—it's hard to recall any particular piece of information if it was processed only hazily to begin with, and has become mixed up with lots of other things after that. On the other hand, rationalization, the tendency to find logical, acceptable ''reasons'' for things, is abetted by a more focused and concentrated cognitive style that teases out often unessential details and makes those the subject of preoccupation, while ignoring the important overall context.

Although this study was an important step toward an integration of psychoanalytic theory with cognitive psychology, it didn't receive the attention it deserves among either academic psychologists or practicing therapists. One exception is in the work of David Shapiro[11] who has adapted the concept of cognitive style in his seminal study of different personality types, different forms of cognitively shaped characterological patterns of adaptation and maladaptation that he terms *neurotic styles*:

> By ''style'' I mean a form or mode of functioning—the way or manner of a given area of behavior—that is identifiable in an individual through a range of his specific acts. By ''neurotic styles'' I mean those modes of functioning that seem characteristic, respectively, of the various neurotic conditions.[12]

What are often regarded clinically as neurotic symptoms or pathological personality traits, says Shapiro, regularly appear in the context of a person's attitudes, interests, intellectual endowments, and even vocational aptitudes and social affinities. That is, the pathological is admixed with the ordinary, the extreme maladaptive or self-defeating or obnoxious aspects of a given person's personality intertwined with the less glaring facets of thought, language, mood, and behavior that together define a person psychologically as a unique individual.

From this perspective, the neurotic person doesn't simply "suffer" a neurosis as one suffers a cold or toothache, but actively participates in it and sustains it. His way of thinking and his attitudes—his *style*, in other words—is an integral part of his neurotic functioning, moving him to think, feel, and act in ways that both confirm and reinforce it. The way a person characteristically organizes his perceptions, thoughts, feelings, and attitudes is in large part determined by his or her particular cognitive style, and this style also influences the ways in which the person deals with life and with his or her own reactions to situations.

Indeed, we recognize this intuitively when we tell someone—perhaps defensively—"Hey, that's my style." And how often have we been intrigued by the way various aspects of thought, speech, desire, and even interpersonal behavior and life pursuits seem to hang together in certain people?

The flighty, self-preoccupied histrionic attention-seeker chooses acting or modeling as a career and gets what she wants from others by florid blandishment and manipulation. The habitual cynic and suspicious scrutinizer of other people's actions and motives becomes an expert in surveillance equipment, subscribes to paramilitary magazines, and develops a life ethic of looking out for Number One. The person forever preoccupied with details and with doing things "correctly" chooses science or finance as a vocation and, like the banker-father in *Mary Poppins*, runs each aspect of his life with the utmost precision. The devil-may-care bon vivant is often admired and envied for his cavalier disregard of ordinary petty conventions and mores, but when this joie de vivre turns into reckless disregard for the rights and safety of others, he's no longer the spirited antihero, but the dangerous psychopath.

And so on. You'll recognize that the above descriptions are stereotypes of psychological trends and tendencies that we all display to one degree or another in different patterns and proportions. After all, accountants and actors, clergymen and comedians don't all necessarily suffer serious psychopathology in the clinical sense of the term. But the paths of life they follow do frequently seem inextricably tied up with their individual patterns of inner talents and weaknesses—indeed, our preception of these individual styles is part of what forms the predictions good-naturedly tendered in high school graduation yearbooks.

It's only when aspects of this pattern occur in the extreme, when they dominate the person's life to the point where other components of a reasonably normal life experience are squeezed out or smothered, that we refer to the style as neurotic or maladaptive. The accountant begins to see every single facet of his life as something to be "balanced." The minister becomes intrusively preoccupied with the morality of his congregants. The actor fails to leave his affected histrionics on the stage or set. In each case, the *content* of his character pathology may have to do with a warped relationship with his mother early in life, but the *form* of the pathology—hysteric, say, or compulsive—is shaped by his cognitive style. It's in these extreme cases—these living caricatures of personality—that we may see the cognitive style patterns in bold relief.

A Word About this Book and the Brain

In the pages that follow, we'll take up the gauntlet thrown down by Freud and his successors at the turn of the century, carried by Hartmann and Goldstein in the '30s, passed to the ego-psychologist researchers and personality theorists of the '40s and '50s, through Shapiro's work in the '60s, and on to the neuropsychological insights gained in the '70s and '80s. In the process, we'll tackle the question of how the brain represents, facilitates, and determines the cognitive and emotional processes that form our identities, that shape our personalities and selfhood. As the following chapters will show, identity and personality are complex *emergent processes* of the brain; no one nucleus or pathway, lobe or hemisphere, is the "site" of any complex personality function such as impulsivity, obsessiveness, or hysterical regression.

Rather, by looking at how the brain handles the cognitive *elements* of action and volition, thought and consciousness, motivation and emotion, we can gain some insight into the broader neuropsychological nature of selfhood and its implications for our daily activities and lifelong potential. This is what I mean by a *neuropsychodynamic* approach: "neuro" because we're dealing with the brain, "psycho" because our interest is in how the brain mediates the workings of the mind, and "dynamic" because we recognize the fluid, everchanging, and interactive nature of brain functioning and eschew a static localizationist approach (more about this in the next chapter). To accomplish this goal, we need to examine neuropsychological functioning and personality dynamics in brain-injured, psychiatric, and normal subjects.

In terms of neuroanatomy, the approach taken in this book is to deal mainly with relatively large structures and subdivisions within the cerebral hemispheres. Many writers have focused their attention and their theories on the microstructure of the brain, the individual cells, synapses, and chemical neurotransmitters that mediate states of arousal, emotion and, more hypothetically, cognition. And while I agree in principle that the bases of thought, feeling, and action depend ultimately on such microneuronal and biochemical complexities and subtleties of brain functioning, our knowledge of these factors vis-à-vis everyday human experience is still in its beginning stages. But the insights and conclusions about how the brain handles complex modular functions like consciousness, thought, personality, and behavior have come mainly from examining the activity of the overall three-dimensional topography of the brain.

Previous attempts to conceptualize whole chunks of human experience in terms of this or that neurotransmitter pathway or synaptic arrangement have largely failed because something as complex as a thought or a perception can't yet be dissected down to this microstructural dimension—we simply don't know enough at this level. But we *do* have enough information, gleaned from decades of clinical research in human neuropsychology, to make conclusions and informed speculations about how different overall regions and systems of the brain modulate the basic cognitive components of personality.

We can observe how individuals who have survived a stroke or gunshot wound or surgery with part of the brain destroyed now perceive and think and feel with their obliterated or weakened powers of language, memory, or recognition. We can study how they use the remainder of their brains to reconstruct reality as best they can, to make sense again of the world they knew. Once we begin to comprehend the broad brush-strokes, we can then proceed to analyze the fine details. And it's precisely these broad strokes that this book will use to elaborate a neuropsychodynamic model of personality. This theory should be viewed, not as the last word, but as a necessary first step.

In the next chapter, we'll examine how differences in personality might come to be organized in the developing brain of the individual person, the single self, and we'll also explore the evolutionary psychological underpinnings of the human race as a whole. In Part II, we'll take a close look at the three pillars of the human neuropsychodynamic makeup—thought, feeling, action—that form the foundation of selfhood. Part III melds the concept of cognitive style with the facts and principles of neuropsychology to form a novel reconceptualization of four of the most common personality types encountered in clinical practice and in daily life. Finally, Part IV applies the neuropsychodynamic model to the outer reaches of the personality and to the timeless questions of illness and vigor, baseness and morality, stagnation and change.

By the deficits we may know the talents, by the exceptions we may discern the rules, by studying pathology we may construct a model of health. And—most important—from this model may evolve the insights and tools we need to affect our own lives, mold our own destinies, change our selves and our society in ways that, as yet, we can only imagine.

CHAPTER 2

THE ORIGINS OF SELF

Brain Development and the Anatomy of Who We Are

The ego is first and foremost a bodily ego; it is not merely a surface entity, but is itself the projection of a surface. If we wish to find an anatomical analogy for it, we can best identify it with the "cortical homunculus" of the anatomists, which stands on its head in the cortex, sticks up its heels, faces backwards and, as we know, has its speech area on the left-hand side.

—SIGMUND FREUD

The soul is the voice of the body's interests.

—GEORGE SANTAYANA

Think all brains are alike? Just look at a few. One of the most striking things about seeing a number of real human brains together (or at least pictures of them) is that they're all different. They *look* different: Even though there are some standard neuroanatomical landmarks that characterize most normal human brains (Fig. 1), the particular configuration of bumps and fissures along the cortical surface of any individual brain is as unique as the pattern of loops and whorls in a fingerprint. Once, during a neuroanatomy course, our lab assistant lost the name tags for the individual containers that housed the brains we'd each been assigned to dissect and study. With very little trouble, each of the eight students in the class was able to identify his or her specimen simply by inspection; having worked with these brains for a couple of weeks, we were as intimately familiar with them as with each other's faces.

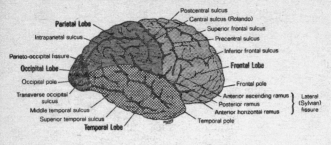

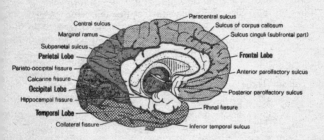

Fig. 1: The dorsolateral (upper-outer) and medial (inner-middle) surfaces of the brain, showing the four main lobes of the cerebral cortex
and the major patterns of sulci (fissures) and gyri (bumps). Each brain
is an individual variation on this general anatomic plan. (From E. L.
House & B. Pansky, *A Functional Approach to Neuroanatomy*, 2d ed.
Copyright © 1967 by McGraw-Hill. Used by permission.)

Brain Maps and Brain Modules

So it's not difficult to imagine that the personalities en-
crypted in the brain's structure might also show a similar
variability. What's more, perhaps by cataloging the relationship between anatomy and behavior, structure and function,
one could eventually predict a person's personality, even
chart one's life's course by studying one's unique pattern of
brain anatomy. And since you can't conveniently get at the

actual brains of living people, examining the rises and depressions of the overlying skull might yield the next best clue. This, of course, you may recognize as the now long-discredited discipline of *phrenology*, with its complicated "brain charts" pinpointing precise regions of the skull (and presumably underlying brain) corresponding to such traits as amativeness, conjugality, approbativeness, and veneration.[1]

While phrenology was certainly wrong in its application, the underlying principle perhaps wasn't so far off.[2] The "father" of the phrenological movement, Franz Joseph Gall, was in fact a serious scientist who made a number of real and lasting contributions to neuroanatomy. Around the time that Gall was developing his interest in the brain and behavior in the late eighteenth and early nineteenth centuries, brain researchers were coming to understand that the organ in question was not a uniform mass, as earlier anatomists had thought. Rather, it was composed of parts and subsystems that had their own unique functions and were responsible for individual aspects of behavior, such as language, perception, and movement.

Gall's fascination with the brain and mental traits stemmed from the time when, as a schoolboy, he believed he could observe a relationship between the mental characteristics of his schoolmates and the shapes of their respective heads. Later, as a working scientist, he made the rounds of prisons and lunatic asylums, carefully cataloging the associations between such traits as acquisitiveness (particularly prominent, to no surprise, in pickpockets) and the various patterns of cranial bumps.

Together with his student and later colleague, Johann Casper Spurzheim, who in fact coined the term "phrenology," Gall popularized the idea that the brain was made up of multiple "organs." Each such organ represented a mental or moral quality or proclivity whose preponderance in the personality depended on the size of the corresponding brain

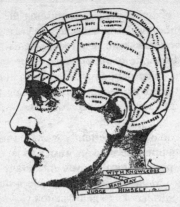

Fig. 2: A typical nineteenth-century phrenological chart, showing the location of the various mental "faculties," according to Spurzheim. Although the system itself is today regarded as patently false, phrenology represented one of the first attempts at localizing complex functions within the brain. (From B. Kolb & T. Q. Whishaw, *Fundamentals of Human Neuropsychology*, 2d ed. Copyright © 1980 by W. H. Freeman & Co. Used by permission)

organ. Since a larger bump of brain needed more room in the cranium than a smaller one, the pattern of a person's intellectual, emotional, and moral life could literally be palpated over the surface of his or her skull.

Gall believed that there were twenty-six or twenty-seven such brain organs, and he based his classification of mental traits on an analysis of actual behavior. No such empirical cautions restrained many of his followers, however. Spurzheim, for example, divided the various capacities of the mind into separate intellectual and emotional categories. As the number of separate, often arbitrarily determined mental faculties multiplied, room in the brain map had to be found for each separate localization until the skull was literally crammed with such traits (Fig. 2). Spurzheim traveled the world, spreading the gospel of phrenology, which didn't catch on in France—Napoleon disliked the theory—but found a warm reception in America, the land of new ideas.

Is that what we're trying to do in this book—come up with new and better brain maps? No, and I'll explain why. Phrenology today exists only as a caricature of pseudoscientific crankism. It couldn't survive as a legitimate approach to brain research because, for one thing, the predictions made about which bumps correspond to which mental traits turned out to be just plain wrong. Also, it's unlikely that a complex personality trait like secretiveness or conscientiousness represents a single, uniform, discrete psychological entity.

What *did* endure is the idea that the brain is composed of subsystems and that these subsystems in their myriad daily interactions are in some way responsible for the way we think, feel, and act. The problem has been less in trying to pin down discrete neuroanatomical loci than in defining exactly what a "function" or "behavior" actually is. The ability to move a joint of your finger has been pretty well mapped out in terms of anatomical pathways from motor cortex, through subcortical loops and subloops of gyroscopic control, to nerve clusters in the brainstem, thence to the spinal cord and ultimately to the nerve branches supplying the muscles of the digit in question. In actuality, if you stop to analyze the inner workings of each link in this chain, it's even *more* complicated than I've made it sound.

And that's just the action itself. What about the *motive* that made you want to raise that finger to scratch your head in consternation, as opposed to using it to grasp a pen or flip someone the bird? When it comes to the brain's role in complex functions and behaviors, we know less about the details and more about the generalities, the broad strokes. As pointed out in the last chapter, we understand through observation and experimentation that certain areas and systems of the brain have more to do than others with sensing and perceiving, with loving and hating, with planning and anticipating, with thinking and analyzing, and so on.

The details, in terms of precise connections and physiological pathways, must await perhaps another generation of researchers with new and as yet unimagined tools and techniques. In this book, we take a top-down approach, examining what we know about the effects of brain injury on broad qualities of the mind, putting that together with the data on cognition and personality and developing a heuristic synthesis—not a detailed map, but a broadly sketched baedeker that can guide future explorations into the intricate landscape of neuropsychology and personality.

As a starting point, let's look at some recent conceptualizations of the brain's role in shaping the personality, viewpoints that have inherited the phrenological emphasis on localization of function, but, I hope, without the gross distortions and oversimplifications of that now defunct school of thought.

Brain Evolution, Personality, and Adaption

Stuart Dimond,[3] the late British neuropsychologist, developed a phylogenetic, or evolutionary, theory that attempts rather directly to integrate personality with brain functioning. Dimond begins by raising a point similar to the one we discussed at the beginning of this chapter. That is, just as people are distinguished by physical differences—height, shoe size, eye color, lung capacity—they also differ with respect to the structure and organization of their brains. This much is true, as we've seen, just for the looking. But, says Dimond, this considerable variation from one person to another in the brain's appearance and physical structure signifies a corresponding variability in the encoding of individual abilities. These could vary quite widely in terms of their localization: differences in structure imply differences in functional organization.

Dimond proposes that basic personality "types" arose early in human evolution because such psychological variations—as much as similar diversity in tooth or limb—suited the purposes of species adaption. Dimond's theory assumes that personality is coded by genetic mechanisms. These either produce some direct effect through built-in ("hard-wired," as neurophysiologists are fond of putting it) features of brain organization or by providing for genetically controlled learning systems that facilitate the "stamping in" of some basic personality attributes rather than others. Hence, human personalities, like other human differences, have their origins in brains that have been molded during the course of evolution, and the personality that each of us now possesses is the psychological scion of that early formative phase of the human species.

Actually, Dimond's theory derives from an earlier hypothesis of Jerre Levy,[4] who suggested that a crucial step in evolution came when our hominid ancestors acquired the genetic capacity to separately program the two cerebral hemispheres for different sets of functions (more about this in Chapter 4). Thereafter, the further evolution that made us truly human was not directed toward selecting one or another basic type of brain architecture and cognitive organization; indeed, no such single prototypical brain-type could adaptively exist.

Rather, evolution was geared toward producing a variety of types. Each of these would contribute to social organization and cohesion by bringing to the group particular sets of abilities, skills, and ways of thinking that would help to form a durable yet flexible fabric of human society. No Platonic psychological ideal, then, best characterizes the human species; there is no one "best" personality-type. Rather, the Levy-Dimond theory says that we are bound together by those differences in cerebral and mental structure that make possible an organized, yet diverse, human society.

It works something like this. If one member of a group spends much of his time looking around in case predators or rivals from another tribe are in the vicinity, we might describe that individual as "anxious." In this case, anxiety is the handmaiden of vigilance. And this form of behavior serves a sociobiologically adaptive purpose, since groups containing a few anxious members can collectively relax and tend to other business: The anxiety of the few results in the protection of the many. Indeed, in many species of social birds and mammals, just such a "lookout" strategy is used. For humans, Dimond suggests that some individuals of the total number are genetically programmed to be "anxious" types or have anxious personalities, because this particular trait promotes the survival of the group as a whole.

In this view, personalities dominated by anxiety or depression or compulsiveness are not so much pathological as simply variations of the normal range of human psychological diversity. Just as people differ in such physical and mental traits as height, strength, intelligence, eye-hand coordination, memory, and so on, such natural differences also characterize personality. And just as natural diversity in other traits probably contributed to the adaptiveness of early human social groups as a whole—some members being better at hunting, some at creating tools and artifacts, others more adept in planning war strategies or chronicling the tribe's history in oral stories or cave pictures—so did natural differences in personality play a crucial role.

For example, while severe anxiety may be disturbing, even debilitating for the individual it afflicts, the intense watchfulness that goes along with it has in the past probably been of great benefit to the social group. As mentioned above, the anxious person carries the burden of such a biologically inherited psychological constitution for the rest of the social group who are less anxious—but his "alarmist" warnings allow the group to avoid or avert danger. Similarly, the compulsive tribesman sticks to a task of toolmaking until it's done and done right. The impulsive group member leaps before he looks: Although he perishes in the quicksand, the rest of the group learns by his example.

Still, it's possible to suppose that too much of an extreme might be *mal*adaptive. The numerous false alarms of the pathologically anxious individual exhaust and debilitate the other group members. The overcompulsive craftsman is so obsessed with perfection that the ax is never completed. The impulsivist's rash behavior disrupts the social harmony of the group or makes it vulnerable to external threat.

Other examples of these "evolutionary personality types" can be found, and Dimond offers some of them: the foresightful or "paranoid," the person who anticipates danger and thus strives to prevent it; the aggressive, capable of defending home and territory; the cohesive, the affiliative person who tends to bind the social group together for mutual benefit and support. All of these personality types would have their adaptive downsides as well, when they occur in extreme form. An overly affiliative person might drain the group's goodwill by his or her clinginess and dependence on approval or affection. The consequences of hyperaggressiveness are obvious, and so on.

A given individual's brain, according to this view, might therefore be seen as being primarily dominated by one neuropsychological system over others. These basic personality types pop up again and again in different ages because they've become genetically programmed into the human gene pool. Within this unabashedly neurodeterministic perspective, Dimond provides his own catalog of possible brain-personality types:

Visualists—brain dominated by looking and seeing.
Audists—brain dominated by listening and hearing.
Sexists—brain dominated by seduction and procreation.
Motorists—brain dominated by movement and action.
Linguists—brain dominated by speech and language.

Spacists—brain dominated by form and image.
Emotionists—brain dominated by feeling and passion.
Aggressists—brain dominated by confrontation and belligerence.

Dimond obviously believes that it's possible to relate differences in certain global personality traits to a more or less whole-hog genetic molding of the structure and organization of the brain. He clearly casts his lot with the view that it's the brain mass of identifiable systems that largely determines the overall differences in human personality. This, I think, flirts dangerously with the old-style phrenology. At the same time, however, Dimond acknowledges that these gross personality types and the brain subsystems that mediate them are only the building blocks of individual accomplishment, and he recognizes that there may be even more important differences between one individual and another in the pattern and relationship of these neuropsychological building blocks. He also seems to recognize—if not elaborate on—the essential point of the present book: that the final structure of the personality is an *emergent property* of the blocks or components from which it's created.

But there's more to the story. Dimond's theory takes a first stab at how individual differences in personality might have emerged with respect to the human species as a whole. Of equal interest, however, is how these subtle psychological patterns are encoded in each individual's nervous system from the moment of conception.

Birth of the Brain

In addition to the genes, there's the environment. Most psychologically-minded people take it for granted that the things that happen to us in our lives, especially early in childhood, produce lasting effects on our personalities. But there's another kind of environment—chemical rather than experiential—an environment that envelops and suffuses the developing brain while the fetus is still cradled in the womb, an environment that may have as great an effect on the eventual person we will be as anything that happens to us subsequently in the world outside.

Norman Geschwind,[5] another great neurobehavioral clinician and scholar who died before his time, believed that the most widely accepted genetic theories of brain lateralization—the differences in structure and function between the left and right cerebral hemispheres—had serious shortcomings. While he couldn't totally discount the role of genes in brain organization, Geschwind's research led him to conclude that the most powerful factors influencing the development of the brain and the range of talents, deficits, and personality characteristics it subserves lay somewhere else, in the internal hormonal environment that begins in fetal life and continues to a lesser extent in infancy and early childhood. Moreover, Geschwind argued, the factors that modify cerebral dominance also influence the development of many other bodily systems, for example, the organs involved in the immune response.

Geschwind's theory, like Dimond's, is a grand one in its attempt to account for a wide range of data in the brain and behavioral sciences that had previously been regarded as unrelated. These include the following well-documented findings:

Left-handedness is more common in men than in women.

Many developmental disorders of language, speech, thought, and emotion, such as stuttering, dyslexia, and autism, are strongly male-predominant.

Women are on the average superior in verbal ability, while men tend to have better spatial skills.

For both sexes, people who are left-handed or who have learning disabilities—and the two frequently go to-

gether—often exhibit a superiority in right-hemisphere
functions such as art or spatial reasoning.

Left-handedness and ambidexterity occur more frequently
in the various developmental disorders of childhood
such as dyslexia and attention deficit disorder.

Finally, certain disorders and diseases are more common
in left-handers and are frequently seen in combination,
for example, migraine, nearsightedness, dyslexia, disorders of pigmentation, skeletal anomalies, allergies,
and other immune-system disorders.[6]

Geschwind notes that the human brain is asymmetrical in
structure even in fetal life, with a pattern presaging that seen
in adults. For example, the Sylvian fissure (discovered by
the sixteenth-century anatomist Jacques Dubois—*Sylvius* in
Latin) is the main cortical crease that demarcates the temporal lobe from the frontal and parietal areas. If you visu-
alize the lateral surface of the brain as resembling something
like a cracked and lumpy boxing glove, the Sylvian fissure
is the main groove that separates the ''thumb''—the temporal lobe—from the rest of the brain surface (see Fig. 1,
page 24).

In both fetal and adult humans, the right Sylvian fissure
has a more sharply upward angle on its posterior end than
the left. Also, the left *planum temporale*, the region around
which the language systems of the brain develop, is larger
on the left than on the right in the majority of both adult
and fetal brains; moreover, this pattern can be observed as
early as the twenty-ninth week of gestation. In the course
of gestational development, the brain's pattern of bumps and
folds develops earlier on the right side than on the left. These
findings suggest that the developing brain is asymmetrical
almost from the start, and that this asymmetry normally
favors the structures around the left Sylvian fissure. However, in many cases, there's something that apparently slows
the growth of the left hemisphere, or parts of it, so that the

corresponding regions on the right side develop more rapidly. And noting how left-handedness, dyslexia, and learning disorder seem to go together mainly in boys rather than girls, Geschwind theorized that this "something" is the male sex hormone *testosterone*.

Let's back up a minute. Every high school biology student knows that the gender of a person is determined by whether he or she received an XX (female) or an XY (male) chromosome pattern. What's less well known, however, is that this is only the beginning of the story and that a human being has a long way to go before he or she achieves normal adult man- or womanhood. The chromosomal endowment is responsible for the development of either male or female gonads—testes or ovaries—and these appear rather early in fetal development, at seven to eight weeks of gestation. The male gonads begin producing testosterone and it's the presence of this hormone that determines whether the body will develop along male or female lines.

For example, the structural potential for either male or female genitals exists during the first few weeks of embryonic development. It's the exposure to testosterone that commits this initially gender-neutral tissue to becoming a penis and scrotum, rather than a clitoris and labia. Without testosterone, the embryo "naturally" develops along female lines, which is appropriate if it's really going to be a baby girl. Problems arise where, for example, the fetus is a chromosomal male, but some abnormality results in insufficient testosterone secretion or the inability of the body to utilize it. This genetic boy may be born with a girl's body type, including female genitals.[7]

And it's becoming increasingly clear that gonadal hormones have a directing influence on the development and functioning of the brain, as well as the body.[8] In addition to the obvious bodily changes accompanying masculinization, there are more subtle organizational changes taking place in the brain, changes that will determine the subsequent course of behavior and personality.[9] Regardless of genetic sex, without the presence of masculinizing hormones, the undifferentiated embryo will develop along female lines in both body and brain, genitalia and behavior. Nature's rule, therefore, seems to be "female, unless stated otherwise." And "otherwise" means testosterone.

What this implies is that embryos destined to become males will necessarily have to undergo more developmental changes than those bound for femalehood. Since nature has to work harder to make a boy, greater stress is placed on the developing male fetus. This sets up the male protobrain to be more vulnerable to any adventitious influences that could affect its growth in the womb.[10]

Geschwind, remember, postulated that the basic pattern of the brain is one with a strong left-hemisphere asymmetry for the neural substrates of language and handedness. One effect of testosterone, Geschwind argued, is to delay development in certain critical areas of the brain, particularly the left hemisphere, and particularly for males, since their gonads produce much more testosterone than fetal females. Such a delay in left-hemisphere growth tends to create brains in which the "normal" asymmetry of these regions is diminished or altered, so that the corresponding areas of the two sides are more symmetrical. And in the world of brain development, symmetry isn't necessarily better.

It works like this: Intrauterine brain development occurs according to an inexorable embryonic timetable that governs the migration and implantation of different clusters of neurons in the appropriate parts of the forming brain. If the development of one part of the brain is suppressed, more binding or attachment sites for the as-yet "free" neurons become available in other areas. In effect, if the growth of one hemisphere is suppressed, the other side has a chance to attract more neurons and thereby to get bigger and more complexly organized. Or, in some cases, certain *parts* of one side are suppressed, so other parts of the *same* side get bigger. Or, various combinations of these patterns of development may occur. Neurons that would have migrated to and made connections with those now-suppressed areas during embryogenesis go to the other areas instead.

In boys, the upsurge of testosterone affects the left hemisphere more than the right and leads to the male pattern of poorer left-hemisphere verbal skills and greater right-hemisphere spatial skills. Sometimes testosterone may really overdo it in terms of inhibiting a left-hemisphere system. Since verbal functions are handled mainly by the left hemisphere, this explains why there's a higher incidence of verbal learning disorders in males and why these disorders are frequently associated with left-handedness (indicating that the right hemisphere has taken over dominant motor control, since the control of motor function is crossed).

But—and here's the important point—since the influences that produce delays in the growth of the left hemisphere will lead to a final greater development of other brain regions, this process may in some cases be a mechanism not merely of disability, but of giftedness. For example, it may account for the high incidence of left-handedness in architects and members of certain other spatially related occupations. In this sense, Geschwind liked to speak of a "pathology of superiority."

We'll return to this issue of talents and deficits in the last chapter as it bears on the topics of creativity and morality. For now, though, Geschwind's theory could explain the presence of certain isolated high talents—the so-called savant syndrome—in many cases of autism, dyslexia, and stuttering, and the common occurrence of superior right-hemisphere functions in dyslexics and their families.

Like Dimond, Geschwind attempted to put a sociobiological cast on his neurodevelopmental theory. If we assume various kinds of cognitive deficits to be maladaptive, why should there continue to be so many cases of dyslexia and learning disorders in the population? Wouldn't natural selection eventually eliminate the hormonal mechanism responsible for such deficits?

Not necessarily. To begin with, something like a reading disorder is only maladaptive in a society where most of the population is supposed to have some degree of literacy. Such societies were rare until only a few hundred years ago and are still far from universal today. Nobody's going to notice "dyslexia" in a rural agrarian community where most of the population doesn't read.

But more than this—and importantly for the neuropsychodynamic orientation of this book—Geschwind's theory stresses the relatedness, even interdependence, of deficit and talent. For example, the high spatial talents of many verbally deficient individuals might counteract whatever evolutionary disadvantage their disabilities confer. While weak verbal communication skills in such people might render them less able to understand or convey certain information useful to the group, their superior ability in negotiating unfamiliar terrain or their heightened sensitivity to environmental nuance would be a definite adaptive plus.

In fact, seeing as how *written* verbal ability would have been virtually useless for most of human history (and for most of recorded history, too, except for small literate segments of the population), we might speculate that a brain pattern favoring high right-hemisphere spatial abilities at the expense of left-hemisphere written-language or calculation skills *has* been the truly adaptive pattern up until the recent rise of industrialized and technologized Western culture where facility with certain kinds of written communication is suddenly (in historical terms) at a premium. Even now, language for its own sake, as opposed to serving some technical purpose, is highly valued only by a literary-minded few—nerds and eggheads are still the butts of popular humor. And statistics show that fewer men than women are regular bookstore customers, attesting to the more nonverbal bias of the typical male brain.

The Geschwindian hypothesis also implies that genetic mechanisms may influence personality and cognition by using the hormonal mechanism as an intermediary. One of the things that might be inherited is the tendency to produce a particular balance of intrauterine hormones, which in turn will affect the developing brain. These hormonal influences could act synergistically with whatever more direct, non-hormonally mediated genetic influences there are that operate on brain structure to produce a final result of exquisite neuropsychodynamic complexity. This substrate is then honed by the individual's psychological and behavioral interaction with his or her environment, an interaction that puts the finishing touches on what we see as a mature personality and cognitive style.

For example, the son of two English Lit professors probably already has at birth a greater genetic brain-bent toward a verbally contemplative life of the mind than his neighbor, the son of a football pro and his artist wife. Add to this a lower level of fetal testosterone, and you have a brain whose left hemisphere is more likely to be unrestrained in its potential, in addition to probably having a greater genetically based potential to begin with. Moreover, this kid is more likely to be raised in a home full of books, rather than on a playing field. All other things being equal, who's going to be the novelist and who the next all-American? Genes, hormones, and environment—all play their role in the development of our talents and proclivities, temperaments, and personalities.

In addition to brain effects, the influence of hormones on skeletal growth and overall body development has a number of important implications. There's a venerable old literature, much of it from the last century, on the association of physical and facial anomalies with disordered behavior. Cesare Lombroso, for example, who is best known as the nineteenth-century promulgator of the ''born criminal,'' or ''criminal type,'' described a high rate of such anomalies—

including asymmetric ears and "beetling brows"—in criminals and so-called mental defectives.

While some recent authors[11] have attempted to revive portions of this discipline, this line of research has generally failed to achieve wide acceptance. One reason is the modern-day sociopolitical explosiveness usually inherent in research into human differences that smack of anything "inborn" or "genetic." Another, more specific difficulty is the observation that many of the same somatic or mental anomalies present in biological and psychological deviates of one kind or another also occasionally pop up in normal or even highly superior individuals. This seems to suggest that such anomalies are uniformly or at least randomly distributed in the population, since they can apparently happen to "anyone."

But *not* anyone. Geschwind's research suggests that such developmental anomalies show what's called a bimodal distribution. That is, a high rate of anomalies occurs at both the very talented and the very disadvantaged ranges, with a lower rate in the more ordinary, middle ranges of the population. This is similar to what seems to apply to hand-dominance: Left-handedness is very frequent both in retarded and learning-disabled subjects at one extreme, and in gifted and talented individuals at the other.

There's also a large body of literature, much of it old and currently ignored, on the association of *somatypes*—body types—with different behavioral characteristics and disorders. Kretschmer[12] proposed that different body types went hand in hand with different forms of mental illness, a concept that has received greater attention among European and British than American behavioral scientists. In the United States, some researchers argued for the association of certain physical characteristics with particular diseases, but this gained little attention, owing largely to the influence of Freudian psychodynamic theory with its emphasis on the primary role of early childhood experience in the molding of personality. Still, it often seems that many intellectual prodigies do seem to fit the skinny nerd caricature—but some are robust jocks. Many violent criminals do indeed resemble Neanderthals—but many could pass for aesthetes and bluebloods.

The prenatal hormonal influence on both body and brain development may help to explain these disparate findings. Variations in brain organization produce special talents in some individuals and deficits in others. Ditto with body types. Further, various patterns of deficits and talents can also be seen in the *same* person. With trillions of possible synaptic arrangements in any given brain, potential individual variations on the basic blueprint of human laterality and localization of function are myriad, depending on the original genetic endowment and the timing and intensity of intrauterine hormonal factors. Exceptions, in these cases, would clearly prove the rule.

On top of this, there's the role of individual personal experience and learning, whose form and direction may themselves be influenced by the type of biologically bequeathed brain-mind-body system the person has to work with. Despite these numerous possibilities, however, certain regularities in brain organization and cognitive style do seem to recur in the human population, and these are what form the basis for the different personality types to be examined in this book.

What emerges, then, from this developmental conceptualization is not a neophrenology but a broad and fluid codex of fundamental human functions as they're plotted out within the three-dimensional structure of the brain. We're not interested in static "maps" here. We're not trying to "pinpoint" psychological functions in discrete patches of brain tissue or in individual synaptic weblets.

Rather, we're now ready to see how the fundamental elements of personality—primarily thought, feeling, and action and the subtleties of perception and communication that tie them together—are understandable in terms of individual differences in cognitive style. And the dimensions of cognition that define these styles are what are encoded in the hemispheric brain systems that will concern us throughout the following three chapters. From personality to cognition to brain, and back to personality—this is the neuropsychodynamic framework that will guide our exploration into the origins of who we are.

PART II

THE BRAIN'S
SELF-SYSTEMS

CHAPTER 3

THE IMPETUS OF SELF

Action and Volition

The will is never free—it is always attached to an object, a purpose. It is simply the engine in the car—it can't steer.

—JOYCE CARY

Our wills and fates do so contrary run,
That our devices still are overthrown;
Our thoughts are ours, their ends none of our own.

—WILLIAM SHAKESPEARE

Psychoanalysis does not set out to make pathological reactions impossible, but to give the patient's ego freedom to decide one way or the other.

—SIGMUND FREUD

An old professor of mine once told our class this true story from his clinical files. A neighborhood butcher, well respected in the community and a cantor at his local synagogue, began over the course of several months to feel and act strangely, although nothing that anyone could put their finger on. He went to work, paid his bills, talked with his family over the dinner table and generally acted pretty normally, or at least correctly. But *something* was just "off" about him, people said. A little less serious, maybe, a little more "casual," but oh well, he's getting old, he's entitled to his eccentricities, his lapses, and so on. Until one day in his butcher shop, a female customer innocently inquired as to the day's best cut of meat. At this, the butcher reached over the counter, grasped the startled woman's bosom and chortled, "How about a little breast of veal?" *This* wasn't normal. One investigation led to another and ultimately a large meningioma (a slowly growing and usually benign type of brain tumor) was found to be pressing on the frontal region of the butcher's brain.

You and I generally act "appropriately" in most familiar situations. Furthermore, we do this virtually without thinking, unselfconsciously, automatically. In forming our plans and carrying them out, we're able to negotiate both the demands of outer reality and the promptings of our inner desires. In this way, we're able to go after many of our goals and still maintain our basic integrity of self. Some of us do this better than others and, as this chapter will show, the differences may be tied to the brain system that specializes in planning, anticipating, acting and evaluating.

The Frontal Lobes, Then and Now

Among neuroanatomical structures, the frontal lobes can claim at least one unique, if dubious, distinction: Even the brain experts don't quite seem to know what to make of them. Neuropsychologist Has-Lukas Teuber[1] called them a "riddle," while for neuroanatomist Walle Nauta,[2] they're a "problem." Why all the perplexity?

We know that damage to different regions of the brain often results in certain identifiable syndromes of impairment. Injury to the language areas of the left hemisphere results in disturbances of speech and comprehension—the aphasias; dysfunction of memory mechanisms in the temporal lobes produces organic amnesias; disease or trauma to higher-order sensory processing areas of the occipital and parietal lobes results in disorders of recognition; and damage to the sensorimotor areas around the central fissure produces paralysis and weakness. But for a long time, neuroscientists were struck by the fact that damage to the frontal lobes, particularly the more anterior *prefrontal*

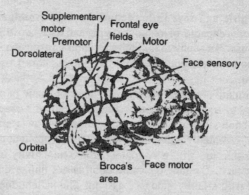

Fig. 3: The *frontal lobes* actually play a variety of roles with respect to regulating thought, feeling, and action, as this modern-day neuropsychological functional map illustrates. Also note that in the human brain the frontal lobe comprises about a third of the entire mass of each cerebral hemisphere. (From B. Kolb & I. Q. Whishaw, *Fundamentals of Human Neuropsychology*, 2d ed. Copyright © 1980 by W. H. Freeman & Co. Used by permission)

regions (Fig. 3) failed to produce any specific syndrome of impairment in the faculties of speech, perception, memory, or motility.

What frontal lobe damage *does* seem to produce, they observed, is more of a disturbance in the overall regulation and evaluation of thought and behavior, a disruption of the superordinate control over otherwise intact faculties of brain and mind.[3] That is, a frontal-injured person may be able to walk around, hold a conversation, and express emotions—in fact, seem pretty normal in the short run. But the goal-directedness, the purposefulness of the activity as a whole is deranged.

Depending on the location and amount of damage to the frontal lobes, there may be a marked poverty of thought, speech, emotion, or action. A kind of behavioral *inertia* seems to have set in. Left to himself, the frontal patient does little and says little; engaged by the examiner, he's perfectly capable of responding, but fails to do so spontaneously. In such cases, the individual's very capacity for autonomous volition seems to have been sucked right out of him.

Alternatively, once a particular behavior, topic of conversation, or train of thought begins, the patient may perseverate endlessly, talking about the same thing over and over again, repeatedly doing tasks long since completed, and being unable to shift appropriately from one activity or topic to the next. Overall, the impression is not unlike that of a robot with a faulty guidance system: The patient does little on his own, but once prompted, seems incapable of stopping what he's already doing or shifting to something else without explicit outside guidance. Again, a problem of inertia. I saw one woman in a nursing home meticulously pack her suitcase, item by item; when she was finally done, she just as meticulously *un*packed it. This cycle was repeated about five times until a unit nurse came and got her for lunch.

Damage to other parts of the frontal lobes produces a somewhat different, but related picture. Here the person seems to have lost all normal adult tact and restraint, and a "childlike" emotional and behavioral lability, or instability, takes over. One minute he's coarse, irritable, petulant, foul-mouthed, and suspicious; a moment later this demeanor is replaced by a cheery and wisecracking one. He may act in a jauntily promiscuous and lewd fashion, and generations of nurses on neurology wards have learned to deftly evade the good-natured gropes and lusty propositions of frontal patients.

Such patients may commit impulsive, inappropriate acts. They may relieve themselves in the physician's office, make puerile jokes about the doctor's baldness, or walk away with something from the desk. But in these cases it's apparently a lack of judgment and impulse control, rather than malice or treachery, that seems to underlie this kind of childishly incorrigible behavior. In such cases, it may seem as if the frontal damage has produced a caricature of the dull-but-naughty child.

The Frontal Lobes and the Regulation of Behavior

Two key dimensions of the frontal lobe syndrome, then, are inertia versus lability, and fixity versus changeability. Emotions as different as night and day can come and go in a flash, just by altering the circumstances. Tell the frontal patient a joke and he'll roar—sometimes well before the punchline. In this case, the mere "joke-telling" *setting* is enough to trigger a mirthful reaction. Mention an unpleasant event or idea in the next breath and, as if by the pull of a switch, anger or tears may supervene. Again, inertia—but in this case involving emotion as much as thought and action. In the frontal patient, the appropriateness of behavior has come to be dictated by momentary, immediate cues. Actions occur in detached isolated snippets, intact in themselves, but unconnected to the overall context of the situation or behavioral goal.

It's observations like these that have led researchers to this main conclusion: Frontal lobe functioning represents the essential neural substrate for organizing intellectual, emotional, and behavioral activity as a whole. This includes the planning and programming of that activity and the moment-to-moment evaluation of its effect on the environment and utility for the person. One of the best descriptions of the behavioral role of the frontal lobes comes from the noted Russian neuropsychologist Alexandr Romanovich Luria:

Preliminary integration of all stimuli reaching the organism and the attachment of informative or regulatory significance to some of this—the formation of the "provisional

basis of action" and the creation of complex programs of
behavior; the constant monitoring of the performance of
these programs and the checking of behavior with comparison of actions performed and the original plans; the
provision of a system of "feedback" on the basis of which
complex forms of behavior are regulated—all these phenomena in man take place with the intimate participation
of the frontal lobes, and they account for the exception-
ally important place of the frontal lobes in the general
organization of behavior.[4]

Similarly, according to Walle Nauta (who thinks they're a
"problem," remember?), the normal role of the frontal
lobes is to facilitate the integration of information about
internal states of the mind and body with input about the
outside environment. Therefore, a main effect of frontal lobe
damage is to produce what Nauta calls an *interoceptive ag-
nosia*. This is a blindness to, or ignorance of, what's going
on inside the person (or, we might say, in the person's "own
mind") in terms of motives, feelings, thoughts, and memories.

Intimate connections exist between the frontal lobes and
the brain's *limbic system*, the subcortical brain network that
links emotion and memory to perception and action. These
connections, Nauta argues, enable the frontal mechanism
to engage in a moment-to-moment, on-line internal self-
evaluation. In this way, feelings, motives, experience, and
knowledge of the current state of the world, as well as the
effects of individual actions, can all be combined for the
purpose of coming up with the right combinations of behavior to achieve the goal at hand.

You can't retain a plan of action in a stable form for any
length of time, says Nauta, unless it's represented in the
brain both as an image of an action to be performed and as
a motive to perform that action. And in frontal lobe damage, the brain loses a major mediator of information ex-

change between sensorimotor and emotional mechanisms. The emotional-motivational impetus that sustains a plan of action through its various component stages is destroyed. This is followed by an impairment of strategic choice making, and also by a tendency for projected action programs to fizzle out or become overridden by stray interfering influences—in short, behavior goes "off the track." Thus, argues Nauta, one of the main difficulties for the frontal lobe patient is maintaining a normal *stability-in-time* of behavior. The individual's action programs, once started, are likely either to fade out, to ineffectually perseverate, or to become deflected away from the intended goal.

This *time* dimension of frontal lobe functioning—the ability to maintain a certain adaptive temporal continuity of experience and behavior—also receives support from the research of Joaquim Fuster.[5] Fuster argues that the frontal cortex, particularly the more forward prefrontal area, plays an especially important role in integrating behavior in the time domain. For one thing, the prefrontal cortex appears to regulate the processes of memory and anticipation, allowing you to form goal-directed and temporally extended sequences of behavior, to link what just was with what is to be. It's also critically involved in the processes of attention that ensure that the behavioral sequences will remain directed toward the main goal, even in the face of internal and external interference.

When you form a plan to do something, and when that plan requires the appropriate execution of a number of different steps, it's important that each step be carried out intactly, in the correct order and at the right time. In addition, your basic plan shouldn't be derailed by momentary diversions produced by whims and urges from within or distractions and tantalizations from without. You should be able to keep your overall plan in mind, not lose sight of the big picture, even when forced to alter the individual steps to conform with unforeseen or unalterable circumstances. This is what defines the temporal-stability domain of the frontal lobes that both Nauta and Fuster describe.

Moreover, it's not for the carrying out of overroutinized, stereotyped behavioral sequences that frontal lobe functioning is most important. As we'll soon see, such daily routines as doing the dishes, getting undressed for bed, walking a familiar route, and so on, can be carried out even in the face of quite extensive frontal damage. Where frontal regulation of behavior seems most important is where the carrying out of a plan requires the ability to flexibly alter that plan's subcomponents in the face of changing contigencies, all the while retaining the overall purpose of the plan intact. That is, the frontal lobes are most important for dealing effectively with situational *novelty*, while preserving the integrity of the goal.

Say you want to fly from New York to Miami to present your business proposal to the main office of a corporation. The primary overall goal of this activity is, of course, to secure for yourself and your agency some important account. Now you find that all New York-to-Miami flights on your regular airline are booked for that particular day and time. So you give up, go home and watch TV, right? Of course not. You try another airline, or you see if a stopover as opposed to a direct flight is available, or you consider driving or taking a train—even calling the corporation to see if the date can be changed.

Note that through all this you're probably consulting, if only "unconsciously," some internal hierarchy of preferable options regarding the goal. Leaving hours earlier to take a train to make the meeting at the scheduled time is probably better than risking the annoyance of the corporate honchos by requesting an appointment change. Still, even this is better than canceling the presentation and blowing the account altogether. And even *that* may yet be preferable to missing an even bigger opportunity that would be lost by messing around with your own tight schedule. In this last case, the original goal itself has changed, or rather has been subordinated to a larger goal: Losing the first account is acceptable if it means bagging a bigger one. That's still okay, because a still greater overriding goal here is to keep your job, rise in the firm, and become a success.

I've used a business example, but you can probably think of other instances from your own experience. Haven't you been forced at times to shuffle priorities, change plans, and reevaluate goals in various affairs of the pocketbook, heart, or personal philosophy? And while it may have been painful or frustrating to have to do this, the fact that you *could* do it at all is due largely to the intactness of your frontal lobes.

The frontal lobes, then, synthesize information received about the outside world (appointment dates, plane and train schedules) and information about the internal states of the mind and body (financial goals, personal values). This provides the means by which your behavior is regulated according to the effects produced by your actions. Your frontal lobes allow you to judge and regulate your ongoing external perceptions and calculate appropriate responses to what it is you're perceiving. Again, the larger purpose of all this is to maintain a certain optimal equilibrium between yourself and the external world. And since for most people, other human beings comprise an important part of that world, optimal negotiation of the *social* environment is crucial.

The Sociable Brain

Stuart Dimond,[6] whose views on brain evolution we encountered in the last chapter, regards the frontal lobes as the very seat of social intelligence for advanced mammals—particularly man. One important function of the frontal lobes, Dimond argues, is to regulate those aspects of species-specific social behavior that are related to self-perpetuation. This involves complex social relations that determine how

animals associate with one another for sex and reproduction
and the behavioral roles through which parental care is administered to the developing young.

Damage to the frontal lobes, according to Dimond, produces a deterioration in the capacity of the individual to
maintain his or her social position. This results from a disruption of the frontal lobe mechanism that normally controls both aggressive and prosocial responses. One way this
has been tested directly is by studying the effects of brain
damage on the behavior of monkeys in monkey communi-
ties.[7] These studies have shown that experimentally induced
frontal lesions often result in a decline in the normal social
assertiveness needed to maintain a monkey's position in the
status hierarchy. However, in some cases, the opposite may
occur—an enhanced aggressiveness, a tendency to fly into
a rage at the slightest provocation, making these frontally
damaged animals generally feared and avoided by other
members of the group. But as is the case for dangerously
volatile individuals in any group, these pugnacious primates
soon come to be ostracized by monkey society and end up
as virtual social isolates.

Here, as in human patients with frontal damage, the injury seems to have produced a heightened *instability* in
emotional reaction and social relationships. The frontal
damage has interfered with the finer-grained modulation of
emotionality and interpersonal behavior that gives normal
social relationships—monkey or human—their stability and
appropriateness. Being assertive, after all, is not the same
thing as being wildly aggressive. The former involves being
able to gently but firmly interact with members of the social
network to get more or less what you want; the latter is just
being nasty. In the first case, your actions may garner at
least some grudging respect; in the second, you're just another badass to be avoided. Thus, to the extent that the frontal lobes can be said to perform an "executive" function
(as is the customary description in many textbooks), Di-

mond contends that they do so for social behavior as a distinct specialization.

The frontal lobe system is certainly important in social behavior, but, for the very reasons cited above, I'd nevertheless argue against the *uniqueness* of this social aspect of frontal lobe functioning. Social appropriateness is only one facet, albeit an important one, of overall behavioral regulation vis-à-vis the environment. Just as maintaining appropriate stability of behavior in *any* domain requires the intact melding of means and goals and an appreciation of the proper context of a given type of behavior, so does *social* behavior involve this maintaining of stability-in-time.

Sociability, in its day-to-day practical application, is not separate in principle from other kinds of ability; all require certain forms of behavior at certain times and in certain ways. People may be more or less socially adroit as they may be more or less skilled in other areas, and we all recognize individuals who are total jerks in social situations, just as we perceive other persons to be clumsy at sports or slow at intellectually demanding tasks. All are forms of behavior and all require a certain degree of frontal lobe mediation and control for optimal performance. Sociability is the form of *adaptive* behavior most appropriate to the *human* environment, and this, its situational adaptiveness, is what I think accounts for its dependence on frontal lobe functioning—just like other forms of adaptive behavior.

The following vignette, involving two patients studied by the French neurologist F. Lhermitte,[8] illustrates the effects of frontal lobe damage on socially adaptive behavior.

The Case of the Frontal Frenchmen

The first patient, whom we'll call Pierre, was a fifty-one-year-old, right-handed engineer who'd been treated for epilepsy since age thirty. Most recently, he'd begun to develop disturbing mood swings. A computerized tomography (CT) scan showed a tumor of the left frontal lobe; in order to get at the whole mass surgically, the left frontal lobe itself had to be removed, after which followed a course of radiation and chemotherapy.

At first, Pierre responded well to this treatment. The clinical disturbances subsided and a six-year period of relative stability followed. Then problems began anew—the CT scan showed a recurrence of the tumor. Chemotherapy was again tried and some improvement was observed for the next fourteen months. However, the tumor relentlessly recurred and despite further treatment, Pierre died twelve months later. Post-mortem examination of his brain showed that the tumor had invaded the entire white matter of the remaining frontal lobe.

The second patient, a fifty-two-year-old, right-handed housewife whom we'll call Marie, had been suffering from progressive apathy and an inability to carry out coordinated movements. In addition, a neurologic exam disclosed a mild right-sided weakness. A look at her CT scan revealed the presence of a tumor in the left frontal lobe and a left frontal lobectomy was undertaken, followed by radiation therapy. She recovered well, returned home, and resumed her domestic chores. But despite normal findings on the neurologic exam, she seemed to show a certain lack of initiative and other disturbances.

For fourteen months, Marie existed in this relatively stable condition, until her tumor, like Pierre's, came back and led to her death eleven months later. Post-mortem examination of her brain showed evidence of the prior left frontal lobectomy, as well as more tumor tissue encroaching on a greater portion of the remaining frontal lobe.

Lhermitte describes several interactions with these patients while they were under his care that illustrate how their frontal lesions affected their behavior, their personalities, their selves. On one occasion, as Marie sat in Lhermitte's office, he placed some medical instruments on his desk. The patient immediately picked up the blood pressure gauge and very meticulously took the doctor's blood pressure. Next, she took the tongue depressor and examined his throat. To complete the "exam," she picked up the percussion hammer and proceeded to test Lhermitte's reflexes. When he asked her what she thought, Marie replied that she was quite satisfied with the state of the doctor's health.

Another time, a buffet had been laid out in a lecture room where there were about twenty people. Pierre entered the room and lost no time in helping himself to food and drink. When Lhermitte offered him some whiskey, he declined, but poured himself a glass of water and drank it down. He behaved overall like a supercilious guest of honor, not thinking to offer anything to Lhermitte or any of the other guests.

When Marie came in to the buffet, she noticed some stacks of chairs and proceeded to set them out side by side. She then took the glasses that were stacked on the buffet and laid them out one by one. This completed, she offered Lhermitte food on various plates and asked him if he wanted any wine. Although the doctor declined, she nevertheless poured some into a glass. Seeing that Lhermitte continued to refuse, she offered him a glass of orange juice instead. Lhermitte indicated that he'd like to clink glasses with her, so she poured herself some water and clinked away. In contrast to Pierre's snobbish behavior, Marie acted like the perfect hostess, as if it were in fact *her* buffet.

One day, Pierre and his girlfriend showed up at Lhermitte's apartment for a visit. After a while, the doctor asked Pierre to come outside onto the landing where the two men stood in silence for about a minute. Lhermitte then said, in a neutral tone, "museum," and opened the door back into the apartment. Pierre strode right in and immediately began examining the paintings on Lhermitte's walls as if he were, in fact, in a museum. This was continued in the other rooms.

Some objects seemed to attract more of Pierre's attention than others, an attitude appropriate for any museum visitor, and he made apt remarks concerning the various "exhibits" he was viewing.

In another room, three paintings had been hanging on a wall, but one had been taken down and put on the floor. Pierre noticed the missing painting at about the same moment he also spied a hammer and nails lying on a nearby table. He proceeded to pound a nail into the wall (one can't fail at this point to admire Lhermitte's forbearance for the sake of science) and mounted the painting next to the others.

On returning to the bedroom, Pierre noticed that the bedspread had been taken off the bed and the top sheet turned back. Immediately, he got undressed, got into bed, pulled the sheet up to his neck, and prepared to go to sleep. A while later, Lhermitte picked up an article of clothing and, as if on cue, Pierre popped out of bed and got dressed.

On another occasion Marie was also a guest at Lhermitte's home. As soon as she saw the unmade bed, she tucked in the covers on both sides. Lhermitte then walked toward the bed wielding his stethoscope in a doctorly manner. Marie lay down on the bed immediately. "Realizing that her clothes were getting in the way," explains Lhermitte with clinical aplomb, "she helped me unbutton her blouse and undo her brassiere, so that her chest was completely bare."

After this, Marie accompanied Lhermitte to a table where various hypodermic syringes were laid out. As the doctor went through the motions of preparing an injection, the patient immediately lifted her dress and pulled down her pantyhose, exposing her right buttock. Later, he showed her the hypodermic syringe, and she took it from him. "When I took off my jacket and shirt," Lhermitte tells us, "she picked up the needle and a cotton ball, which she soaked in antiseptic, then bent down to my buttock to give me the injection." The doctor is uninformative about what transpired next.

On another occasion, Lhermitte seated Pierre at a table on which women's makeup had been placed. The patient looked at the items and then glared angrily at Lhermitte, as if greatly annoyed that the doctor should regard him as some kind of cosmetological transvestite, or worse. Not long after this, Pierre noticed a magazine-loaded pistol and a revolver on a table. He got up and made directly for them, with a gesture of intense delight. He spun the bullet chamber of the revolver, looked for the box of cartridges, and found it. Seeing that these cartridges were the wrong caliber for the revolver, he picked up the pistol instead, pulled the magazine back, and loaded the gun. "The experiment," Lhermitte notes dryly, "was then stopped."

Next, Lherimitte walked into the bathroom. Pierre followed and washed his hands. Seeing an electric shaver, the patient proceeded to shave. On approaching the toilet bowl, Lhermitte lifted the seat. For about fifteen seconds the patient made the characteristic "psii, psii" sound until Lhermitte commented that Pierre didn't seem to want to urinate. The patient replied that, no, he really didn't, and both men left the bathroom.

Marie, upon catching sight of the cosmetics on the table, smiled and immediately began using the powder and eye makeup. She'd just gotten up to put on the lipstick and to check herself in the mirror when she noticed some balls of yarn and knitting needles lying about. Apparently forgetting about the makeup session, she began to knit. This activity was in turn abandoned when she spotted sewing needles, spools of thread, and pieces of fabric, whereupon she put on her glasses and began sewing. In the kitchen, she noticed a broom and proceeded to sweep the floor. She then saw dishes in the sink, so she washed them.

What are we to make of these two people who'd suffered

considerable frontal lobe damage? Lhermitte, for his part, describes these as examples of what he has termed the *environmental dependency syndrome*. There was nothing wrong or improper about any of Pierre's or Marie's isolated activities: cosmetics were applied, guns were loaded, food was served, and paintings were hung, all in the correct manner. Someone watching each of these activities in isolation would have had to conclude that here were two perfectly normal people doing what people normally do.

But not *exactly* normal. What was glaringly absent in these cases was any sense of the appropriate *context* for the actions. Rather than a particular behavior sequence being embedded in a temporally contiguous, goal-directed overall plan, the patients' momentary states of activity were dictated by the cues of the moment.

You and I don't treat our friends' home furnishings like museum exhibits. That's because, as fascinated as we might be by a particular gewgaw, we know that in the overall context of the situation, the appropriate behavior is that of a visitor, not a spectator. A turned-down bed is not an automatic cue to go to sleep, because we know it's still daytime, it's not our house, we're not tired, and so on. We *know* all these things because we're able to take in and analyze input from the environment—where we are, who we're with, what time of day it is, who says what—as well as from our internal thoughts, images, feelings, and actions. This, in turn, we utilize—quite effortlessly and unselfconsciously in most familiar situations—to guide our behavior in ways appropriate to both our own motivations and the situation at hand.

The frontal-damaged patient, however, seems to have lost this sense of overall behavioral context. He or she appears to be a virtual slave to isolated contextual cues—the word "museum," the sight of a stethoscope, a raised toilet seat, and so on. When questioned by Lhermitte about the reasons for their actions, Pierre and Marie were puzzled; they felt they'd reacted perfectly normally, did what they were *sup-*

posed to do. No sense of subjective compulsion, no "driv-enness" against their will, accounted for their objectively in-appropriate behaviors. From these patients' own disjointed vantage points, they could no more fail to act as they did than you or I could fail to act the way we do. It *was* their "will" to do what they did; by their blinkered lights, they were act-ing normally, appropriately.

Recall the point made earlier that the effects of brain damage almost always occur against the background of the person's total personality. Lhermitte notes that his patients' preillness personalities and experiences formed an integral part of their own particular idiosyncratic manifestations of the more general environmental dependency syndrome. For example, Pierre, an educated man from a high social back-ground, behaved like an entitled guest at the buffet, and in the "museum" expressed intellectual curiosity about the "exhibits," making otherwise appropriate comments and observations. Marie, from a humbler provenance, was more interested in the plainer and utilitarian aspects of Lher-mitte's apartment and was quite content doing domestic chores, such as serving food at the buffet and washing the dishes in Lhermitte's kitchen.

Cases like these illustrate how intimately tied to brain functioning—and how fragile—is our sense of autonomy, our notion of free will and our ability to decide on and dictate our own courses of action. Lhermitte points out that a decision made of one's own "free will"

depends on two different groups of forces, the first im-plicit in the environment and the second dictated by the psychological state of the subject. These two forces com-bine to form a dynamic balance that is constantly shifting, and which determines the subject's behavior at all times.[9]

In Pierre's and Marie's cases, it's that second aspect, the

internal psychological state, that seems to have been stripped of its motivating and guiding force by frontal lobe damage.

Remember the naughty butcher at the beginning of this chapter? That case, too, underscores the fact that even with quite extensive frontal damage, most isolated or overroutinized aspects of behavior can be preserved for a long time. After all, it wasn't his well-practiced butchering that was affected by the growing frontal tumor. Moreover, the butcher's admittedly grievous lapse in propriety (groping a customer) was not done without some degree of wit, albeit of a puerile, junior-high variety. And even Pierre wasn't so out of it as to be fooled into performing a patently gender-incongruent act—how *dare* Lhermitte suggest he put on makeup! Again, it's an example of the *elements* of behavior remaining intact, but the ability to deal flexibly with the *context* of that behavior—the larger picture—that's askew.

We can conclude that one fundamental aspect of ego autonomy inheres in the frontal lobes' stewardship of the goal-directedness and appropriateness of behavior. This is *not* the same as saying that the ego is "in" the frontal lobes or that the frontal lobes are the "seat" of the self. The point bears repeating that no one brain site or structure alone controls any higher mental function. Rather, the frontal lobes have a primary role in mediating the ability to form a plan and stick to it, in facilitating the evaluation of one's own behavior with respect to that plan's goal and to the situation as a whole. These are, after all, components of what we ordinarily regard as *volition*. And a sense of inner-directedness, of volition, is basic to our sense of self.

As later chapters will show, the problems of impulsivity and compulsivity that dominate certain personalities probably have to do with developmentally based variations of frontal lobe functioning, similar in type to that of Pierre and Marie, if not in origin or severity. But first, there's a little more to the frontal lobe story.

The Language of Self-Control

Just *how* do the frontal lobes help keep behavior on an even keel? In his studies of patients with frontal lesions, Luria noted that they were easily distracted by irrelevant stimuli and had particular difficulty keeping their attention focused on a definite plan. We've already encountered these phenomena as familiar components of the frontal lobe syndrome. But Luria noticed something else. The problem many of these patients had in regulating their attention and behavior seemed to have to do with their inability to properly use *language*.

Neuroscientists can measure a certain type of brain wave activity, called the *orienting response*, which occurs whenever a person actively pays attention to a demanding task. In normal subjects, this orienting response can be elicited by presenting them with some problem to solve or some particular instruction to carry out. But in Luria's frontal patients, this electrophysiological response to a spoken instruction was markedly deficient, even though the specific language areas of the brain were unscathed. Somehow the brains of these frontal patients didn't register the verbal cue as an event to be taken notice of. In fact, if directly queried, some patients might actually acknowledge that they'd heard and understood the cue, but it nevertheless seemed to have no spontaneous effect on their behavior.

Luria took this to mean that one of the primary tasks of the frontal lobes concerns the higher-order regulation of attention. To most people, attention may not seem like such a complex, sophisticated cognitive function, but without the ability to properly direct, focus, and shift attention, it's hard to make sense of incoming information or to create complex plans of action. Just remember the last time you tried to concentrate on a job or study for a test while you were upset or distracted and you'll realize that information in the environment doesn't just passively flow into the senses; it has to be grasped and assimilated by an active and flexible attentional process.

But even more important, said Luria, in man it's the unique faculty of language that facilitates the brain's focusing of attention in an adaptive way. This is what lets us elaborate plans of great complexity and in turn permits our complex behavior to be guided by these preformulated plans of action. Language, the faculty that has sprung up so recently in our evolutionary history, is enlisted by the modern human brain for the purposes of greatly enhanced behavioral self-regulation.

Luria further pointed out that this regulation of attention and behavior by the brain's language system is ill defined in the child, develops progressively in early adolescence, and appears in stable form only at about age twelve to fifteen. Interestingly, this is also the period when the frontal lobes are beginning to play a more intimate part in higher voluntary attention and behavior control. And to Luria, the role of the frontal lobes in directing and modulating the adaptiveness of behavior is inextricably tied up both with language and with the role of social forces in human development.

Bear in mind that Luria did the bulk of his research and clinical work under the postwar Soviet regime, so it's not surprising that numerous references to socialistic concepts, principles, and examples (including even a quote by Lenin) dot his writings in neuropsychology. However, rather than letting politics overrule empiricism as did many of his comrades in science during those Stalin-Khrushchev days, Luria creatively absorbed the metaphors of socialism into his evolving neurobehavioral model.

Thus, the normal socialization of the growing person, said Luria, is facilitated by language and permits the growing child to assimilate and internalize self-directed verbal control of behavior. This takes place first as a literal talking to oneself, as you've no doubt seen small children do. Later, it occurs as a true internalization of the linguistic codes guiding mature behavior in the social world, a sociodevel-opmentally fostered verbal mediation that governs all-around adaptive behavior.

Just think of Pierre and Marie with their abnormal susceptibility to behavioral capture by cursory visual and verbal cues (the sight of an unmade bed, the word "museum"). They had ceased to be the masters of their fate in a very literal and poignant sense: Even when asked to explain their behavior, they were unable to use language as a tool for abstractly stepping outside themselves, for maintaining a certain distance from, and perspective on, their own behavior. Instead, they justified their actions as perfectly normal—and by their own limited powers of self-discernment they were right. As later chapters will show, this kind of attenuated introspection and stunted self-evaluative capacity is hardly limited to the organically brain-damaged. Other people, other brains, vary in their individual organization with respect to the powers of looking inward and forming judgments about themselves and the world.

Recall the role of the frontal lobes in social interaction that Dimond was so concerned with. In Luria's view, this is related to the role of the frontal lobes in attentional scanning and emotional evaluation. The socially adroit individual is sensitive to both internal motivation and external information. He reads the nuances of his various interpersonal interactions in all their verbal, attitudinal, behavioral, and insinuative shadings. He's in touch with the effects of his own words and deeds on those around him and he can modulate his behavior accordingly. In short, he's *onto* himself and this gives him a greater edge in being onto those around him. And he does this partly intuitively, but also—albeit quite automatically—partly through the use of internalized codes of language.

So for humans, a linguistic component is suffused through virtually everything we do. In human development, language from the first guides and motivates the progressive internalization of certain standards, certain regularities. It's on the basis of these regularities that our behavior achieves a measure of *intra*personal predictability and stability, as well as adaptiveness to a wide range of everyday situations, both routine and uncommon. Through language we build up Nauta's stability-in-time and forge Fuster's cross-temporal links. These enable us to judge our own behavior in relation to both the environment and ourselves, with respect to past, present, and future. Luria's "signal function of speech" for the processes of attention and social behavior becomes progressively internalized in development, and it is in this process that the frontal lobe system plays a crucial neuropsychodynamic role.

Let me make this clear: Ego autonomy is not *in* the frontal lobes, as some narrowly localizationist viewpoints would have it. Rather, the frontal lobe system is crucial for providing the on-line search-and-analysis mechanism that enables you to harness your own complex array of talents and abilities and direct them toward realizing the goals you think are important. The frontal lobes do this by enlisting *language* as a guiding, structuring, and controlling tool of the self-system. Insofar as ego autonomy requires a realistic self-image of our own capacities and limitations, our powers of volition and will, our self-efficacy, the frontal lobe system plays a critical role.

Again, some of us are better off in this regard than others, because we all have differently organized brains. But, except at the extremes of brain impairment, most of us still possess sufficient volitional leeway to direct ourselves toward productive and valued goals. Just as a mildly elevated blood pressure doesn't necessarily doom you to certain early death from heart disease, a relative weakness in the frontal lobe substrate for autonomous action and self-control doesn't absolve a person from all personal responsibility. We'll return to this issue in the final chapter.

As you've probably realized by this point, self-control implies a certain degree of self-awareness. And the issue of self-awareness raises the question of consciousness and the further roles of language and imagery in both facilitating and limiting our self-knowledge. How does the brain generate consciousness—especially self-consciousness? How much insight into our own behavior is neuropsychodynamically possible? How are thought, language, and imagery related to the capacity to understand our selves—indeed, even to define our selves? It is to these questions that we now turn.

CHAPTER 4

THE AWARENESS OF SELF

Thought and Consciousness

The world of thought and the world of perception—both of which are among the ego's regulating factors and are elements of that adaptation process which consists of withdrawal for the purposes of mastery—need not always coincide. Perception and imagination orient us by means of spatial-temporal images. Thinking frees us from the immediate perceptual situation (memory and imagination are of course its precursors in this), and its highest form—in exact science—strives to exclude all images and qualities from the world. Still, images do have, in many situations, a regulative role in human action. Both these worlds have a specific relation to action: not only thought implies an action tendency, the image does, too, albeit a primitive one.

—HEINZ HARTMANN

An idea, like a ghost, according to the common notion of ghosts, must be spoken to a little before it will explain itself.

—CHARLES DICKENS

Are you a "whole-brain thinker"?

As popular culture frequently usurps the paradigms established by the mainstream arts and sciences, so does the self-help industry seem quick to seize upon the latest trappings of scientific—and pseudoscientific—trendiness. The recent popularization of brain lateralization and cerebral hemispheric asymmetry has spawned a veritable cottage industry of entrepreneurial books, lectures, workshops, and seminars, all promising better living through hemispheric integration.

For example, one program[1] assures you that learning to

use both sides of your brain will send you peeling out ahead of your half-brained colleagues on the road to corporate success. The Japanese are such savvy businessmen, we're told, because they make better use of right-brain thinking than American executives do. On the other hand, it's minority groups' "right-brain values" that keep them from improving their station in life. And John DeLorean's financial troubles were attributable to his being stuck in a right-brain rut. Simple, huh?

In the self-help biz, though, theories without practical application don't feed the proverbial cat. So a recipe is offered for discerning the brain-dominance ratios of your officemates: task-oriented, well-organized types are high in left-brain dominance; emotional, aesthetic, and creative types are more right-brained. By "training" your own brain to achieve peak interhemispheric integration, you can psych out these lesser, half-headed types and become king of the hill.

Don't you wish it were that easy?

These ideas and programs have great popular appeal in part because they do contain some kernels of empirically documented truth. Unfortunately they also contain a lot of tortured distortion and oversimplification in order to whip up some of the more tasty morsels of data into a marketable froth that will appeal to many people's desire for quick-fix solutions.[2]

What's the real story about the cerebral hemispheres and the human mind? Is the left brain really more verbal, rational, and conscious, the right more artistic, creative, and repressed? And what are the implications for human consciousness, identity, autonomy, and personality? This is a key issue, not just for the present chapter, but also for the guiding assumption of this book: that the brain encodes personality in terms of the subelements of thought, feeling, and action. How the two cerebral hemispheres contribute to the handling of these subelements is therefore of great importance.

Left Brain, Right Brain—
The Long and the Short of It

Neuropsychologists continue to study and debate the roles of the two hemispheres in thought, emotion, and behavior. But what's becoming clear from hemispheric laterality research—indeed from neuropsychological research in general—is that very few aspects of brain-behavior functioning are strictly either-or. In normal mental life, the two cerebral hemispheres interact with each other in a constantly oscillating, reciprocally balanced relationship. As such, even those cognitive functions believed to be the domain of one hemisphere are aided, altered, and shaped by the operations of the other. This occurs in both normal and abnormal behavioral states. And you do this naturally; you don't need "brain-training." However, bearing this in mind, we now have enough data to allow us to make some general statements about the two hemispheres' individual and respective roles in higher mental processes[3] (Fig. 4).

For most people, the *left hemisphere* is specialized for linguistic processing and for logical, descriptive analysis. It also plays a special role in the interpretation of the syntactic (grammatical), semantic (informational), and literal qualities of communication. That is, your intact left hemisphere makes it possible for you to comprehend both the grammar and content of the paragraph you're now reading. It also allows you to convey this information to others, perhaps using a different form of expression—colloquial speech, say—all the while retaining the basic meaning and relating it accurately to what's gone before.

Similarly, you're able to make sense of this passage because you can analyze the sequence of information and determine that it follows some logical, purposeful course, that

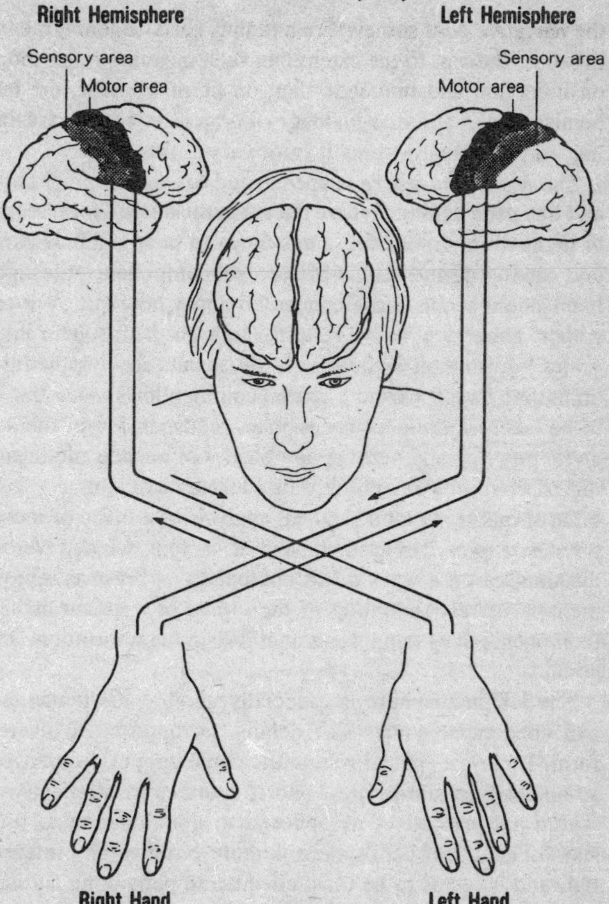

Fig. 4: The two cerebral hemispheres. Motor control and sensory pathways between the brain and the rest of the body are almost completely crossed. But for more sophisticated functions like language, spatial reasoning, and emotional expression, the relationships become more complex. (From S. P. Springer & G. Deutsch, *Left Brain, Right Brain*, rev. ed. Copyright © 1981 by S. P. Springer & G. Deutsch. Used by permission of W. H. Freeman & Co.)

the narrative *goes* somewhere and thus has a coherent meaning to it. Indeed, to the extent that such meaning relies more on inflection and innuendo than on literal content, the left hemisphere is at a disadvantage—one reason why "explaining" a joke usually ruins it (more about this shortly).

The *right hemisphere* is specialized for spatial processing and imagistic coding. Where the left hemisphere's forte seems to be analysis—breaking things down to their smallest parts and cataloging the details of each subcomponent—the right hemisphere seems more concerned about how things fit together, about synthesis, gestalt. The right hemisphere integrates information in the spatial dimension, leaving the time domain to its left partner. Spatial coding allows many things to be taken in at once, necessitates a suspension of the analytic process, and permits new shades of nuance and meaning to color the incoming data. Just as explaining a joke often spoils it, so a mechanical analysis of a piece of music often strangles the aesthetics of it, a long-winded verbal disquisition on a work of art confounds its sensorial enjoyment, a literal recounting of the events of a dream or hallucinogenic drug trip loses something in the translation, and so on.

The left hemisphere is especially good at the perceptual and conceptual analysis of details, as opposed to overall form. It plays a special role in the perceiving of differences, as opposed to similarities, and it operates most effectively within a consecutive, as opposed to a simultaneous, time frame. The right hemisphere is more intuitive and inferential, and it seems to be most effective in perceiving similarities based on broad qualitative features. This may explain why facial recognition ordinarily involves a mere holistic glance, rather than a painstaking analysis of distinguishing features. Try to *explain* to someone what a stranger's face looks like and you'll understand why one picture is worth a thousand words (and why police departments employ artists to facilitate suspect identification).

Yet a form of interhemispheric pinch-hitting often comes into play after unilateral brain injury, as the following example shows. People who've lost the ability to recognize pictures or faces after right-hemisphere damage are unable to tell one figure or person from another by an overall comprehension of countenance or form—they cannot recognize these things "at a glance." They *can* nevertheless utilize cues to identify different individuals by zeroing in on just a small aspect—a detail—of the different percepts: the shape of her eyes, the trim of his beard, the distinctive squiggle in the corner of a drawing, and so on.

That's because the preserved left hemisphere's preoccupation with details facilitates this compensatory "tagging" form of recognition. Even so, mistakes are possible. By altering a salient feature—putting on glasses, shaving off a mustache—you can "fool" the left hemisphere by eliminating the one important tag it so desperately relies on for recognition.

And all of us normally utilize a combination of holistic and detail-orienting recognition for faces or other complex visual forms. That's one of the reasons you recognize a familiar person dressed in a Santa suit, first as Santa Claus—boots, beard, red hat—and at the same time as your friend, because of the particular shape of his eyes or lipline behind the ersatz whiskers.

Arithmetic calculation is often regarded as a quintessential "left-hemisphere" function. That's because most forms of calculation require you to rapidly, sequentially, and cumulatively manipulate precise numerical quantities and relationships. And the handling of discrete, exact details and precise relationships over time is a special province of the left hemisphere. But even here there are exceptions: Geometry and certain kinds of written calculation that require you to align columns of figures (as in long division) may depend as much or more on intact right-hemisphere functioning. Although such calculations are certainly "mathematical,'' they nonetheless depend on a spatially related kind of problem solving.

Or take the ostensibly verbal task of interpreting and analyzing the meaning of a paragraph such as this one.[4] This too can be disrupted by right-hemisphere damage, but not because of any particular difficulty in phonetic-linguistic analysis. Instead, the problem may be a more global derangement in the right-hemisphere ability to integrate complex units into coherent wholes, whether those units be components of written language or something else. And, as pointed out above, the converse is also true. That is, the ability to recognize complex visual forms may preferentially involve the left hemisphere in instances where such form perception depends on first picking up and discriminating important details before synthesizing the image into a recognizable gestalt.[5]

Here's another example: Morse code, to the untrained ear, is processed like any other pattern of possibly interesting, but semantically barren sounds—that is, largely by the right hemisphere. With growing proficiency, however, the telegrapher becomes familiar with what is essentially a new language. The dot-and-dash patterns have come to possess meaning—syntactic and semantic meaning—and it's the left hemisphere that now plays the dominant role in their interpretation.

And this language aspect of Morse code may be affected by brain damage in much the same way as other aspects of language, as the following case illustrates.[6] A fifty-four-year-old ham radio operator suffered an injury to the left temporal lobe as the result of a fall. He wasn't knocked unconscious and, aside from some hesitation in speech, he seemed to be essentially intact—except that his ability to send and receive Morse code messages was reduced from a prior level of forty words a minute down to seven a minute.

Does this prove that there's a ''Morse code center'' in the brain? Not likely. Rather, the ability to process Morse code at forty words a minute requires a high degree of auditory discrimination. It also requires the ability to detect quick temporal sequences of discrete bits of information—in this case, the rapid-fire progression of dots, dashes, and pauses that comprise the grammar and content of Morse code. This is a talent that the language regions of the left hemisphere are especially good at. The disruption of one basic left-hemisphere function—rapid and efficient processing over time—may have had its greatest effect on that particular form of language—Morse code—in which temporal processing is the major feature.

Even music, a traditionally "right hemisphere" function, is handled more by the left hemisphere than the right in trained maestros. If you've had formal musical training, you know that you often just can't *help* yourself from analyzing the component notation or individual melody lines when hearing a piece of music. Music has become for you another language and thus, in large part, a left-hemisphere task. The opposite, predominant right-hemisphere processing, occurs in musical novices who are unschooled in the formal aspects of music theory but who may nevertheless "know what they like."

The experienced musician may delight in a score even more than the casual listener because a more detailed analysis permits a higher level of synthesis. That's one of the reasons, after all, that people take "music appreciation" courses. Similarly, the great painter begins not with his masterpiece, but with laborious drawing and sketching exercises. This is for the purpose of breaking down and mastering the individual components of his art in order to later reconstitute and embellish with his own creative touch. The same with the athlete. And the scientist: The researcher learns his craft by replicating the past experiments and assimilating the acquired data of others; only at a certain level of mastery does it all begin to come together and new ideas spring forth. Indeed, good research designs are frequently said to be "elegant," and new fields or discoveries on the cutting edge are described as "sexy"—all reflecting this interhemispheric melding of the rational with the aesthetic.

That most of us so freely interpose and combine these different ways of apprehending the world is due to the fact that we're normally able to switch flexibly between the two hemispheric modes of cognition. The composer can use precise musical notation to plot out the separate instrumental lines of an orchestral score, then sit back and listen to how the whole thing "sounds." The scientist can let intuitive hunches guide his first forays into a theoretical problem area and then apply the detailed and painstaking rigors of the scientific method to design and carry out the appropriate experiments.

The rest of us, too, need little help from the entrepreneurial "brain-trainers" in applying our innate capacity for interhemispheric multimodal thinking to life's tasks and problems. We're all different in our relative abilities to do this, just as we differ in terms of other strengths and weaknesses. But it's the neuropsychodynamically impoverished person indeed who relies exclusively or predominantly on one or the other style of cognition. Yet, as later chapters will show, there *are* people who seem to do just that—with unfortunate consequences for their overall autonomy, their selfhood.

The Cerebral Hemispheric Basis of Consciousness

I have a cheap plastic imitation-wood plaque hanging in my office, the kind you pick up for a buck at those roadside gas and coffee establishments. It says, "There Are Very Few People Who Think What They Think They Think." Profound, huh? But it shows that we all—philosopher and pump jockey alike—recognize and accept a certain indeterminacy of our mental processes.

We live with the fact that some of our desires, fears, and

motives are beyond the ability of our rational self-reflective consciousness to explain. It's probably safe to say that without the idea of an *unconscious*, there would be no psychodynamic personality theory. Clinical research and common observation both testify to the fact that people frequently behave in certain ways—do certain things, make certain utterances, even harbor certain beliefs—for reasons other than what they *think* those reasons are. Freud[7] recognized this early in his work with neurotic patients. Further, he came to understand that in certain people, an unconscious wish, fear, or conflict could insidiously worm its way into the grain of the personality, only to emerge, perhaps years later, in the form of a symptom or behavior disorder. In addition, Freud[8] came to recognize the role of language in mediating consciousness, and the importance of stripping an idea of its verbal representation in order to keep it repressed.

Before we go on, it should be understood that the term "consciousness" is being used not in the sense of being awake or asleep, but rather in terms of *awareness*. Thus, to be *un*conscious of something is taken here to mean not having access to that thought, feeling, or memory within oneself. This is the way psychoanalysts, the Freudians, use the term, as in "unconscious" motives, wishes, impulses, or conflicts.

Building on the concepts of hemisphericity described earlier in this chapter, a number of modern investigators have begun to apply them to broader questions of consciousness, thought, motivation, and emotion. In so doing, they've often picked freely from other branches of the behavioral sciences, as well as from psychodynamic personality theory.

For example, David Galin[9] regards certain aspects of right-hemisphere functioning as congruent with the type of thinking commonly associated with "unconscious" thought. That is, the right hemisphere figures things out by a nonlinear mode of association, rather than by stepwise logic, and its solutions are based on multiple converging lines of information rather than on a single causal chain of reasoning. The right hemisphere is superior to the left in part-whole relationships, that is, grasping the concept of the whole from just a part.

Conversely, what we ordinarily call conscious "rationality" is viewed by Don Tucker[10] as being associated with the kind of logical, verbal-analytical cognitive representation that requires the left hemisphere's linear and sequential operations. From a neurodevelopmental perspective, Rhawn Joseph[11] regards the very process of thought itself as a left-hemisphere internalization of self-directed language. This, Joseph argues, corresponds to the increased maturation of structures and fiber pathways interconnecting different regions of the cerebral cortex, as well as linking cortical regions with the subcortical brain systems that mediate emotion and motivation.

According to Joseph, thought can be seen as a cumulative integration of action, language, feeling, and motivation. It also involves the progressive development and maturation of the commissural, or interhemispheric fiber pathways that carry information between the two halves of the brain, a process that's not entirely complete until late adolescence. Joseph argues that what we call "thought" is thus a means of organizing, interpreting, and explaining the impulses that arise in the nonlinguistic portions of the nervous system so that the language-oriented regions may achieve understanding.

The left hemisphere's linguistic, self-explicatory ability forms the neural basis for what Stuart Dimond[12] has termed the *generative mechanism of self*. This system interprets and directs the purposive activity of the individual, has special control over most aspects of the conscious self and has a major concern with the individual's interactions with external reality.

Like Joseph, Dimond views mental life as being normally dominated by an ongoing inner monologue, a self-articulation

which is closely linked to the aspects of language functioning that form the basis for the generative mechanism of self.
Right-hemisphere thinking, by contrast, appears more concerned with aspects of *intra*personal reality, the perception
of one's own physiological state and body image. It's less
involved in the negotiation of the individual's needs with
the demands and constraints of the objective, external world.
Thus, says Dimond, self and identity are expressed in what
the person says and does and this has a primarily left-
hemisphere basis.

Dimond's argument is supported by some recent data. One
investigation[13] involved 342 Vietnam War veterans who were
part of the Vietnam Head Injury Study being conducted at
the Walter Reed Medical Center in Washington, D.C. The
original purpose of the study was to examine the relationship between the site of brain damage and whether or not a
soldier experienced unconsciousness or amnesia for events
surrounding the injury.

Each veteran was given a thorough workup, which included a neurologic exam, neuropsychological assessment,
hearing tests, EEGs, and CT scans. The results showed that
injury to the left hemisphere was more likely to have been
associated with a loss of consciousness than injury to the
right. When the right hemisphere was damaged, the preserved wakefulness in the face of brain injury seemed attributable to the intactness of memory processes associated
with the preserved left hemisphere. The left, this study suggested, is more indispensable for consciousness than the
right.

Further evidence comes from the study of a generally less
serious, but more common brain affliction: migraine. Several previous studies had suggested an association between
frequent migraine attacks and memory impairment. So one
team of investigators[14] decided to examine whether there
was a connection between side of headache pain and type
of memory deficit—that is, verbal or visuospatial. To study

this, a group of migraineurs and another group of nonmi-
graine controls were given a battery of tests designed to
assess different aspects of verbal and visuospatial memory.
You'd expect that individuals with left-sided pain (indicating, presumably, that the migraine pathology was on that
side) would show greater memory impairment for verbal
material, while right-sided sufferers would demonstrate
greater visuospatial memory impairment.

The results showed that, compared to controls, migraineurs did indeed demonstrate a memory deficit. But, contrary to expectation, both verbal and visual memory were
impaired in cases of left-sided headache. When the left
hemisphere was not affected, memory for both kinds of material seemed to be relatively intact. Here, as with the head-
injured veterans, there seems to be something unique about
the left hemisphere that renders it especially important for
handling memory processes in general—so crucial, in fact,
that its impairment results in deficits in consciousness and
memory for which the right hemisphere doesn't seem readily
able to compensate.

The explanation probably lies in the left hemisphere's
"verbalness." Alexandr Luria,[15] as we saw in the last chapter, argued that human consciousness and self-control come
to be progressively organized on a verbal basis. Language
guides our awareness and feelings about ourselves and our
world. When this faculty is damaged with injury to the left
hemisphere, a crucial mediating process of consciousness
and memory is impaired. This may explain why the Vietnam vets with damaged right hemispheres, but preserved
left ones, were able to retain consciousness and memory for
the injury event. They were able to encode their experiences
in a verbal, self-explicatory form that rendered the events
more articulable and accessible, both to their own minds
and to others.

Granted, a blow to consciousness caused by a shell frag-
ment ripping through the brain may not be exactly equiva-

lent to a psychological conflict being unconscious due to repression, but the laterality effects suggest that similar mechanisms could operate in both cases. To retain something in "consciousness" implies the intact functioning of a dynamically flexible memory encoding and retrieval system. After all, without a stable memory system, the continuity of consciousness could hardly be ensured. Could failure to verbally encode experiences—especially early childhood experiences—have something to do with why they're so infrequently remembered, why they're in effect "unconscious"? (Scholars of psychoanalytic theory will recognize this as the problem of "infantile amnesia.")

Divided Brains, Divided Selves

Epilepsy can be a crippling disease when it wracks the body with convulsive seizures and impairs the mind through frequent neural storms. Typically, epilepsy begins with a small area of abnormally excitable brain tissue that discharges wildly at varying intervals. The disorganized neural firing can spread to adjacent brain tissue and in some cases may cross the massive fiber bridge between the two hemispheres, the *corpus callosum*, to involve the other hemisphere as well. It's when this happens that a grand mal convulsion usually occurs.

In most cases epilepsy can be controlled or managed by medication. But sometimes even the strongest drugs don't work. Then the task becomes to keep the seizure activity confined to one side of the brain where its effects can at least be lived with. This means surgery. The corpus callosum and often other smaller, less well-known cerebral commisures are severed. The strategy is essentially to "blow the bridges" to keep the invading epileptic army from overtaking the entire territory of the brain. For some, it's the only relief.

This type of surgery, called *commissurotomy*, typically

results in the now-famous *disconnection syndrome* in which information received and processed in one hemisphere cannot directly be utilized by the other.[16] This kind of surgical intervention is not done cavalierly, and so there are only a handful of these "split-brain" cases around to draw conclusions from. Nevertheless, neuropsychologists have learned a great deal about human consciousness by studying these unique individuals.

Following the operation and an adequate period of postsurgical recovery, a curious interhemispheric "competition" frequently manifests itself in which a spontaneous habitual gesture or emotional reaction generated by the right hemisphere will be reported as ego-alien—that is, not part of the self—by the self-articulatory and verbally communicative left hemisphere. For example, the commissurotomized patient may observe his left hand (subserved by the right motor cortex, since motor pathways are usually crossed) to be engaged in some behavior whose origins are unknown to the disconnected left hemisphere. The patient, speaking from his left hemisphere, may then express surprise or alarm that the hand seems, as it were, to have a "will of its own."

By and large, however, these split-brain patients function pretty normally in daily life. In part, this is because they quickly learn to utilize various compensatory cross-cuing strategies to keep the two hemispheric entities in touch with each other. After all, the two eyes can still *see* what each side of the body is doing, so the brain receives feedback from this channel. It's usually only under the experimental constraints of the neuropsychology lab that the two hemispheres are kept in the dark about each other's activities. And that's when things get interesting.

Consider the following experiment, described by Michael Gazzaniga,[17] one of the best-known researchers of disconnection phenomena. The two hemispheres (now disconnected, after commissurotomy) are each presented separately but simultaneously with a different picture on a split viewing screen. The left hemisphere sees a picture of a bird's claw, the right is shown a snow scene. In front of the patient is a series of cards containing such pictures as a rake, lawnmower, apple, toaster, shovel, chicken, and so on. The patient's task is to indicate which card goes with the picture he's currently "seeing" on the viewing screen. The "correct" answer card for the left hemisphere (shown the bird's claw) would be the chicken; the "correct" answer for the right hemisphere (viewing the snow scene) would be the shovel (Fig. 5).

One of Gazzaniga's commissurotomized subjects pointed to the chicken card with his right hand and the shovel card with his left. So far, so good: this "split decision" is what you might expect from a split brain. But when asked to explain the reason for his choices, the patient (speaking, remember, from an isolated left hemisphere), replied, "Oh, that's easy. The chicken claw goes with the chicken and you need a shovel to clean out the chicken shed." Gazzaniga comments:

Here was the left half-brain having to explain why the left hand [subserved by the right hemisphere] was pointing to a shovel when the only picture it saw was a claw. The left brain is not privy to what the right brain saw because of the brain disconnection. Yet, the patient's very own body was doing something. Why was it doing that? Why was the left hand pointing to the shovel? The left brain's cognitive system needed a theory and instantly supplied one that made sense, given the information it had on this particular task.[18]

In some cases, where an image is presented to the right hemisphere only, it may be sufficient to induce an emotional reaction. But without access to the self-explicatory system of the left hemisphere, the individual can't explain the emo-

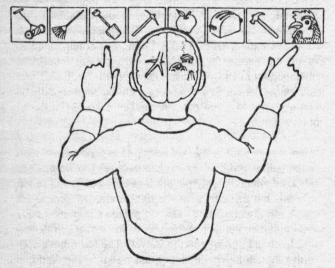

Fig. 5: Gazzaniga's experiment showing how the two disconnected cerebral hemispheres process information in different ways. (From M. S. Gazzaniga & J. E. LeDoux, *The Integrated Mind*. Copyright © 1978 by Plenum Press. Used by permission)

tional reaction either to himself or to anyone else. This was the case for the morally proper commissurotomized woman who was presented with a racy nude scene to her right hemisphere. She blushed, giggled, acted embarrassed, and implied that there might be something perverse about the projection machine. However, for the life of her, she couldn't figure out the actual ''reason'' for her bemused discomfiture. Another patient, responding to a task with her right-hemisphere–controlled left hand, exclaimed, ''I know it wasn't me that did that!''

Cases like these have important implications for the unity of consciousness and the coherence of self. When confronted with confusing or conflicting information that their dissociated hemispheres are unable to handle, the patients don't just sit there inert, but give *some* response, *some* answer to the problem and, most important, *some* post-hoc justification for their behavior. They either *disown* (''It wasn't me'') or *rationalize* (''There's something wrong with the projector'') their reactions, the reasons for which may be obvious to the experimenter but are, as it were, ''unconscious'' to the split-brain patients themselves.

''It wasn't *me*'': How many times have you come up with explanations for your own reactions or behaviors, only to realize later that you were totally off base? All of us fool ourselves this way from time to time; indeed the ability to be aware of our own motives is what we ordinarily refer to as ''self-insight.'' But virtually everyone has two hemispheres whose interactive dynamics almost certainly vary from person to person. Could the differences in people's relative abilities to see into themselves be due to individual variations in functional interhemispheric coherence? And could some people—those, for example, with pitiably small levels of self-insight—resemble split-brain patients in function, if not in structure?

Gazzaniga himself develops this idea in the direction of postulating separate ''modules'' of the mind that can operate independently and often at cross-purposes with one another. But I want to carry this further, to show how the neuropsychology of consciousness revealed by studies of hemispheric asymmetry can form one of the pillars of our neuropsychodynamic theory of personality.

These studies of surgically commissurotomized patients suggest that the isolated right hemisphere can sustain a whole range of emotional responses and goals separate and divergent from those of the left. Klaus Hoppe[19] goes even further in proposing that commissurotomy produces an interhemispheric interruption of the preconscious stream of thought, the kind of mentation that goes on just beyond the fringe of awareness. This, he argues, results in a separation of "word-representations" from "thing-representations," words from images, a distinction first made by Freud.[20] In addition, commissurotomy results in a predominance of unanalyzed unconscious activity in the right hemisphere, since access to conscious linguistic-analytic cognition is interrupted.

Hoppe believes that in some otherwise intact individuals a *functional commissurotomy* may develop by an as yet undetermined form of cross-callosal inhibition. This inhibition or blocking occurs, not as the result of actual surgery or organic brain damage, but as a form of "functional" alteration in neuropsychological processing. Unconscious mental events can then develop a life of their own and thereby form the basis for what is observed clinically as repression.

More important, such a process may be associated with a more general inability to develop fresh insights into one's own behavior and ways of relating to the external world. Functionally disconnected from the right, the verbal left hemisphere cannot articulate to the self the nonrational, imagistic, and emotionally charged content of the right hemisphere's mental activity; this activity, then, remains for all intents and purposes "unconscious."

Galin provides an example of how this kind of functional disconnection syndrome might underlie the repression of psychological conflicts. Suppose a mother presents her child with a positive verbal message (''What a good boy!''), but at the same time delivers a negative nonverbal one (she says it with a scowl or a sarcastic inflection). If the interhemispheric communication system is dysfunctional or inadequately developed, each hemisphere will perceive and interpret the separate aspects of the mother's message. Since the left hemisphere constitutes the self-articulatory system, the verbally identified self—or ego—will react to and behave in accordance with the verbal message. At the same time, however, the emotional reactions elicited by the nonverbal aspects of the message will continue to operate ''below the surface.'' This is because the right hemisphere has processed this information in its own way, but is barred from communicating with the left. This leaves the mental content without benefit of conscious-verbal consolidation.

In future situations where female or parent-like authority figures provide a certain type of communication the person will experience a negative emotional reaction. But because of inadequate interhemispheric transfer and consolidation at the early stage of development, the basis for this confusion has remained unanalyzed, unarticulated, nonego-integrated and therefore ''repressed.'' In these situations, the hapless person may experience waves of anguish without any consciously recognized cause and will thus undergo what the clinician labels as ''conflict.''

The Development of Consciousness and Self-Awareness—The Role of Language

Rhawn Joseph has approached this problem from an explicitly neurodevelopmental point of view. Recall that Joseph views thinking as a left-hemisphere internalization of language that allows self-articulation and thereby selfconsciousness to develop. Joseph emphasizes both the motivational and, like Luria, the sociodevelopmental aspects of speech-thought development. Accordingly, the earliest forms of communication, and thus social speech, are embedded in emotional activity, since emotional speech provides a context within which meaning-laden associations may be formed and value systems developed. Language slowly develops from the association of these sets of vocalization-experience pairings.

As the left hemisphere continues to mature and develop, a second aspect of language emerges, one that arises through interactions and associations with the external world. This Joseph calls *denotative speech*. Although it emerges out of relationships originally having an emotional basis, denotative—or social—language is concerned with naming functions and statements of fact, belief, and assertion. As such, denotative language is closely bound with cognitive activity and the eventual expression of one's thoughts. What we ordinarily regard as mature human thinking, however, doesn't actually appear until much later in development. Moreover, it remains influenced by social-emotional language throughout life. And, as pointed out earlier in this book, what we say, as much as what we do, is virtually always tied to some complex web of short- and long-term plans, motives, and aspirations.

Following the Russian psychologist Lev Vygotsky[21] (who also strongly influenced Luria), Joseph describes *egocentric speech* as the linguistic structure from which thought will arise and which always appears in a social context. Egocentric speech is actually the first self-directed form of communication, which in turn heralds the first attempts at self-regulation. You've seen this—it's the kind of cute, self-directed ''baby talk'' that young children often engage in when they're wrapped up in some play activity or other engaging task.

In later childhood and adolescence, egocentric speech develops into truly *inner speech*, the kind of mature self-articulatory language that we use for autonomous self-regulation. Inner speech occurs largely internally and for most people relatively automatically. For example, when you reflect on some problem or plan, you usually don't sit there saying strings of sentences in your head. Rather, your use of inner speech is covert, automatized, and becomes overtly expressed in syntactic language only when your mental activity hits particularly rough territory. In such cases you then "think out loud," resorting momentarily to egocentric speech to help you clarify some of the more difficult material; or you may write it out, which is essentially the same thing. Most heavy-duty intellectual work requires the flexible oscillation between these different types of thinking, but virtually all are ultimately tied to the faculty of language.

Thus, with regard to consciousness, egocentric speech may be a function of the left hemisphere's attempt to organize and make sense of behavior initiated in part by the right half of the brain. Because early in life the child's interhemispheric communication is incomplete, the left hemisphere uses language to explain to itself the behavior in which it observes the child-person as a whole to be engaged. As the commissures mature and intra- and interhemispheric information flow increases, the left hemisphere also acts to linguistically organize its internal experiences.

As the child further develops, interhemispheric information exchange continues to grow and the left-hemisphere language substrate increasingly acts to organize, as well as to inhibit, sensory-emotional right-hemisphere experiences and behaviors. Rather than passively observing these sensory-emotional actions as they occur, the left hemisphere now actively engages in the formulation of behavior, achieving understanding *prior* to the occurrence of that behavior.

It's almost as if the growing child does a split-brain number in reverse. Or is it the other way around—does commissurotomy force a neuropsychological reversion to a more developmentally primitive state of consciousness? At first, the child's left hemisphere has to overtly explain to itself what the right hemisphere is doing, thinking, and experiencing, in similar fashion to the cross-cuing that commissurotomized patients employ. Later, the maturing of the interhemispheric pathways allows this intrabrain communication to occur internally and automatically.

For the growing child, then, an important stage in development comes when the interpretation or evaluation of an incipient behavior *precedes* its execution. Behavior no longer has to be carried out, and its effect on the environment overtly observed, in order for self-awareness and self-regulation to occur. Vygotsky saw this process as corresponding to the transformation of egocentric speech into true inner speech. In Joseph's neuropsychological formulation, it represents the maturation of the left-hemisphere mechanisms responsible for self-articulation.

What this means is that you don't have to wait passively for an event to happen and you don't actually have to carry out some activity before being able to evaluate its potential effects. Rather, by using self-explicatory language, you can plan actions and anticipate consequences *before* they occur. Most important, self-explicatory language enables you to integrate these plans, projections, and anticipatory activities into your evolving self-concept. Since the ability to do this depends on the development of adequate language functioning, which in turn depends on a certain level of interhemispheric maturation, it's clear why our search for identity—for selfhood—is rarely consolidated before adolescence or early adulthood.

Evidence suggests that the neuropsychological substrate for the linguistic-rational capacity of the left hemisphere matures later in life than does the substrate for the right hemisphere's spatial and emotional functioning. The young child, then, has insufficient left-brain wherewithal to verbally self-articulate and integrate the desires and passions generated by its own needs and by its interactions with the physical and social worlds. To compound the problem, the cerebral commissures themselves are insufficiently developed, so that what little interhemispheric integration might yet occur in the mature brain is further inhibited from operating. In this respect, Joseph goes on to say,

> The curious asymmetrical arrangement of function and maturation may well predispose the developing organism to later come upon situations in which it finds itself responding emotionally, nervously, anxiously or "neurotically" without linguistic knowledge, or without even the possibility of linguistic understanding as to the cause, purpose, eliciting stimulus or origin of its behavior. Instead, like the egocentric child, the individual may be faced with behavior that he may explain only after it occurs: "I don't know what came over me."[22]

Or "It wasn't *me* that did that."

And so, consciousness—in the sense of being "aware"— is a process that appears to depend inextricably on the language system of the left hemisphere and its interactions with the more experiential and less reflective right. It's not that the left hemisphere is conscious and the right unconscious. Rather, the verbal self-articulatory facility of the left hemisphere allows the *person* as a whole to function as a reflectively self-conscious being, to conceptualize both external events and inner states in ways that "make sense" and are relatively predictable. This, then, forms an important basis for a stable identity—a self.

On the other hand, the diffuse awareness processes of the right hemisphere allow consciousness to have a broader beam, to apprehend outer events and inner states that have no easy verbal-conceptual representation. This, too, is integrated into the self-system to help form the shadings and colorings of the individual personality, to give the personality a certain degree of spontaneity, charm, and even mystery.

And what gives the overall interhemispheric system its

dynamic impetus with respect to personality functioning is its interaction with the frontal lobe action-volition system described in the last chapter. According to our neuropsychodynamic model, the construction of a personal identity involves the elaboration of self-generated and reflectively evaluated self-schemas, as well as the integration of these schemas into a cohesive personality framework.

In this view, the left-hemisphere verbal self-articulatory system operates, with frontal lobe guidance, both to guide behavior and to appraise feedback from that behavior's impact on the physical and social worlds. In this way is self-knowledge progressively developed and an identity hewn from the consciousness-emotion-activity mélange of successive life experiences. The increasingly volitional control of the verbal articulatory capacity also enables the person to explicitly communicate, with progressive degrees of refinement, facets of identity—feelings, desires, perspectives—to *others*, even as *self*-communication evolves correspondingly. This process further facilitates the development of a unique personal identity and so imbues behavior with the volition necessary for truly autonomous action.

Problems arise when extreme maldevelopment or imbalance occurs in the frontal-interhemispheric system, where one hemispheric "style" of processing abnormally predominates or recedes. Then, rather than simply resulting in a pleasantly eccentric variation in personality, the person's neuropsychodynamics may produce internal misery or drive him into destructive confrontations with his fellows. As we'll see in Part III of this book, too concentrated and rationalistic an internal focus may be associated with obsessive-compulsive or paranoid personalities; an overreliance on whim or impulse may be the mark of the psychopath or hysteric. And in later chapters we'll explore the implications of the frontal-interhemispheric system—the interfacing of action and volition with thought and consciousness—for human creative potential and its failures.

But first we must encounter one more brain system—the final pillar of our basic neuropsychodynamic model—a system that's essential for the full expression of human identity and personality. This is the system that deals with feelings, with needs and wants, with passions.

CHAPTER 5

THE PASSIONS OF SELF

Motivation and Emotion

Without passion, man is a mere latent force and possibility, like the flint which awaits the shock of the iron before it can give forth its spark.

—HENRI FREDERIC AMIEL

All emotions are pure which gather you and lift you up; that emotion is impure which seizes only one side of your being and so distorts you.

—RAINER MARIA RILKE

Was she going crazy?

The patient, a fifty-three-year-old woman we'll call Mary, seemed to be suffering from a very strange affliction. At thirty-three, she'd had a seizure, her first. Thereafter, she began experiencing what she described as "mild spells," the main feature of which was a disturbing feeling of "fullness" in her head. Her doctor put her on anticonvulsant medication and she did fine until, twenty years after the first attack, she appeared at a Canadian neuropsychiatric clinic complaining that the spells were back. In addition, she was now experiencing bizarre sensations of movement and pressure that, she said, were making her "go crazy." When she was examined, her mood was found to be depressed and her thoughts suicidal, although many of the typical features of clinical depression, such as appetite disturbance, were absent.

At the clinic, a medical team headed by neurologist Trevor Hurwitz[1] used the latest neuropsychiatric research technology to study Mary's condition. This included a combination of EEG brain-wave recording and simultaneous videotape monitoring, the idea being to try and catch both the electrophysiological and the behavioral manifestations of the seizure at the same time.

What they found was that Mary was depressed, all right, but not simply as a psychological reaction to her disturbing condition. Instead, the mood and thought disturbances were part of the seizure syndrome itself. Moreover, abnormal neuroelectrical discharges from the two sides of Mary's brain were producing distinct psychological and emotional symptoms.

For example, following left-hemisphere seizures, Mary became depressed and agitated, couldn't sleep, and considered killing herself. Voices told her she was "bad" and the phrase "googli googli" seemed to emanate from her radio. Following right-sided attacks, her mood switched to elation and her behavior became flighty. She danced in her bed and made seductive advances toward the hospital staff. Shades of Eve and Sybil! It was as if the left side of Mary's brain had a different mood—even a different personality—from the right. Why?

The Brain's Organization of Moods and Motives

As we saw in the previous chapter, the two cerebral hemispheres share the workload of daily cognitive tasks involving language, memory, imagery, and abstract thought. To recap: For most people, the left hemisphere is specialized for language, for numerical calculation and for sequential, logical analysis and problem solving. The left is good at perceiving details and particulars and at making literal, descriptive, and coldly logical interpretations of information and events. By contrast, the right hemisphere is specialized for spatial processing and for the synthesis of images and forms. The right brain is also more intuitive and inferential and generally takes a more symbolic and associational approach to information processing.

Normally, the two hemispheres operate cooperatively so that, for example, the consummately successful scientist or business executive is the one who not only shows proficiency in making quick calculations and implementing complex, orderly programs, but can also marshal a certain degree of intuitive insight, of nonrational experiential "edge." This allows him or her to appreciate and deal with the wider implications of a particular experiment or marketing strategy and to gauge the reactions of coworkers or the public at large.

But while these left-brain–right-brain differences in *cognition* have been fairly well established, only more recently have neuropsychologists begun to train their clinical and empirical armamentarium on the question of *feelings*. This research is yielding valuable clues as to how emotions and motivations, passions and fears, might be understandable in terms of brain organization.

Actually, since before the turn of the century, neurologists had noted that left-hemisphere damage resulting in disorders of movement, and sometimes speech, was often accompanied by what came to be called the *catastrophic reaction*. Unable to verbally express frustration over his disability, the left-hemisphere stroke or head-trauma patient would suddenly explode into tears, yelling, cursing, and sullenly refusing to cooperate with therapists and caretakers. Sometimes the reaction was less violent, showing itself merely as an agitated depression or stony muteness. Complaints of disability well beyond the degree expected from the objective nature of the injury were common. Added to this was a bleak hopelessness about future prospects for recovery or readjustment to a normal life. The overall impression seemed to be one of pervasive disconsolateness over the patient's deficits and the presumed dire implications for life ahead.

By contrast, injury to the right hemisphere, producing

equivalent physical disability, was more likely to be associated with a strange indifference to impairment, an often bland, sometimes even jovial repudiation of even the very *idea* that anything might be wrong. In extreme cases, such patients might actually deny that the paralyzed limbs belonged to them, attributing their ownership to the next patient or even to the doctor. When directly confronted with the fact of his disability, a patient might respond with all manner of facile evasion: "I'd like to raise my arm for you, Doc, but I'm a little tired right now." Or, "Whaddya mean move this leg? It isn't even my leg."

On occasion, a hemiplegic patient—paralyzed on one side of his body—might attempt to walk on nonfunctioning limbs or a neurologically blind patient might try to navigate through the hospital wards. This denial of or indifference to illness came to be known as *anosognosia* and most typically is seen as a consequence of right-hemisphere damage.[2]*

Thus it seemed that cases of left-hemisphere injury were prone to produce a morbid overconcern with disability, while damage to the right hemisphere often resulted in a blithe imperturbability, an incongruent cheeriness. This emotional reaction occurs in addition to whatever physical or sensory disability is produced directly by the brain damage and it colors the patient's perception of and attitude toward these objective deficits.

However, observations such as these generally remained at the level of individual clinical description until only recently, when Italian investigator Guido Gainotti[3] carried out one of the first controlled studies on the hemisphericity of emotion. In a group of patients with unilateral brain damage, Gainotti carefully recorded the side of the damage, as

---

* Historical note: Woodrow Wilson is reported to have suffered from this syndrome (the result of a stroke) in the last days of his presidency.

well as each patient's speech, emotional reactions, and general behavior.

He found that depression and anxiety, in some cases profound enough to qualify as catastrophic reactions, occurred far more frequently when the injury affected the left hemisphere, especially if there were also disorders of speech and communication. The right-damaged patients, by contrast, casually denied or made light of their deficits and joked offhandedly about their condition. In some cases, in true anosognosic form, they vehemently denied owning the affected limbs; it sure wasn't *their* arm or leg that was paralyzed—this dead appendage must belong to someone else. Thus, Gainotti was able to carefully document the changes that until then had been reported only anecdotally.

But, as with cognition, the cerebral organization of emotion seems to involve more than just a left-right hemispheric dimension; there's an anterior-posterior aspect as well. More recently, this has been extensively researched by Robert Robinson and his colleagues,[4] who've discovered a definite relationship between the side of the brain lesion and its proximity to the frontal pole. That is, not only the laterality, but also the "front-backness" of the injury within a given hemisphere is important.

In one study, stroke patients whose lesions were localizable by CT scan were given a comprehensive set of physiological, neuropsychological, psychiatric, and mood measures. The most severe depressive reactions were found to occur in patients with lesions in the anterior part of the left hemisphere. The closer the injury was to the frontal pole, the more likely there was to be an emotional effect. Moreover, while left-frontal damage seemed to result in depression, right-frontal damage produced an undue cheerfulness, a blasé attitude toward the disability.

In the light of the lessons of the previous two chapters, could this have something to do with the role of the frontal lobes in using inner speech for self-evaluation and anticipation of future consequences? That is, are the frontal lobes necessary for self-evaluating and self-identifying not only thoughts and actions, but feelings? Before trying to answer these questions, let's consider another important aspect of emotion—emotional communication.

Talking Blues, Silent Screams: The Languages of Feeling

Neurologists have long known that left-hemisphere damage can produce the varied forms of language disorder collectively known as *aphasias*. In some cases, this involves an inability to understand the speech of others. In other cases, speech comprehension may be relatively intact, but the ability to spontaneously produce spoken language is impaired. Still other patients with more extensive brain damage may be affected in both capacities. More rarely, certain other syndromes may occur, for example, an inability to repeat phrases spoken by the examiner, despite relatively preserved spontaneous speech and comprehension. Or the opposite: Repetition is intact and may even have an imitative, echo-like quality, but either comprehension or spontaneous speech is impaired. In yet other instances, reading or writing may be preserved, while oral language functions are affected—or vice versa.

These aphasic syndromes occur with sufficient frequency that neuropsychologists have been able to extensively catalog and study them. In most cases, they occur as the result of left-hemisphere injury, particularly when it occurs around the middle portion of the hemisphere. But *right*-brain damage can also lead to problems in communication of another, more insidious kind.

During the last decade or so, neuropsychologists began to note that damage to the right hemisphere, which left basic language functions intact, could nevertheless produce disorders of prosodic communication. *Prosody* refers to the inflective, tonal, and emotional quality of spoken language, the aspect of speech that enables the listener to determine if a particular statement (such as ''You're the boss'') is meant to be declarative or interrogative, serious or sarcastic, happy or sad, bland or charged with emotion. Much of the communicative richness of social speech is carried by these nuances or prosody. The same words can bite, caress, or tease, depending on how they're uttered and with what accompaniment of facial expression and body language. (In writing, such qualities are usually conveyed by punctuation, context, or the skillful arrangement of the words themselves; this is partly what we mean when we talk about a writer's ''style.'')

Elliot Ross and his colleagues[5] have studied a class of emotional-communication disorders that they've termed the *aprosodias*. These are found in association with right-hemisphere damage. Just as aphasics have trouble communicating or understanding the verbal content of conversation, aprosodics' problems are with the emotional tone normally conveyed through changes in voice inflection and emphasis. This difficulty occurs even though the raw linguistic content may be preserved in a sort of emotionally disembodied state. Thus, a right-hemisphere patient's complaint ''I feel like hell, I wish I were dead'' may be delivered in a flat, deadpan, aprosodic manner. Because of this, the examining clinician may not take such a complaint too seriously, even though inwardly the patient is really profoundly depressed.

Oliver Sacks[6] has provided a vivid account of the differences in comprehension problems experienced by two types of patients—one apparently a group of aphasics, and another patient, seemingly aprosodic—while listening to a TV speech by former president Ronald Reagan. In Sacks's account, the aphasics, unable to comprehend the verbal content of the speech, laughed uproariously at what they obviously took to be the exaggerated and insincerely prosodic political posings of this former thespian, this "Great Communicator." These patients' intact perception of affective tone, standing out much more keenly in the absence of the usual blending with grammatical and informational content, made them especially sensitive to the studied histrionics of the political speech. This they found wildly amusing, and Sacks speculates that, in this sense at least, "one cannot lie to an aphasic."

Another patient was a former English teacher, whose life-long devotion to formal exactness in language had, if anything, only been intensified by a right-hemisphere aprosodia that left her dumb to inflective nuance. Her sense of the syntax, semantics, and organization of speech was unusually sharp, and she was watching the same speech with obvious dismay. The president "is not cogent," she remarked. "He does not speak good prose. His word use is improper. Either he is brain-damaged or he has something to hide."

What can we conclude? For one thing, we tend automatically to think of cerebral damage in terms of deficit, as necessarily obscuring or distorting reality. Yet cases like these remind us that it is we—the ones with the ostensibly healthy brains—who may at times be more susceptible to the blandishments and subterfuges of others. It seems that it's actually the normal semantically-prosodically integrated faculty of speech understanding that may mislead; dissected by brain damage into its constituent elements, spoken communication lies naked and exposed—insincere orators become objects of derision. How much of reality, then, do our brains manufacture out of the elements of experience in order to allow us to function in what we *believe* to be the "real world"?

And remember Mr. Spock? His coldly analytical, non-emotional cognitive style affords him a superior level of bullshit-detection only insofar as he can extract the true semantic meaning from the emotional medium in which it's embedded. But when the medium *is* the message, when the impact of the communication relies on picking up the nuances of emotional coloring, Spock is like an aprosodic patient listening to a comedy stand-up routine: He just doesn't "get it," and must defer to the prosodically facile humans to interpret the message.

Those who prize rationality above all else should realize that two left brains would no more facilitate true human communication than two right hands would make a better ballplayer. Yet, as we'll see in later chapters, in some cases the problem may actually be in the other direction: Many people aren't rational *enough*. Again, it's the *balance* that's important, and this brings us back to emotion and *its* balances.

Balances of Brainpower

It doesn't necessarily take a major brain trauma like stroke or head injury to produce problems in emotional regulation. In people suffering from certain forms of epilepsy, emotional disorders may be one component—sometimes the only observable component—of the seizure syndrome.

Seizures occur when neurons in one or more regions of the brain become intensely excited in an abnormally prolonged and indiscriminate fashion. The symptoms vary widely, depending on which parts of the brain are affected and to what extent the seizure activity spreads over the rest of the brain. In most cases, the particular form of the attack is typical for a given individual. If motor regions are affected, twitches and convulsions may result. Involvement of sensory areas may produce tinglings, flashes, or strange noises. Abnormal stimulation of subcortical limbic system structures involved in emotion and memory may result in dreamy states, déjà vu, feelings of fear or rage, or even mystical experiences. In many cases the site of the disturbance, called the *seizure focus*, cannot be reliably determined; sometimes this is complicated even more by the tendency of the electrophysiological disturbance to spread to other brain regions.

Which brings us back to Mary's case, which opened this chapter. While most seizure sufferers have only one focus of abnormal or unstable electrical activity, Mary seems to have been blighted with *two* such trouble spots—one in each hemisphere. What may have been going on, Hurwitz and his team of investigators suggest, is that the seizure in the left hemisphere disrupted its modulating influence on the right. The right hemisphere may have an innate emotional bias toward experiences and expressions of negative emotion, toward a worldview of gloom and doom. Consequently, the disruption of cross-callosal modulation by an electrophysiological storm in the left hemisphere would have left the right side free to express its exaggeratedly baleful emotional style. Conversely, Mary's right-side seizures stymied that hemisphere's ability to control the left, releasing, in exaggerated fashion, what appears to be the left hemisphere's inherently cheerful, impulsive, and manic-like emotional style.

This might also explain the effects of unilateral brain injury discussed earlier. That is, a stroke or gunshot wound to the left hemisphere "releases" the right hemisphere's anxious-depressed emotional style, and this is what accounts for the clinically observed catastrophic reaction. Conversely, right-hemisphere damage sets free the cockeyed optimist that lives within the left hemisphere, accounting for the often cheery denial of disability and facile disowning of impaired appendages.

It seems, then, as if the two sides of the brain normally act in a mutual cross-modulatory relationship, a state of what neuropsychologists have termed *reciprocal inhibition*. Each side keeps the other's innate response bias in check so that the result in a healthy brain is a smooth pattern of interhemispheric coordination. The effect of unilateral damage is to remove this modulation from one side of the equation with a resulting exaggeration of the emotional style of the opposite side—rather as if unilateral hemispheric disarmament leads to dominance by a cerebral co-power. Rather than one hemisphere being emotional and the other rational as many used to think, it seems rather that the two hemispheres are specialized for different *kinds* of emotion, just as they handle different kinds of cognitive skills (Fig. 6).

And to see this effect, you needn't look only at the brain-injured. Geoffrey Ahern and Gary Schwartz[7] hooked up a group of college students to an apparatus that measures EEG waveforms indicating different states of brain activity. The subjects were asked a series of sixty questions, each designed to elicit one of ten different psychological states. These varied according to what kind of mood they evoked and whether they involved verbal or spatial thinking.

They found that not only did there appear to be genuine hemispheric differences in emotional and cognitive brain dominance, but that this dominance depended on the kind of psychological function in question and the part of the brain involved. The emotional component—left hemisphere for happy, right hemisphere for sad—occurred in the region of the brain's frontal lobes, a finding that corroborates Robinson's studies with stroke patients. The cognitive aspect—left hemisphere for verbal, right hemisphere for visuospatial—were found in more posterior areas of the brain, which handle complex perceptual analysis.

For ordinary people, then, the pattern of hemispheric dominance for emotion seems to be like that found in brain-damaged subjects. That is, the left hemisphere is more specialized for positive emotions and the right hemisphere for negative feelings—but, it would appear, this holds true only (or at least mainly) when the brain's frontal lobes are involved. This further underscores the idea that normal emotional experience and expression depends on an interaction between the anterior-posterior and left-right dimen-

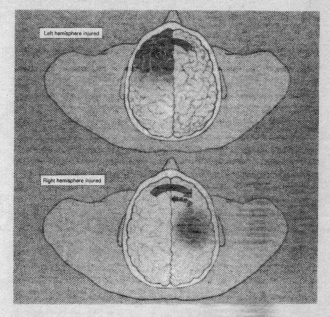

Fig. 6: The principle of interhemispheric cross-modulation as it applies to the control of emotion. When the left hemisphere is injured, depression often results. Injury to the right hemisphere often produces indifference or euphoria. Some neuropsychologists propose that in normal states, the left and right hemispheres mutually control one another's emotional tone; disturbance of one hemisphere allows the opposite's emotional bias to predominate, thus coloring the person's whole mood. (From L. Miller, ''The Emotional Brain,'' *Psychology Today*, February 1988. Used by permission of *Psychology Today* magazine. Copyright © 1988 by PT Partners, L.P.)

sions, that neuropsychodynamics play themselves out within a complex three-dimensional framework.

Sadness and Beyond: Lessons from Depression

For some people, unfortunately, negative emotional states don't have to be artificially induced as part of an experiment. They're depressed enough on their own, their gloomy worldviews graying out life's highlights of color, which most of us take for granted. Schaffer and colleagues[8] administered the Beck Depression Inventory to a group of college students and selected those who scored as most characteristically depressed. Compared to nondepressed students, the depressed subjects showed heightened EEG activation over the right frontal region of the brain. Could this mean that in chronically depressed individuals, the morose right hemisphere is working overtime?

Yet these students, angst-ridden though they may have been, were still functioning more or less adequately in their everyday worlds, despite their gloomy states. For some people, however, depression is more than an annoying disturbance of mood; it's a crippling affliction that saps the will and disrupts even the most basic human functions. If hemispheric imbalance plays a role in this syndrome, perhaps an understanding of its nature could lead to more effective treatments.

For example, one approach to the psychotherapy of depression emphasizes helping the patient to restructure his perceptions of his illness and of the world in general. This *cognitive therapy*, pioneered by Aaron Beck and others[9] focuses on how the depressed person thinks about various issues affecting his life. By encouraging the patient to develop different perspectives on the various problems, cognitive therapists hope that a new, healthier way of functioning will emerge. In some cases, this therapy has been shown to be as effective in improving mood and motivation as antidepressant medication.[10]

But what if the depressive illness *itself* inhibits the very neuropsychological bases for such important cognitive skills as reasoning, understanding, and perspective-taking? The biochemical changes in depressive illness, like physical damage to the right brain itself, seem to impair some of the basic cognitive skills that might otherwise help the depressed patient to effectively deal with the illness and its effects. *Unlike* physical brain damage, however, the effects seem to clear up when the depression does, at least to some degree. This suggests that one fruitful direction of neuropsychological research might be to find out what kinds of therapeutic strategies work best in compensating for the psychological deficits seen while the person is clinically depressed and consequently at a cognitive disadvantage.

If, for example, the depressed patient has difficulty using certain right-hemisphere cognitive strategies like intuition or empathy, perhaps a more concrete, logical, left-hemisphere form of therapy would be more effective. The application of neuropsychological principles to the development of more effective treatment strategies is an exciting, but as yet virtually untapped, area for future study.

The Emotional Brain—Multiple Dimensions

As we've seen, the brain's control of emotion can be conceived of as depending on a system of interhemispheric checks and balances. According to this view, each hemisphere's activity serves to keep the other's in line. Disturbances in mood occur either because one hemisphere gets too excited, overriding the opposite's control, or because the other hemisphere's functioning falls abnormally low, in turn "releasing" the contralateral, or opposite-side, hemisphere.

Harold Sackeim[11] goes even further. He suggests that neuropsychological control over negative moods is *by nature* greater than over positive moods—which is another way of saying that the brain's intrinsic organization naturally predisposes humans to feel sadder rather than happier, and that's why more control is needed over the gloom-and-doom mechanism. Under normal circumstances, a combination of internal and external factors operates continuously to keep these mood fluctuations more or less consistent with our changing life's situations.

Indeed, we sometimes go to impressive lengths to preserve the state of optimum emotional equilibrium we feel most comfortable with. If a particularly rotten piece of luck befalls us we tell ourselves it's just a fluke, so don't worry about it. If we make total fools of ourselves, do something we know is wrong, or take advantage of someone in a way that violates our ethical values, we rationalize: Nobody noticed, it wasn't *really* stealing, the schmuck deserved it, and so on. In this way we keep ourselves from feeling too guilty, too disappointed, too out of control, too brought down.

It works the other way, too. When we're feeling especially good about ourselves, proud of an accomplishment, excited by a new prospect, we allow ourselves to revel, but still manage to keep some kind of reasonable lid on it. Don't get carried away, we tell ourselves, maintain a perspective on the situation, keep both feet (okay, at least one foot) on the ground. Thus, for most of us, the optimal emotional state is a sort of contented equanimity. *Too* much of either elation or melancholy is perceived as unnatural. It's as if there's some ideal standard of emotional homeostasis that we're continually trying to self-tune through our thoughts, actions, and relationships with other people.

Still, we tend to avoid bad feelings more vigorously than good ones. As we'll see in a later chapter, people who are into drugs typically choose substances that make them feel better, not worse. This tendency toward trying to keep ourselves in a positive frame of mind may be a reaction to the brain-based negative emotional bias that Sackeim postulates—a bias that's inherent in the nature of the mutual reciprocal-inhibition system of the two cerebral hemispheres.

Accordingly, anything that jars the neural system as a

whole—injury to the brain, the biochemical disruptions of a depressive illness, the experience of a traumatic loss, and so on—is going to have a greater disinhibiting, or releasing, effect on negative emotions, since they're the most "primed" to burst forth in the first place. People who develop depressive illnesses, says Sackeim, aren't necessarily inclined to feel sadder than the rest of us. Instead, it's a matter of recovery time. Whereas you or I may become temporarily totaled by fortune's occasional slings and arrows, we usually bounce back pretty quickly and intactly. Not so with the depressed patient. He or she seems to suffer from an inability to inhibit the depressed reaction, once it gets started. The more depressed the person becomes, the more he or she suffers from this kind of emotional hemispheric disinhibition; the greater the disinhibition, the greater the depression, and so on in a positively accelerating vicious cycle. "Depressives," says Sackeim, "have faulty brakes."

But this mutual hemispheric watchdog system may not be the whole story. Robert Robinson's group has recently been studying patients with injury to *both* cerebral hemispheres. If it were simply a matter of reciprocal hemispheric disinhibition, the effects ought to cancel one another out—the patient with damage to both hemispheres shouldn't seem appreciably happier or sadder than before the injury. Instead, preliminary research suggests that it's the left hemisphere that dominates in the overall coloring of mood. When both sides of the brain are damaged the subjects become depressed, much as in the case of unilateral left-hemisphere damage—it's as if the coexisting right-hemisphere injury just didn't count.[12]

According to Don Tucker,[13] in fact, Robinson's findings could be viewed as evidence *against* the reciprocal-inhibition hypothesis. Instead, such research suggests that, in some cases at least, a brain lesion might disinhibit its *own* hemisphere's functioning. The frontal lobes, after all, are the chief brain system involved in the regulation of behavior as a whole, and this includes emotional behavior. In Tucker's model, the frontal portions of the brain normally exert control over the emotional mechanisms mediated by more posterior brain regions. Thus, according to Tucker, the main division of the brain may be a front-back one, rather than a left-right dichotomy—an *intra*hemispheric control system.[14]

But there's even more to the story. Remember, our neuropsychodynamic concept of the brain is a three-dimensional structure, not a flat map. Tucker believes that the relevant dimensions of emotional control include not just left-right and anterior-posterior, but cortical-subcortical aspects as well. That is, to understand the brain's role in emotion and motivation (and probably in most other functions as well), we have to take into account how the front-back and left-right dimensions of the cortical parts of the cerebral hemispheres interact as well with the up-down perspective.

The relevant subcortical systems consist of structures in the *limbic system* and elsewhere (Fig. 7) that lie deep within the brain and that arose early in evolution to regulate the basic functions of movement, attention, perception, motivation, emotion, and memory. In mammals, especially humans, the overlying cortex has progressively evolved to elaborate, extend, and fine-tune the workings of these subcortical structures. We still carry these "primitive" brain systems within us, but their functioning has been shaped in a human direction by their interactions with the cortex that evolved out of them over the eons. Overall, this allows for a tremendous increase in the range and variety of brain-based capacities like learning, communicating, and perhaps also feeling.

Tucker hypothesizes that the left hemisphere may have a general *activation* role in behavior, a function that is neuroanatomically tied to frontal mechanisms and with subcortical structures located ventrally, that is, at the base of the brain. On the other hand, right hemisphere-mediated *arousal*

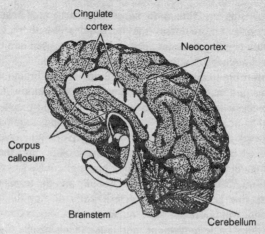

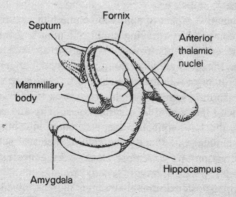

Fig. 7: This drawing of the *limbic system* shows its major component structures and how it fits into the rest of the brain. The limbic system plays an important role in emotion, motivation, learning, and memory. (From J. Winson, *Brain and Psyche: The Biology of the Unconscious*. Copyright © 1985 by J. Winson. Used by permission of Doubleday, a division of Bantam, Doubleday, Dell Publishing Group, Inc.)

mechanisms are linked to subcortical structures that are posterior and more dorsal (that is, topside). Whether a given emotion is pleasant or unpleasant is superimposed upon this three-dimensional activation/arousal framework.

According to this model, left-anterior-ventral brain mechanisms are associated with movement and motivation— hence their activating or "drive" function—and their emotional concomitants can include either happy anticipation (positive) or anxious trepidation (negative). When you're activated in the positive sense, you're looking into the future, ready to move, focused on a plan or activity and filled with anticipation. You feel "motivated" and the terms used to describe people who characteristically display this type of cognitive-emotional style reflect the intimate connection with more basic movement-motivation mechanisms: She's a "go-getter," we're "on the move," he enjoys "the thrill of the chase," and so on.

The negative aspect of activation comes out in ruminative fear, a compulsive worrying about potential outcomes and implications, an anticipatory trepidation about events to come or the possible dire consequences of our behavior. Positive or negative, the emphasis is on *action*, past, present, or future, something which we've seen is intimately tied in with the frontal lobe system of activity and volition. In man, the left-hemisphere aspect comes into play when we use language to specify the contingencies of activation and motivation: We *articulate* plans, *voice* concerns, *speak* our minds, *express* motives, and so on.

The right-posterior-dorsal system is more involved in perception and awareness—arousal in the sense of a holistic "taking in" of the environment. Positive emotional aspects of this would include relaxed elation, or being at peace with the world and oneself. Some drugs of abuse are prized precisely because they induce an "amotivational" state; for many of us, vacations serve much the same function. In such states, you don't have to plan, have no cause to anticipate, needn't worry about consequences. Overall, the emphasis is on taking it all in, not giving out, being passive rather than active.

The downside of this emotional-cognitive style often manifests itself as depression, a sense that the world is against you and that you're powerless in the hands of a cruel and inexorable fate. There's no anticipation of better days because this is how it's always been and always will be. Activity seems futile, helplessness sets in—why do anything, nothing's any good. A free-floating feeling of general unease may occur, a nonspecific, unfocused, queasily agitated arousal that's not tied to any particular situation or idea: The pain is there, but there's no clear tormentor to lash out at. Whereas the adverse consequences of activation involve frenzied overextension and anticipatory worry, the negative expression of arousal includes helplessness, hopelessness, and despair.

Most of us enjoy a balance between activation and arousal; that's why we work pretty ambitiously most of the time, yet relish the occasional opportunities to lie back and enjoy vacations, parties, or the occasional nip and toke. But as the following chapters will show, for some people these brain-behavioral systems of the self occur in exaggerated, stunted, or distorted form.

We've all met people who seem to be "functional" aprosodics, whose compulsive behavior embodies activation to its most self-debilitating degree, or whose moods shift like the wind so as to render their behavior maddeningly unpredictable. And as we'll now see, these personalities, these variations of self, have their roots in the subtle and fluid interplay of the neuropsychodynamic systems we've just explored: action and volition, thought and consciousness, motivation and emotion.

PART III

BASIC NATURES

CHAPTER 6

THE CONTROLLING SELF

The Obsessive-Compulsive Style

My candle burns at both ends;
  It will not last the night;
But, ah, my foes, and oh, my friends—
  It gives a lovely light!

—EDNA ST. VINCENT MILLAY

We may say that hysteria is a caricature of an artistic creation, a compulsion neurosis a caricature of a religion, and a paranoiac delusion a caricature of a philosophic system.

—SIGMUND FREUD

Admit it.

Sometimes you'll go back to check if the door is locked or the gas is turned off, even though you *know* you already covered this on your way out. You probably feel a little silly doing it, but something tells you you *have* to check one more time—just to be sure.

Or maybe it's something else. Do you have some little daily ritual—say, the weekday morning's order of events for getting ready for work—which, if interrupted for any reason, fills you with a mild, but nevertheless gnawing sense of unease? Wrapped up in an important problem—doing your taxes, preparing a homework assignment or job presentation, going over a condo contract, picking out the right birthday present—haven't you ever become so caught up with details that you find you've drifted away from the "point" of what you're doing, begun to lose the overall picture?

Sure you have. So have I. All of us at one time or another

have had experiences like these where a preoccupation with trifles seems to get in the way of larger issues or just basic peace of mind. But for most of us, under most circumstances, these are transient phenomena: You perceive your own state of overfocused bemuddlement, laugh at yourself, shrug it off, and get back in the race.

Or maybe some particular item of compulsive thought or activity has become an obdurately fixed part of your life. Okay, you just *can't* resist counting the telephone poles as they whiz by on the road, or you *have* to compare all the prices on all the brands of detergent so you can make the "best" purchase. In such cases, you've probably learned to accept it, to live with it. Most of us have enough adaptive flexibility, enough ego autonomy, to allow space in the psyche for the little peculiarities we can't explain or control. This is part of my personality, you tell yourself, a small annoyance but no big catastrophe, even part of my unique "color," and, anyway, this should be the *worst* thing I ever have to worry about, right?

But for many people, obsessions and compulsions *are* the worst thing. For them, the overriding need for structure and control clamps a constraint on spontaneity of thought, feeling, and action that no amount of logical persuasion or good-natured cajolery can undo. In some extreme cases, this need expresses itself in the form of ultimately self-destructive compulsive habits.

Examples include the housewife whose cleaning ritual lasts from dawn to dusk, every single day, year in and year out, making her quite literally a prisoner of her own fastidiousness. Or the businessman who spends so much time getting every detail of a presentation or report exactly right that he misses the deadline, then eschews any kind of rest and relaxation before plunging into the next project. All too frequently, this obsessive-compulsive style works its way into and around every activity that the person engages in. In some cases, it may improve the overall efficiency of many activities, in others it may fritter it away on trifling details. But in almost every case, this style ends up robbing life of its spontaneity, its flexibility, its "fun."

Obsessive-Compulsive Psychodynamics

Freud's[1] early formulation of obsessive-compulsive phenomena began with the observation that some of the ideas, wishes, or memories that many people harbor are simply too painful or repugnant to be acknowledged. One way of dealing with this unacceptable material is to repress it from consciousness. But according to Freud's psychodynamic theory, that which is chased away from one precinct of the psyche eventually turns up in another, bearing with it all manner of "neurotic" manifestations.

In some cases, the repressed material becomes transformed into an hysterical symptom, a kind of somatically "symbolic" representation of the buried psychological conflict or idea; we'll consider this in more detail in Chapter 8. In other cases, however, the idea itself may remain in consciousness, but it becomes divorced from the intense feelings that ordinarily accompany such conflict-laden material. Remember, however, that nothing in the psychodynamic realm just disappears, so now this dissociated emotion, this "free affect," as Freud called it, has to latch on to *something*. And that something is frequently an otherwise neutral mental content, some idea or plan or activity that's ostensibly inappropriate for any kind of obsessive concern.

Thus, in a seemingly paradoxical but psychodynamically deterministic way, all the preoccupation, fretfulness, and morbid overconcern related to the painful idea or memory is split from the original source and reattached to a relatively neutral, albeit symbolically related, idea. It's psychodynamically "easier" to agonize obsessively about whether the salmonella outbreak you read about in the morning paper has crept into your chicken salad sandwich than to worry about the real, unconscious source of the contamination phobia—a source that may hark back to a series of painful psychosexual experiences and developmental traumas of childhood.

In later elaborations of the theory, Freud[2] outlined the various symptoms that were expressions of this form of cognitive splitting and reattachment. These include obsessive brooding and rumination, compulsions to question and test everything, "doubting mania," and a veritable catalog of penitential and precautionary rituals, like handwashing, repeating phrases, and so on.

But even Freud recognized that there might be features of some people's mental makeup, of what we are here calling *cognitive style*, that predispose them to obsessive-compulsive (as opposed to, say, phobic or hysterical) manifestations of their repressed conflicts. It remained for later psychoanalytic writers to try to determine what features of cognitive style predispose to and shape the form of obsessive-compulsive and other symptoms. And only after this type of consideration can we today begin to build a truly comprehensive neuropsychodynamic model of character disorder, personality, and neurosis.

The Obsessive-Compulsive Cognitive Style

Recall our discussion in Chapter 1 of David Shapiro's application of the concept of cognitive style to his own work on "neurotic styles."[3] Shapiro describes one of the crucial features of the intellectual rigidity that typifies the obsessive-compulsive style as a *special restriction of attention*. That is, the obsessive-compulsive's attention is always narrowly concentrated and sharply focused, never relaxed or just diffusely aware.

We all frequently have periods during the day when we're forced to mobilize attention, to concentrate hard in order to deal with challenging tasks and important problems. Just as frequently, though, we allow ourselves to relax this state of vigilance, to let our minds wander, think of nothing in particular, take things as they come. This latter condition allows for a sort of free-floating awareness that facilitates a sensitivity to events around us in a general way. It's a flexible scanning function of the mind that lets us zoom in momentarily on individual elements of our perception as they seem important, and—the significance having passed—just as easily refocus the lens of our consciousness to again take in a broader field.

This flexibility of mental focusing is what the obsessive-compulsive seems to lack. His is a cognitive style of continual concentration, of maximal mobilization of mental effort to deal with even the merest of exigencies. In the obsessive-compulsive mindset there are simply no small matters. Choices that most of us make easily, even whimsically—what tie to wear, which restaurant to have lunch in—become an agony of decision, often dealt with by a set of ritualized protocols governing every foreseeable situation. On Tuesdays wear the blue suit, eat at Joe's Diner, and do the vacuuming when you get home. Even slight forced deviations from this regimen (Joe's is closed for remodeling) create anxiety, so much so that many obsessive-compulsives have already developed, overlapping contingency plans for dealing with such "emergencies" (if Joe's is closed, buy dinner at the supermarket; if the supermarket burns down . . . and so on).

An overfocused style of cognition may actually be quite appropriate for specific tasks that require sustained, concentrated work. And, interestingly enough, obsessive-compulsives *do* frequently gravitate toward professions and avocations that involve this kind of concentration—the stereotype of the uptight, rigid schoolmaster, accountant, or scientist isn't totally bogus. But such a style also carries with it a marked limitation in the overall mobility and range of attention in daily activities, a cognitive lifestyle pattern of missing the forest for the trees. These people, says Shapiro, not only concentrate, they seem always to be concentrating. And some aspects of the world are simply not to be apprehended by a sharply focused and concentrated attention. Specifically, this is a mode of attention that seems unequipped for the casual or immediate impression, that more passive and impressionistic sort of cognitive experience that can include in its notice or allow one to be "struck" by even that which is peripheral or incidental to its original, intended focus of attention or that may not even possess a clear intention or sharp focus in the first place. These people seem unable to allow their attention simply to wander or passively permit it to be captured. Thus, they rarely seem to get hunches, and they are rarely struck or surprised by anything. It is not that they do not look or listen, but they are looking and listening too hard for something else. Thus, these people often seem quite insensitive to the "tone" of social situations. In fact, they often make a virtue of necessity by referring with pride to their singlemindedness or imperturbability.[4]

For most of us, the fact that certain areas of life are within our control and other areas aren't presents no special problem. You may not *like* the fact that some things that affect you deeply lie beyond your control, but that's how it is, so you deal with it, make the best of it and hope you're wise enough to discern what you can do and what you can't. In fact, it can be decidedly unpleasant to feel you have to be in control of *everything*: freedom from onerous responsibility is one of the things that define relaxation. Most of us actually cherish the opportunity to periodically unwind, decompress, be "ourselves." That's because a normally developed sense of autonomy and volition allows room in the personality structure for whim, playfulness, and spontaneity of expression. If your sense of self is secure, you can afford to abandon constant conscious direction of yourself; you can "let go."

This the obsessive-compulsive cannot do. The tight, rigid, consciously volitional control sought over all aspects of life belies an inner fragility of autonomy, a sense of self so shaky that any prospect of relaxation of control is inextricably fraught with the danger of ego dissolution. Letting go means to risk falling apart.

So there must be rules and rules and rules. The obsessive-compulsive must always remind himself of some objective necessity, some overarching imperative or higher authority that alone can supersede his personal choice or wish and provide some external guide for his actions. Nothing is done just because he feels like it; there has to be a well thought-out intellectual, philosophical, religious, or moral "reason" for every decision and act. These strictures and directives, though weighing down on him like a psychic stone, are nevertheless indispensable for the obsessive-compulsive's internal cohesion. They provide an external, authoritative framework of guidelines within which he can function comparatively comfortably and without which his fragile autonomy is threatened with disintegration.

Ironically, despite all the hesitation and contortionistic juggling of pros and cons, the actual decision or action will often be made quite abruptly. It's as though embedded in the rigid structure of obsessive control is a mirror-function of *impulsivity*, a total abandonment of control. As a later chapter will show, the seemingly opposite traits of compulsivity and impulsivity are in fact tied together by their relationship to another quality of mental functioning, *reflectivity*, the capacity to take perspective, to see things in their larger context.

Another thing the obsessive-compulsive appears to lack is the normal experience of "rightness" or conviction. That's because a sense of conviction about the world—a sense of "truth"—involves a certain breadth of attention, an interest in and sensitivity to the shadings and proportions of things, and the capacity for a direct response to these feelings. In order to have convictions, you need sufficient autonomy so that your own belief system is perceived as something that comes from within *you*—not a tacked-on set of externally imposed imperatives that lock you into the song of your life like a phonograph needle in a record groove.

True conviction, true choice and volition, demand a certain requisite degree of ego autonomy. What might be the brain systems that contribute to this flexibility of attention and action, thought and feeling? And how might perturbations in these systems be related to the obsessive-compulsive cognitive style and the genesis of obsessive-compulsive symptoms?

The Obsessive-Compulsive Brain

In 1917, Constantin von Economo[5] first described what at that time seemed to be a new disease called *encephalitis lethargica*. During the next few years this illness took on pandemic proportions and involved tens of thousands of victims, leaving an estimated one-third of them with permanent, progressive, and often bizarre neuropsychiatric symptoms. The original outbreak overlapped with the 1919 influenza pandemic and for a long time these two disorders were confused with each other, although today many medical historians consider them to have been separate entities.[6]

What especially intrigued clinicians about this outbreak was that many of the survivors' symptoms involved disorders of impulsivity and compulsivity. These included conduct problems, hysterical and hypochondriacal syndromes, psychosis, depression, and obsessive-compulsive disorders—all phenomena that were considered to be well within the purview of the predominant Freudian psychogenic mental model of the times. These "neurotic" symptoms, seemingly produced by an organic disease, forced clinicians to take a closer look at psychological disorders, including obsessive-compulsiveness.

One such observation came from Paul Schilder[7] who wrote extensively on the similarities between organic obsessions and compulsions due to epidemic encephalitis and those of so-called "neurotic" origin. Schilder noted that in patient after obsessive patient, careful examination frequently turned up organic signs similar in kind, if not always in degree, to those found in the aftermath of chronic encephalitis—even in patients with no history of the disease.

Rather than attributing all cases of obsessional neurosis to hidden encephalitis, Schilder took another tack. If it could be shown that organic disturbances lead to a specific compulsive symptomatology, then it was reasonable to infer that cases which show a near-identical symptomatological picture have disturbances of impulse and will with a similar etiology. This need not be a frank instance of brain damage due to encephalitis or other easily recognized illness, but any organic factor that could affect the brain, no matter how subtle, no matter how difficult to pinpoint by the usual medical diagnostic methods.

According to Schilder, the encephalitic process, and by implication the seemingly "functional" alterations in brain physiology that produce equivalent symptoms in "neurotic" compulsives, disinhibit or *release* motor impulses and motor innervations. Release phenomena of this kind could include eye muscle spasms, repetition of speech (called echolalia), tics, writhing choreic motor movements, and hyperkinetic impulse disturbances. For Schilder, these phenomena of heightened motor activity had their psychological equivalent in impulses that reinforce hostile and aggressive attitudes. In fact, Schilder observed, impulsive actions of a sadistic character were common in postencephalitic cases, and when these impulses were inhibited, the result was often the appearance of compulsions—a very psychodynamic, or "Freudian," conceptualization, but with a basis in brain functioning.

A similar pattern of findings was subsequently presented

by Grimshaw,[8] who in studying a group of obsessional neurotics found that many suffered from neurologic illness or the neurological aftereffects of systemic disease. The range of disorders associated with the obsessive-compulsive symptomatology included Sydenham's chorea, epilepsy, encephalitis, meningitis, poliomyelitis, diphtheria, and others. Interestingly, Grimshaw observed that "the obsessional character is the antithesis of the uncontrolled, antisocial and wayward disposition of the postencephalitic patient," a theme we'll return to in a later chapter.

More recently, four cases of obsessive-compulsive disorder in previously normal patients were observed to follow traumatic head injuries.[9] In all cases, the obsessive-compulsive symptoms appeared within twenty-four hours of the head injury and were preceded by a period of increased anxiety or agitation. The investigators suggested that this state of heightened emotional arousal might be a necessary prerequisite for obsessions to intrude into consciousness, a position not unlike Freud's, as we saw at the beginning of this chapter.

So, obsessionality is often associated with overt cerebral injury or disease, but certainly not in every case. Where such brain pathology cannot be identified by traditional neurodiagnostic methods, some authorities have reasoned by analogy that there must be a more subtle, as yet undetectable impairment that's responsible for the similar symptoms.

But must this always be the case? Indeed, most obsessive-compulsive individuals have no standard neurologic illness, and the disorder is often regarded as the prime example of a nonorganic or "functional" or "neurotic" psychopathology. Yet subtle signs of cerebral disturbance may sometimes peek through. The question is whether these represent a pathological process, per se, or a normal variation within the realm of brain-related individual differences.

Consider the case[10] of a thirty-four-year-old woman with a lifelong obsessional disorder, including dread of the dark, washing and toilet rituals, a compulsion to act like a dog, and an obsessional fear of murdering her mother with an ax. These symptoms had progressed to the point where the patient needed to be hospitalized. While there, she was found to have abnormal EEG activity that seemed directly correlated with the obsessional state. That is, when her obsessions were upon her, the brain waves were abnormal; less-disturbed behavior was associated with a normalization of the EEG. Otherwise, neurological findings were normal, and there was no evidence of epilepsy, encephalitis, or any other brain disease.

What might be the significance of an abnormal EEG in obsessive-compulsive individuals? Rather than reflecting "brain damage" in the usual sense of a stroke or head trauma or cerebral infection, could the EEG abnormality reflect some subtle and unique pattern of brain organization that's tied to the normal, characteristic cognitive and emotional functioning of obsessive-compulsives?

This question was examined by Pierre Flor-Henry and colleagues,[11] who compared a group of obsessional patients with a matched group of normal controls. The subjects were evaluated by means of a power-spectral EEG, which measures the amount of electrical activity generated by different brain regions during different psychological states or levels of cognitive activity. In addition, the subjects were given a lengthy series of neuropsychological tests to assess their level of performance on a variety of cognitive tasks known to reflect the participation of different brain areas.

The neuropsychological test findings suggested that the obsessional syndrome in these patients was associated mainly with impairment in frontal lobe functioning; moreover, it was the left frontal lobe that was implicated. Perturbations in left-hemisphere functioning were also suggested by the EEG findings, although areas other than the frontal lobes seemed to be implicated.

Overall, the bulk of the findings supported a primary left-frontal dysfunction as the neuropsychological basis of the obsessional syndrome. This might account for obsessionals' frequent inability to inhibit the ceaseless verbal ruminations that so often torment them. That is, deficient frontal modulation of more posterior left-hemisphere language areas would result in the release of that region's overratiocinative tendencies—a breakdown in the kind of *intra*hemispheric control discussed in earlier chapters. In addition, the investigators hypothesized, the area of the frontal lobe probably most affected is the *cingulate gyrus*, which has rich connections with the brain's emotional limbic system, accounting, perhaps, for the emotional concomitants—anxiety, agitation, and sometimes depression—of obsessive-compulsive states.

Unfortunately, the situation may not be so clear-cut. An attempt to replicate this study was undertaken by Thomas Insel and his colleagues,[12] who, in addition to neuropsychological tests and EEG recordings, also employed CT scan measurements of their obsessive-compulsive subjects' brains. The investigators found that the obsessives' CT scans couldn't be distinguished from scans made on the brains of nonpsychiatric control subjects. In addition, the EEG recordings showed only mild, sporadic anomalies of uncertain significance. Worse for theory, the neuropsychological test findings didn't point to any specific pattern of impairment, certainly nothing that would single out left frontal lobe dysfunction. If anything, the only consistent finding—impairment on a tactual visuospatial task for half of the subjects—suggested a possible disturbance of right-hemisphere functioning, hardly a vindication of the original hypothesis.

Another study[13] tackled this problem by also employing a combination of CT scanning, EEG recording, and neuropsychological testing, this time on a group of adolescents with obsessive-compulsive disorder. First of all, no consistent EEG findings were noted. Further, in contrast to normal controls, the obsessive-compulsive subjects were found to have enlarged brain ventricles, usually considered a sign of cerebral pathology or possibly an anomaly of development. Also, these subjects exhibited a peculiar pattern of neuropsychological deficits, involving the inability to rotate themselves in space and to discern and follow unstated rules and patterns during maze learning—a pattern known to frequently occur with right-hemisphere and/or frontal lobe impairment.

Thus, the findings were partly similar to those reported in the two previous studies: some signs of frontal involvement and some evidence of right-hemisphere compromise. The curious thing about the adolescents in this latter group, however, was that the ventricular enlargement and neuropsychological impairment didn't correlate. That is, the subjects with the larger ventricles weren't necessarily the same ones as those with the impaired neuropsychological profiles, and vice versa. Could there be, perhaps, two kinds of neuropsychologically-based obsessive-compulsive syndromes—one involving observable anomalies of brain substance but not necessarily cognitive impairment, the other showing such impairment, but in the presence of a structurally normal brain?

Newer research with newer technologies may be on the verge of answering questions like these. Lewis Baxter and colleagues[14] studied fourteen obsessive-compulsive patients by means of positron emission tomography (PET scan) and the fluorodeoxyglucose (FDG) method. In this technique, the subject is given a radioactively labeled compound, glucose, that is easily metabolized by the brain. As the glucose is used up, the PET scanner records the radioactivity given off. The more active a particular brain area is, the more fuel it will need, and so the more radiation will be released from the radioactively tagged glucose as it's "digested." The PET scanner then transforms this profile of glucose utilization into a visual display of activity in various brain regions. If we assume that different psychological and behavioral functions are subserved by different brain regions, then the PET scanner affords us a glimpse of living brain-mind or brain-behavior interaction. The technique has already been used to study such functions as motor planning, sensory processing, attention, emotional awareness, and schizophrenic thinking.

In Baxter's experiment, the obsessive-compulsive patients were compared with normal controls, as well as with a group of depressed patients. This was to check out whether the observed differences, if any, had to do specifically with obsessive-compulsive disorder or were just a nonspecific result of suffering from *any* kind of mental disorder. What the investigators found was that the obsessive-compulsive patients, unlike either the depressives or normal controls, showed greater activity in the left frontal lobe and especially in a subcortical brain structure called the *caudate*.

The caudate is a member of a group of structures called the *basal ganglia*, which are important for the coordination and programming of movement and action. The caudate seems to be involved not just in the execution of a particular movement but in the planning and programming of that movement, the evaluation of that movement's appropriateness in the context of the person's overall momentary state of motor activity and intentionality, and the linking of that movement with sensory and motivational factors.[15]

In fact, if this description sounds familiar to that given earlier for the role of the frontal lobes, it's because the caudate in fact has strong connections with the frontal cortex and interacts with it in the planning, execution, and evaluation of behavior. The two roles, however, can be roughly distinguished: The caudate, in conjunction with other basal ganglia and limbic structures, is responsible for the appropriateness of actions in a moment-to-moment context. For its part, the cortex of the frontal lobes deals with the larger picture, with the determination of broad patterns of actions—*activities*, really—in the context of the individual's overall goals and plans, behaviors that transcend the immediate and that retain their integrity and continuity over time, as we saw in Chapter 3.

In obsessive-compulsive disorders, the goal-directedness of behavior appears to have undergone a sort of psychological hypertrophy, so that a virtual caricature of volitional intentionality now exists. Activities that would normally seem appropriate—checking one's bank balance, cleaning one's apartment, making decisions about what to wear or which job offer to accept—now become exaggerated to the point of grim parody: The bank balance is checked again and again and again; the apartment is scrubbed and polished beyond the demands of even the most fanatical drill sergeant, and so on. Every conceivable contingency related to every decision, major or minor, is gone over with such exacting detail that the overall momentum of the activity as a whole becomes paralyzed.

And this may be what's being reflected in the hyperactive left frontal lobe and associated subcortical structures of obsessive-compulsive patients. The normal function of intending, of planning or forming adaptive behavioral strategies, gets tangled up and hung with its own rope. This is not due to the avolitional inertia that's sometimes seen in the frontal-damaged patient, but quite the opposite: *too* much planning, *too* much taking things into consideration, *too* much attention to detail ruins the overall adaptiveness of the larger sphere of activity—the very losing-the-forest-for-the-trees that is the hallmark of the obsessive-compulsive cognitive style.

To summarize: The neuropsychological evidence so far seems to suggest that while a specific ''center'' for the obsessive-compulsive style has by no means been definitively pinned down, there's probably an association with disor-

dered frontal lobe functioning, including that of at least one
of its underlying subcortical structures, the caudate. This
seems to involve either a lack of modulation of posterior
brain regions leading to *linguistic* rumination, or perhaps a
subcortical-frontal hyperactivity that results in a *behavioral*
preoccupation with discrete, moment-to-moment details,
rather than with more comprehensive plans and goals, the
larger picture. In the obsessive-compulsive, the frontal lobe
system may be doing its job not wisely, but too well.

Whether this involves mainly left- or right-hemisphere
predominance is not settled. Bearing in mind our neuropsychodynamic model developed in earlier chapters, this is
probably not an all-or-none affair. That is, there may be
different ratios of hemispheric activation associated with different degrees or types of obsessive-compulsiveness.

For example, verbal obsessionalizing may be linked to left-
hemisphere disinhibition, imagistic preoccupations to the
right. Additional factors, such as native intelligence or other
psychological traits, may also influence the results of such
neuropsychological studies. An instructive example of "pure"
organically induced obsessive-compulsiveness would be
someone without any previous significant disturbance of personality or cognition, who first developed problems following
damage to a relatively localized region of the brain. It is to
such a case that we now turn.

The Case of the Obsessional Professional

The story of "Evan," a patient studied by neurologists Paul
Eslinger and Antonio Damasio,[16] begins happily enough
with an uneventful childhood, normal developmental mile-
stones, and no serious illnesses. The oldest of five children
raised on a farm, Evan excelled in school and had many
friends. After high school he married and worked his way
through two years of business college. By age twenty-five,
he'd landed a job as a staff accountant in a building firm,
was raising two kids, and was active in church affairs. He

steadily advanced in his career, achieved promotion after promotion, and was considered by his brothers and sisters to be the role model of the family. All in all, one couldn't ask for a better living illustration of self-efficacy, ego autonomy, optimal adaptation, and realized potential.

Such a life, alas, was apparently too good to be true. At age thirty-five Evan began to experience visual disturbances and behavioral changes. Medical investigation led to the discovery of a brain tumor, a meningioma, the same kind of tumor that afflicted the butcher at the beginning of Chapter 3. Recall that meningiomas are actually tumors of the fibrous coverings of the brain, the meninges, and are typically not malignant—that is, the cells don't directly invade the healthy tissue of the brain or other parts of the body.

However, since the tumor expands within a closed space—the skull—it compresses and may destroy the brain tissue under and around it. In Evan's case, the tumor arose from the anterior base of the skull and was pushing up from below onto the lower surface of his frontal lobes. Naturally, the tumor had to go. But it's often difficult to operate in or around brain tissue—especially at the underside of the brain—without affecting that tissue itself. So virtually all of the orbitofrontal cortex (the lower, basal part of the frontal lobe) of the right lobe, and a good part of that on the left, was sacrificed as well.

Characteristically, Evan toughed out the operation, recovered uneventfully, and was discharged from the hospital two weeks later. After an appropriate three-month convalescent period, he dutifully returned to work. That's when the trouble began. Evan soon became involved in a business deal with a former coworker of shady reputation, who'd earlier been fired from the company where Evan worked. Despite warnings from friends and pleas from his family, Evan sank his life savings into this dubious partnership, which promptly led to bankruptcy and disrepute.

It got worse. After losing his position with the company,

Evan drifted through several jobs, getting fired from each one for tardiness and disorganization—all the more strange, since even those bosses who canned him were forced to acknowledge that Evan's basic skills, manner, and temperament were generally appropriate. Similar difficulties at home led to marital problems and eventually to divorce. Unable to hold a job and separated from his family, this once proud, happy, self-reliant and self-made man was compelled, like a child, to move in with his parents.

Reevaluation two years after the operation showed no recurrence of the tumor, and a neurologic exam was normal, except for an inability to smell. This is not uncommon after bilateral orbitofrontal damage, because the two olfactory nerves to the brain each sit in a groove on the lower surface of the frontal lobe and can be easily damaged along with the lobe itself.

Interestingly, the operation had not left Evan stupid. His verbal IQ was found to be in the superior range and his performance IQ (which involves mainly nonverbal, spatial-manipulative kinds of reasoning) was solidly in the average range; from these scores, we can estimate that Evan's full-scale IQ was in the overall high-average category. A memory test likewise showed that his ability to recall was well above average, and assessment with a standardized personality test revealed no significant psychopathology. Confronted with these test scores alone, any trained psychologist might reasonably conclude that they came from a normal, bright, and well-adjusted individual—actually, an apt description of Evan prior to his illness and operation.

However, the record of Evan's continued troubles told quite a different story. He still couldn't keep a job. A month after his divorce, and against the advice of relatives, he remarried and that marriage in turn broke up two years later. But the striking feature during this time was the remarkable contrast between Evan's poor judgment and lackadaisical manner with important matters of job and family, and his seemingly pathological obsessiveness over trifles.

For example, Eslinger and Damasio describe how

> he needed about two hours to get ready for work in the morning, and days were taken up entirely by shaving and hair-washing. Deciding where to dine might take hours, as he discussed each restaurant's seating plan, particulars of menu, atmosphere and management. He would drive to each restaurant to see how busy it was, but even then he could not finally decide which to choose. Purchasing small items required in-depth consideration of brands, prices and the best method of purchase. He clung to out-dated and useless possessions, refusing to part with dead houseplants, old phone books, six broken fans, five broken television sets, three bags of empty orange juice concentrate cans, 15 cigarette lighters and countless stacks of old newspapers.[17]

Reevaluation at a private psychiatric hospital six years after the operation showed "no evidence of organic brain syndrome or frontal dysfunction"; if anything, there seemed to be an actual improvement in test performance. This time, both verbal and performance IQs were clearly in the superior range and memory continued to be well above average. He was also given a comprehensive neuropsychological test battery and showed average to superior performance on every subtest. Again, personality functioning was assessed to be normal.

Based on these test results, the psychological evaluation team concluded that Evan's adjustment problems were not the result of organic problems or neurological dysfunction. Rather, they reflected emotional or psychological factors and were therefore amenable to psychotherapy. It was reported further that Evan could return to work after appropriate retraining. The diagnostic classification Evan received was a

dysthymic disorder in a patient with a compulsive personality style.

Well, compulsive yes, that much seemed clear. And since
psychotherapy was so heartily recommended, it was tried—
with dismal results. It was at this point that Evan was
referred to Drs. Eslinger and Damasio.

One of the first things they did was a CT scan. The findings showed a low-density area in both frontal lobes, corresponding to the extensive surgery that had involved all of
the orbitofrontal cortex on the right side and part of the
orbital cortex on the left. Conclusion: This patient had had
a considerable chunk of brain taken away from him. So much
for the exclusively "psychogenic" hypothesis of the earlier
report.

But even more important, a particularly careful neuropsychological and behavioral assessment showed that the
original sets of test results, while not wrong in any technical
sense, had failed to pick up certain subtleties of Evan's impaired cognitive functioning. Specifically, the picture
emerged of a marked dissociation between intact individual
cognitive abilities measured by standardized tests, and the
poor *utilization* of those abilities in real-life environments.

For example, formal tests of language, memory, visual
perception, constructional abilities, abstraction, calculation, and orientation all yielded high-average or superior
scores. Personality testing once again showed nothing remarkable. Engaged in abstract political, social, financial,
and philosophical discussions, Evan's reasoning was logical
and his comprehension and responses appropriate. But when
called upon to act on the real-life equivalent of these hypothetical situations, things went all to pieces.

He typically took the wrong action in the wrong way or
at the wrong time, often with disastrous results. He'd learned
and used normal patterns of social behavior before his brain
lesion, assimilated a lifetime of experience in interpersonal
interaction, but although he could recall such patterns when

questioned about their applicability in hypothetical situations, real-life circumstances failed to evoke them. Specifically, Eslinger and Damasio were struck by how Evan rarely acted on impulse, but rather seemed to spend an inordinate amount of time reviewing often irrelevant details of a proposition without keeping the whole problem in perspective—missing, that is, the forest for the trees.

In their neuropsychological conceptualization of this case, Eslinger and Damasio point out that Evan's intellect was normal, even superior. Furthermore, his performance on even complex conceptual classification tasks—usually quite sensitive to frontal lobe impairment—was excellent. The intactness of this performance, the doctors speculated, was probably due to the preservation of other regions of the frontal lobes, such as the upper, or dorsal, surfaces that seem to play a special role in such "pure reasoning" tasks. But the areas of the frontal lobe that are richest in emotional-motivational limbic connectivity—the lower, or orbitomedial, regions—were destroyed.

The orbitomedial frontal lobe serves as integrator and intermediary between limbic drive systems, sensory and memory mechanisms, and the planning and response operations of the dorsolateral frontal cortex—recall Nauta's point from Chapter 3.[18] Thus, although the neurological substrates of both motivation and response may have been independently intact in Evan's brain, the orbitomedial integrating mechanism was destroyed, resulting in a dissociation of drive and action. Behavior—especially abstract forms of behavior, such as talking about situations rather than doing them—was "appropriate." But when circumstances required the actual application of behavior to real life—situations that one ordinarily gets "involved" in—behavior deteriorated into obsessive preoccupation with details. When explicit external guidance and structure were not forthcoming, behavior fell into an aimless, drifting pattern.

Thus, this man who could engagingly discourse on the most abstruse intellectual matters, couldn't pick an item off a restaurant menu. He might describe very well the various courses of action one might take in all sorts of different situations, but placed in those circumstances himself, he foundered. In normal everyday life, too, we make distinctions between "doers" and "thinkers," people who are "armchair" philosophers, sportsmen, entrepreneurs, and so forth, and those who are able to put their money where their mouth is. What Evan's case most clearly illustrates is the importance of the frontal lobes for choosing a strategy and following it through to its correct completion. Disturbances in this ability cause a person to become abnormally fixated on trifles or to meander aimlessly, perhaps with the "best of intentions," but unable to transform these intentions into a workable plan of action.

And—as Shapiro has pointed out—compulsively deliberated decisions are often, in the event, made quite impulsively. It's as if there were some mental rubber band that, stretched beyond endurance by compulsive rumination, bounces back reflexively in abrupt impulsive action. Unable to make an "informed decision," the strained obsessive-compulsive cognitive style paroxysmally plunges into impulsive capitulation.

Conclusions

As is typical in any multidisciplinary field, it's difficult to expect total uniformity in neuropsychological studies of personality. However, despite differences in the type of patient groups being studied (psychiatric, brain-damaged, "normal") and the diversity of measures used (neuropsychological tests, EEGs, CT scans, PET scans), it's encouraging to see some consensus emerge.

Several of the case reports and experimental studies reviewed in this chapter seem to point to anomalies of activation and arousal that are associated with the obsessive-compulsive cognitive style. Schilder, we saw, referred to the release of motor inhibition that characterized his patients with obsessive-compulsive symptomatology. And obsessiveness in a group of head-injured patients developed in the context of anxiety and emotional arousal. Significant EEG abnormalities have also been observed in obsessive-compulsives.

Carey and Gottesman[19] have noted that many patients whom clinicans call "neurotic" are subject to chronic over-arousal and anxiety-proneness. Hans Eysenck[20] has described a tendency for such individuals to show increases in arousal on repeated presentation of feared stimuli, instead of the normal getting-used-to-it response, called habituation, that's usually associated with a decrease in arousal. According to Samuel Turner and colleagues,[21] if obsessive-compulsive patients are congenitally overaroused, this might explain their tendency to worry excessively and to overrespond to threatening stimuli, as well as the ability of such stimuli to elicit anxiety responses. In vulnerable individuals, such a process could be set off under stressful circumstances, including the ubiquitous interpersonal conflicts that humans characteristically create and endure.

Overall, the evidence for cerebral localization is far from conclusive, if what is being sought is some sort of "obsessive-compulsive brain center." But the evidence does seem to suggest that frontal lobe mechanisms play an important role in the onset or at least the maintenance of the obsessive-compulsive cognitive style and obsessive-compulsive symptoms. Moreover, it may be the left frontal lobe that's especially implicated when the obsessive rumination has a verbal-ideative bias—although, again, other evidence suggests there's probably more to the story.

Flor-Henry's hypothesis of a deficiency in left-frontal inhibition of left-hemisphere verbal processes (intrahemispheric dysregulation) is consistent with the evidence for such neuropsychodynamics presented in Part II of this book. Thus, normal regulation of more posterior left-hemisphere thought, language, and calculation processes may depend on the evaluation of situation-appropriateness by frontal mechanisms. Dysfunction in this frontal control system could result in disinhibition of posterior left-hemisphere verbal and attentional mechanisms and the consequent hyperrational and superfocused cognitive style that Shapiro has attributed to obsessive-compulsives.

Additional disturbances might occur in the reciprocal connections with the right hemisphere and other brain regions subserving emotion, memory, and holistic perception. As seen in Chapter 4, disrupted access to these forms of processing (or the failure of these forms to develop normally in the first place) could prevent any kind of compensatory emotional or intuitive approach from softening the obdurately hard-headed rationality of the obsessive-compulsive cognitive style. The inability to inhibit verbal representations—to keep oneself from *always* taking a rational approach—could thus be one expression of this cognitive style.

This would have its neuropsychodynamic foundation in frontal-to-posterior intrahemispheric disinhibition within the left hemisphere itself, combined with limited access to the possible moderating effects of right-hemisphere intuition and imagery. And again, the symptoms we see hacked out in bold relief by brain damage might be etched more subtly, more "functionally," more "normally" in many other people, contributing to their own idiosyncratic versions of the obsessive-compulsive style.

Although this book's focus is on broad aspects of cerebral cortical localization, what we've discussed in this chapter also underscores the importance of taking subcortical structures into account when describing the brain-behavioral dynamics of lobes or hemispheres. Baxter's work has focused on the caudate, but even the deeper subcortical structures known to be affected by encephalitis have intricate connections with other parts of the brain that we know to be important for human behavior and personality.

Thus, the obsessive-compulsive cognitive style depends—as do all such styles—upon a particular arrangement in the psyche of a variety of subcomponents of cognition and feeling. These subcomponents, in turn, are represented in the complex three-dimensional pattern of brain functioning that gives each of us our distinctive personality, our individual self.

The obsessive obsesses because his particular neuropsychodynamic pattern predisposes him to concentrate, focus attention, analyze, and verbally dissect. But there's another type of personality, another cognitive style, in whom these qualities are even more magnified, more intense, more distorted, and more disruptive. It is to this that we now turn.

CHAPTER 7

THE GUARDED SELF

The Paranoid Style

There is nothing makes a man suspect much, more than to know little.

—FRANCIS BACON

I hold it cowardice,
To rest mistrustful where a noble heart
Hath pawned an open hand in sign of love.

—WILLIAM SHAKESPEARE

Here's the setup: You walk into a room where several people are talking. One of them looks over in your direction, then turns to her friend and says something in her ear. Both smile, then turn around and greet you with big, friendly hellos. *Were they talking about me? What were they saying?*

The reaction is natural, and rare is the person who hasn't had a similar experience. So what do you do? You might conclude that the "conspirators" have been spying and plotting against you all along, that their cheerful greetings are merely further proof of their disingenuous treachery and that you should be on your guard at every moment, taking note of every suspicious detail of speech and behavior, ready to mount a preemptive counterattack at the first sign of escalation.

But that would be *crazy*, wouldn't it? I mean, that's just *paranoid*, a label we use in common speech to denote defensive actions or attitudes that seem to have no grounding in reality. Reality as *we* perceive it, that is. But what if the two whisperers in the above example really *do* have it in for you, based on hard evidence you've accumulated through painstaking surveillance and research. How do you know what's a true sign of malice and what's simply an innocent remark or gesture? How do you put the evidence of your perceptions together to come up with some working model of the motivations of those around you?

Most of us don't spend too much time mulling over such things because we have a relatively stable "sense" of what's going on around us in our interactions with other people. In some cases we may overtrustingly be taken in by some smooth operator who turns out to be only after our money or body or whatever. Or we may at first too harshly judge the intentions of someone because they just rub us the wrong way or bear an unfortunate resemblance to some bastard who's burned us in the past. If this person actually turns out to be a nice guy, we're likely to change our opinion, even feel a little silly for having jumped to so hostile a conclusion.

The point is that in making judgments about the social environment we use a combination of evidence and emotion, logic and intuition. We usually don't focus our attention on a single feature of appearance and behavior, form a definite conclusion, close our minds completely and use all further evidence to back it up. Instead, we're *flexible* about the kinds of information we utilize to form opinions and ideas about the people around us. When such flexibility is absent, when the faculties of attentional focus and analysis become entrained by a narrow tractor beam of perception, our relations with our fellows take an insidious and ultimately self-destructive turn.

Paranoid Psychodynamics

Freud's original formulation of paranoia[1] sought to place it within the framework of the other defensive personality styles that foster the repression of painful or unacceptable

thoughts, feelings, and impulses. While the hysteric trans-
mutes conflictual material into a physical symptom by means
of conversion (discussed in the next chapter), and while the
obsessive substitutes an ostensibly neutral object or topic
for his preoccupation, the paranoid utilizes the process of
projection, the attribution of his own motives, usually hostile, but not consciously acknowledged, to someone else.

There's a price to pay for this, however. The psychic con-
tortions that the paranoid requires to maintain this defense
necessitate a certain loss of reality; the defensive process at
this point becomes *delusional*, severely threatening the stability of the ego and the mental constitution as a whole.

In a later work, Freud[2] delineated his now famous, if much
debated, psychosexual connection between paranoia and
male homosexuality. Paranoia begins, according to this formulation, with homosexual fantasies that the person finds
unacknowledgable. "I love him" is thereby defensively
turned around into "I hate him" and further to "He hates
me." In this way, the paranoid's own hatred is rationalized
into "I hate him because he persecutes me." Although many
later psychodynamic theorists have continued to subscribe
to the homosexuality-paranoia connection,[3] only recently
have attempts been made to elucidate the features of cognitive style that might predispose someone to this kind of
defense complex.

The Paranoid Cognitive Style

David Shapiro[4] describes two main variations of the paranoid style. These, of course, are only two differentiations
of a more general style, and, as with most personality
"types," sharp distinctions are the exception, blends and
combinations the rule.

The first type is exemplified by the furtive, constricted,
apprehensively suspicious individual that we're all familiar
with. This is the person who reveals little about himself,

forms few close relationships, and has hardly any close friends. Although he may act in an ostensibly sociable manner, people around him always feel that he's holding back a large part of himself, that his interactions with his fellows lack spontaneity and ease. Indeed, we may occasionally even feel sorry for someone who seems to have to hide so much of himself, to forgo so much of the pleasure of normal human companionship, in order to feel secure and unthreatened.

The second type of paranoid style is less benign. This is the rigidly arrogant, more aggressively suspicious, even megalomaniacal person who *always* watches his back, trusts *nobody*, and *knows* that everyone's really out for Number One and that the sonsofbitches'll stick it to you if you don't stick it to them first. Human sentiments of affiliation and benevolence are dismissed as disarming crap and the people that display them are seen as chumps at best, dissembling tricksters at worst.

This philosophy of cynicism pervades every facet of the paranoid's human interactions, even though many of them are skillful at putting on a façade of ordinariness, at blending in with the crowd while searching for weaknesses and determining the best opportunities to exploit. For many, however, this is a lost cause: They're convinced that they're so obviously superior in their perceptions and talents that other people just can't *help* but envy them and plot to undo them.

Whether in its extreme or more common form, says Shapiro, the paranoid cognitive style is characterized by an extremely tense and rigid directedness of attention. In principle this isn't really different from that of the obsessive-compulsive style discussed in the last chapter, but in the paranoid it's more severe in degree. For these people, the tense, rigidly directed attention is always on the alert, always looking for something, always in a searching mode. This mental search beam is perennially on the move, narrowly focused in its search for "evidence," for "clues" to validate the paranoid's own suspicions. As a result, the paranoid has little difficulty imposing his own particular conclusions anywhere.

We've all encountered people like this, who may in fact be quite correct about the raw content of their perceptions. They see, hear, and experience the same things we do, such as a news story or personal conversation, perhaps observe things in an even more acute and detailed fashion because of their intensely focused attention. But they're way off in their interpretations, in the conclusions they draw from these perceptions and experiences. Chance remarks, incidental rumors, innocent glances are all processed with the same keen analytic machinery used for the weightiest of problems, the most urgent of emergencies.

Worse, the paranoid almost always interprets such events as attacks, as challenges, as confrontations, overt or implicit, which require the mobilization of his entire defensive armamentarium and the redoubling of his intelligence-gathering efforts. This tendency to perceive things in an overaccurate way, but to skew one's interpretation of them in accordance with preconceived ideas of attack and defense, is what Shapiro describes as the epitome of *bias*, the virtual psychological opposite of the suggestibility and impulsivity seen in the hysterical and impulsive cognitive styles.

Like the obsessive-compulsive, the paranoid is ever on the lookout for "clues" from which to construct his subjective world. But the clues and indicators that interest the paranoid are far narrower than those that capture the obsessive's attention, and are, moreover, tied to the paranoid's specific biases or preconceived notions. If he thinks communism is a global threat to human freedom, then every international incident is seen as the work of communists, all events are interpreted in terms of communist plots and evidence to the contrary is dismissed as a smokescreen obscuring the true underlying communist origins. Or if not communists, capitalists; or if not capitalists, certain ethnic or racial groups, and so on. The choice of target may vary from individual to individual, but what really matters is the intensity with which these biased views are held and the wracking tortures that logic is subjected to in defense of the skewed outlook.

Indeed, we're sometimes astounded by the degree to which such a person interprets *everything* in terms of his uniquely constrained weltanschauung. "How can this guy function in the real world?" we ask ourselves. And, as Freud pointed out, the paranoid's loss of reality is much greater than that of the obsessive-compulsive. For example, whereas the obsessive may be preoccupied with certain technical data, for the paranoid the whole *world* is one big technical problem, much along the lines of a military campaign: No detail is too trivial, nothing is to be overlooked, lest his guard be relaxed for that one crucial instant which would allow the adversary—however well identified or ill defined— to seize the advantage.

Thus, the paranoid's construction of his subjective world has two important aspects: first, a biased abstraction of "significant" cues and clues from their context; and second, a loss of appreciation of that context itself. Context, remember, is what ordinarily gives individual cues their overall meaning, their actual significance in terms of the larger picture. And the narrow, ferociously concentrated attentional mode of the paranoid precludes the wider span of apprehension that makes sensitivity to context part of the normal experience of reality. The passive experience of the perceptual world—just letting go and taking things in as they occur—is anathema to the paranoid cognitive style. Accordingly, so much of what for most of us gives reality its varied shades of meaning is lost to the paranoid, shut out from his consideration.

This may also explain another frequently observed feature of paranoid persons, their general humorlessness. Certainly, they can crack wise as well as the next guy; in fact, a certain cutting, sarcastic, hostile type of joking often characterizes their interactions with people. Certain stand-up comedians of the "nasty" variety use this attitude to good effect in their acts. But the reason we, the audience, laugh is because we know it's an act. In the case of the person with a paranoid cognitive style, however, this is real life.

The use of a predominantly snide brand of humor betrays a deeper fundamental cheerlessness that pervades the paranoid personality. "Show me a man who knows what's funny," Mark Twain said, "and I'll show you a man who knows what's not." The ability to take perspective, to mentally stand at a distance and smile at the inanities we often get ourselves so worked up about, is part and parcel of the capacity to perceive what *really* has to be taken seriously, what's *not* all a big joke. As we'll see in the final chapter, most genuinely altruistic and socially conscious people have a well-developed sense of humor. True humor implies an appreciation of the broad view, a multidimensional perception and understanding. A true sense of humor is cynicism's worst enemy. But when all of life is construed as a desperate struggle against devious adversity, very little is truly funny; the paranoid is rarely "amused."

Even the obsessive, caught at an off moment, may be able to step back and chuckle at himself and his foibles, if only in the wry, existential manner of the chronically overwrought. This ability to impose even a modicum of distance between oneself and the reflective observation of oneself, to attempt to regard one's own behavior from a different point of view, to "see ourselves as others see us," à la Robert Burns, is alien to the paranoid. The faculty of *perspective*, the capacity to flexibly shift perceptual stance so as to facilitate the apprehension of context, is laser-blasted aside by the paranoid's beam of intensely focused attention on incriminating details.

It's no surprise, then, that the rigid cognitive style of the paranoid leads to a loss of autonomy even greater than that of the obsessive-compulsive. Says Shapiro:

> In the paranoid person, even more sharply and severely than in the case of the obsessive-compulsive, every aspect and component of normal autonomous functioning appears in rigid, distorted and, in general, hypertrophied form. While the normal person is capable of purposeful, intentional activity, he is also capable of abandonment. But the paranoid person is totally mobilized; all action is purposeful, directed toward an aim (for example, a defensive aim) with an intensity close to what is normally reserved for emergency. Nothing is done playfully, whimsically, for its own sake or with abandon. This mode of functioning, pervaded by tension, certainly does not represent a greater degree of the normal person's autonomy. It reflects, rather, an exceedingly frail autonomy, one that, because it is so frail, can be maintained only in this remarkably rigid and exaggerated form.[5]

Ordinarily, you feel more or less free to exercise your will, to be generally self-directing, in charge of your life, master of your fate, and so on. And you feel this, moreover, without any sense of struggle or inordinate mental exertion. But the paranoid person is continuously occupied and concerned with the threat of being subjugated to some external control or infringement of his will. So piteously fragile, after all, is the paranoid's autonomy that he's obsessed with "control" on every level and in every sense of the word.

Paranoids are, as a rule, exquisitely aware of power and rank, who's on top and who subordinate, who must take orders from whom, who's in the position to dish out humiliation and who has to eat it and grin. Everything is politics, motives are to be mistrusted, everyone's got an angle and a hustle, and watch out for your own behind.

Many paranoid characters find that, as a result of this do-

it-to-them-before-they-do-it-to-you philosophy, they're always involved—subjectively, if not actually—in some form
of defensive and antagonistic engagement with one or another authority figure. The paranoid might be the dissimu-
latively ingratiating toady who turns around and stabs you
in the back, not out of the sheer mean-spiritedness of the
psychopath nor from some overriding compulsion of acquisitive greed, but because of the genuinely urgent necessity in his own mind of protecting his flanks, of striking a
defensively preemptive blow.

The discussion of behinds and flanks, incidentally, brings us
back to the Freudian theory of paranoia and homosexuality,
introduced earlier. In Shapiro's formulation, the sexual
component may actually be secondary to the dominance-
passivity connotations of homosexuality, considerations that,
as we've seen, weigh heavily on the paranoid's mind. Any
temptation toward passive surrender is guarded against
mightily by the paranoid. Inasmuch as passivity at times
may carry with it a sexual component—and one imagines
this may be as much true for heterosexuality as for homosexuality—it may in fact be sexuality that's occasionally the
focus of the paranoid's defensive posture.

So it's not necessarily the "sexual" aspect of sex that the
paranoid fears and loathes, but the giving-in aspect, the
abandoning, even temporarily, of rigid control that normal
reciprocal sexual relations involve. "Losing oneself" to a
moment of passion, which for most of us makes sex so fulfilling, so much fun, represents for the paranoid a literal
losing of the self, a dissolution of the ego that the paranoid
cannot tolerate. Sexual passivity, homo or hetero, is out of
the question for the paranoid, as is any other kind of passivity, because it constitutes a capitulation of the self, an
obliterative surrender of the personality.

Paranoid characters almost always seem a little "off";
perhaps colorfully eccentric if possessed of some redeeming
technical expertise, otherwise just obnoxious or weird. Sha-

piro observes that elements of psychosis—a more serious loss of reality—frequently creep into the paranoid personality makeup. Indeed, it's difficult to view the world in such an idiosyncratically skewed and one-dimensional way, to have such a constricted range of emotion and style of relating interpersonally, and not seem at least a little "crazy."

In the more subdued cases, the paranoid manages to keep his conspiratorial agenda to himself; he doesn't let it be known that he's on to everyone or that he's taking advantage of seemingly innocent interactions to collect espionage data for later use. His is not usually the florid delusional preoccupation with fantasied persecutions by bizarre enemies: he sees no spacemen or commies under his bed and he knows his boss doesn't really work for the CIA, or is not literally trying to read his mind.

In short, he's not psychotic—"crazy"—in the usual psychiatric sense and, as mentioned above, may actually have an unusually keen perception of reality, may in fact see through other people's pretensions and motives with near-clinical perspicacity. Again, it's the interpretation that's the problem. The distinguishing feature is his constant alertness to threat and challenge, a general "philosophical" suspiciousness and preoccupation with control, which often goes hand in hand with an adherence to punitive absolutist theological beliefs, for example, or coercive political ideologies. Other paranoids may actually go off the deep end, may become crazy to the point of having to be periodically hospitalized or otherwise restrained. Still, the degree and nature of the psychosis is typically different than that of the more deteriorated mental state seen in nonparanoidly delusional chronic schizophrenics.

Scratch a paranoid, Shapiro suggests, and you may find that his underlying nature turns out to be an obsessive-compulsive one. Indeed, in extreme cases, the boundaries between obsessiveness, paranoia, and delusional psychosis may blur together. Certain other conditions fall intermediately between the two states. Sometimes described as overideational, "preparanoid" states, these are conditions in which obsessional and paranoid features seem to intermingle and shade into one another.[6] In such cases it may be difficult to say whether all the elaborate intellectualizing should be regarded as obsessional or paranoid.

Thus, according to Shapiro's conceptualization, the paranoid style may in many cases represent a more primitive transformation of the obsessive-compulsive style. When an obsessive-compulsive person decompensates—"loses it"— it's often in a paranoid direction. As control appears to be slipping away, the person may search for "reasons" or "causes" to justify his increasing self-dissolution. It must be *somebody's* fault, *somebody's* doing. And the plot thickens.

The Paranoid Brain

Is the paranoid's habitual style of "looking for trouble" only one extreme variation of a more basic human tendency to anticipate consequences and prepare for them? This idea forms the basis of Paul MacLean's intriguing conceptualization of paranoid thinking.[7] Unlike many creatures, MacLean points out, man relies primarily on *teloreceptive* sensory systems—those that detect things at a distance, that look ahead.

It's quite remarkable, really, how many mammals depend mostly on smell and touch to gather information about the world around them—think of all those large snouts and whiskers. But primates—monkeys, apes, and especially man—rely much more on hearing and particularly vision to deal with the environment at large. And regarding the world at several removes may have been what gave rise in human evolution to the psychological function of *perspective*.

When things are perceived unclearly, natural wariness is aroused. Repeated exposure to something that cannot be clearly seen creates a setup for this wariness to evolve into chronic suspicion. And "given the seed of suspicion," says MacLean, "the human mind is capable of developing any kind of paranoid hybrid."

A particularly important manifestation of this "unseen" that besets us is the poorly outlined and uncertain picture of future events that a highly evolved human prefrontal cortex strives to envision in an almost continual state of wary anticipation. Recall our discussion in Chapter 3 of the importance of the frontal lobes in mediating time extension and the ability to anticipate. Humans are almost always looking ahead. Our projected roles in possible tomorrows are in fact what help define our identities. But uncertain tomorrows breed anxiety. "As the future is always generating more 'futures' ad infinitum," MacLean goes on to say, "it is apparent why its uncertainties are responsible for most of man's chronic forms of suspicion."

Since the paranoid cognitive style reaches its most extreme and noticeable form in paranoid psychotic syndromes, most neuropsychological studies have involved this clinical group. Also, since most studies of this type have relied essentially on "captive audiences"—that is, hospitalized inpatients—it's not surprising that the more severe cases comprise the typical research samples, since they're the most likely to wind up in institutions of one kind or another. These caveats in mind, we'll endeavor to apply the principles and conclusions generated from these "tough cases" to the more everyday paranoid personalities we deal with in our normal lives.

From his psychophysiological studies of psychiatric patients, John Gruzelier[8] has advanced a theory of paranoid and nonparanoid schizophrenic syndromes based on a hemisphere typology. According to this view, the full-blown paranoid syndrome typified by exaggerated self-concepts, pressure of speech, flight of ideas, and increased motoric arousal reflects an enhancement of the dynamic activation properties of the left hemisphere. The left hemisphere is implicated because of the predominance of verbal processing, however idiosyncratically organized.

The paranoid's problem, says Gruzelier, is that he's "locked in a left-hemisphere processing mode," resulting in an overly intellectualized orientation. This, in turn, impairs his ability to flexibly adapt to various life situations, since characteristically adopting an extreme position precludes flexibility in thought or action. Conversely, the nonparanoid psychotic syndromes, typified by loss of self-confidence, reduced speech, slow muddled thinking, motor retardation, and blunted emotional responsiveness, suggest a reduction in normal arousal functions and therefore reflect a diminution of left-hemisphere activation. In fact, a number of neuropsychological studies have shown just such a verbal deficit syndrome to be part of the nonparanoid schizophrenic process.[9]

Peter Magaro and Diana Chamrad[10] have approached the hemisphericity issue of paranoid versus nonparanoid schizophrenia from the vantage point of what is known as *hemispheric "metacontrol."*[11] This neuropsychological concept begins with the observation that different kinds of cognitive tasks are handled preferentially by one or the other of the two cerebral hemispheres, as discussed in Chapter 4. Given a particular task—for example, letter recognition—an individual generally "prefers" to use the hemisphere most appropriate for the task, in this case the left. That is, the person has some control over which hemisphere does the task, thereby affecting the brain's higher-order control—metacontrol, or "control of control"—over cognitive performance. In most cases, according to the theory, people can adaptively direct this sort of metacontrol, albeit usually without conscious awareness of doing anything more than trying to apply the right kind of thinking to the problem at hand. In this way, they can influence the proficiency by which their brains handle the various jobs of the day.

However, some people may characteristically opt to use the "wrong," or less proficient, hemisphere to solve certain tasks, even though this results in less than optimal performance. The reason for this may be that other aspects of the preferred hemisphere—its overall cognitive style—may be relied on for more general features of personality functioning. These people get "used to" using one hemisphere for everything, as it were, so they can't flexibly switch hemispheric "gears," when changing circumstances demand it.

So, for example, the paranoid person may prefer nonstop differentially greater left-hemisphere activation, since this is the mode most suited for the detection of discrete pieces of information and for analysis of things into their constituent components—the hallmark of the paranoid cognitive style. Never mind that continual reliance on this overfocused, overscrutinizing mode bars from consideration the more subtle shades of context and intuition—more in the domain of right-hemisphere functioning—that give much of human experience its overall meaning and significance. The paranoid has no use for that; his analytic machine is in constant maximal overdrive.

It stands to reason, then, that the paranoid's biased hemispheric metacontrol might interfere with the performance of certain cognitive tasks requiring the ability to shift to a right-hemisphere mode. What Magaro and Chamrad did to test this hypothesis was to use a task that's known to reliably assess hemispheric differences in processing style.

Four groups of subjects—paranoid schizophrenics, non-paranoid schizophrenics, nonschizophrenic psychiatric patients (to control for the effects of having any kind of psychiatric illness) and normal controls—were given a viewing task using a *tachistoscope*. This is a device that permits visual stimuli to be presented to one hemisphere or the other at a time. The stimuli consisted of a letter-recognition task, known to be handled better by the left hemisphere, and a face-recognition task, which the right is typically better at.

The results showed that for the letter-recognition task, both the paranoid and nonparanoid schizophrenics used their left hemispheres in the usual way to handle this verbal- and detail-based information. However, the paranoids recognized far fewer faces when these were presented to the right hemisphere. Apparently, the paranoids' overreliance on a left-hemisphere serial search strategy for all kinds of activity bollixed their appreciation of information that simply can't be handled well by the left hemisphere: human faces.

Whether this represents a metacontrol preference for pervasive left-hemisphere processing or some arrested development of right-hemisphere capabilities, or both, can't be answered by this kind of experiment. But it does seem to show that one single style of thinking, one rigid approach to all situations, can be woefully maladaptive for even the relatively simple experimental tasks of the neuropsychology lab.

How much more so, then, must this inflexible cognitive style bode poorly for the carrying out of life's myriad responsibilities. If being locked into a left-hemisphere processing mode deprives the paranoid of the all-important avenues of understanding normally provided by way of context, innuendo, shifting perspective, gut reactions, inflective nuances, facial expression, and body language, then is it any surprise that these people—even those you wouldn't describe as obviously psychotic—seem so removed from the ordinary human world, so brittle of character as to seem, well, at least a *little* "crazy"?

Acquired Paranoia: Left Versus Right

The hemisphericity dimension of the paranoid cognitive style is starkly illustrated by the following two cases, each representing a different manifestation of paranoia. The first case[12] involves a patient—we'll call him Fred—who suffered a left-hemisphere stroke. The stroke spared most of the speech processes, so that Fred was able to communicate relatively intactly. But he soon developed a paranoid delusional syndrome as florid as any seen in a long-term paranoid schizophrenic. Fred's family, he believed, was in cahoots with the hospital staff to steal his money and possessions. No amount of persuasion or reassurance could disabuse Fred from his conviction that all about him were schemers and plotters.

The experience of the second patient[13]—whom we'll call Jim—began with a brain tumor in the right hemisphere. The neurosurgeon, to get at the whole mass, couldn't help but damage some of the surrounding tissue. Again, paranoia developed, but of a decidedly different kind. Recall from Chapter 5 that right-hemisphere damage sometimes results in a distortion of body sense, in a hemi-neglect syndrome where the patient denies owning his left-side limbs.

In Jim's case, this took a bizarre twist. The appendages on his left side weren't part of his "true self," he insisted; no—they were agents of the devil, sent to deceive and torment him. The right side of the body (subserved, remember, by the intact left hemisphere) represented to Jim his good, true self, while the left side (subserved by the damaged right hemisphere) was evil incarnate, and furthermore, in mortal conflict with the "good" right side.

Both Fred and Jim developed organic delusional paranoid syndromes as a result of their unilateral brain injuries, but with important differences. Fred's delusion involved an external persecutory cabal, outside enemies who were ganging up on him. Jim's ordeal was even more sinister—in every sense of the word. His tormentors came from within, even if acting as messengers of Satan himself.

Recalling the neuropsychodynamic lessons of Chapter 4, Fred's problems might be seen as involving impaired self-articulation of external social cues owing to left-hemisphere damage. Even though overt speech seemed to have been largely preserved, the crucially important self-explicatory function of language seems to have suffered as the result of his left-hemisphere stroke. Unable to fully make sense of what was going on around him or to properly use internal language as a self-explanatory guide, Fred's interpretive options were limited. Under the emotionally charged circumstances surrounding his illness and hospitalization, he seized on what at the moment seemed to explain his lack of comprehension, namely, that people were deliberately fooling him.

In Jim's case, on the other hand, the right-hemisphere damage produced a violation of the very fabric of corporeal apperception, so that even though the autoexplicatory left hemisphere seems to have been intact, this interpretive capacity was unsuccessful in mitigating the primary body-image disturbance. In fact, the left hemisphere, forced to make some sense of the left hemi-body's lack of normal sensibility, and released by the damaged right to express its overideative bias to the fullest, elaborated this Satanic persecutory delusion into a whole quasi-religious system.

In both Fred and Jim we see exemplified Kurt Goldstein's primary principle of brain functioning.[14] A damaged brain just doesn't sit there with a psychic hole in it: It tries its damnedest to make sense of the world any way it can. Often the sense it makes is wrong—just as it may be with someone whose brain is structurally intact. But healthy or not, we all try to impose some kind of structure on our own selves. Sometimes this structure is a sound one; other times it stands quivering in mortal danger of imminent collapse.

Conclusions

The hypervigilant, superfocused, suspicious cognitive style of the paranoid may have its neuropsychodynamic substrate in left-hemisphere overactivation or overutilization that's even more pronounced than that of the obsessive-compulsive. Could part of the reason for this relate to an overcompensation for deficient right-hemisphere processing skills? At this point it's hard to say, although as we've seen in Chapter 2, differential hemispheric ability may relate to factors in early life, in the womb or in the genes.

A frontal component to the paranoid cognitive style is suggested by MacLean's conceptualization of paranoia in terms of a forward-looking, ever-searching bias in the absence of sufficient feedback from environmental context to make such a searching strategy effective and responsive to reality. The frontal lobes, as we've seen, guide important aspects of search behavior that are important for normal daily activities, and paranoids are *always* searching, whether or not there is in fact anything to search for. What we need for further research are clear cases of localized frontal lobe damage that produce paranoid syndromes.

The obsessive-compulsive also scans the environment, is sensitive to detail. Yet his grasp on the reality of that environment, albeit in a rigid and truncated form, is essentially intact. The obsessive is thrall to a vast occupying force of internal and external constraints, but he does not always fully embrace its directives. As noted, many a compulsive person is baffled and dismayed by his inability to simply relax and let things be, to suspend the search mode and give himself a break. Some even manage to accomplish this for a while, and obsessive-compulsive symptoms and behavior are known to wax and wane over time.

But so concentrated and unrelenting is the search mode of the paranoid that reality itself may be distorted or abandoned in favor of maintaining a rigid focus on "important" details. The overt manifestations can range from mild idiosyncratic weirdness to out-and-out psychosis. Thus, the obsessive-compulsive agonizes over the fact that some things don't seem to "fit"; the paranoid *makes* them fit, if necessary by Byzantine mental twists and turns that may involve a hyperrational, but ultimately unrealistic, reconstruction of reality.

In our neuropsychodynamic model, the left-hemisphere overparticularization of reality that occurs in the obsessive-compulsive is abetted in the paranoid by an even greater abnormal release of frontal search mechanisms. The hypertrophied scanning mode finds significance in the smallest of things; the merest of cues is taken apart and analyzed as the most critical pieces of "evidence." The left hemisphere-frontal lobe mechanism of rational thought, ordinarily indispensable for the maintenance of reality, becomes in the paranoid, its nemesis.

CHAPTER 8

THE AMORPHOUS SELF

The Hysterical Style

> If the mind, which rules the body, ever forgets itself so far as to trample upon its slave, the slave is never generous enough to forgive the injury, but will rise and smite its oppressor.
>
> —HENRY WADSWORTH LONGFELLOW

> How strange are the tricks of memory, which, often hazy as a dream about the most important events of a man's life, religiously preserve the merest trifles.
>
> —SIR RICHARD BURTON

> Hysterics suffer mainly from reminiscences.
>
> —JOSEF BREUER AND SIGMUND FREUD

"Don't get hysterical," we tell someone when we want to forestall some particularly angry, lachrymose, or otherwise messy emotional display. This commonplace, colloquial use of the word "hysterical" retains the connotation of histrionic flamboyance that we associate with people who habitually act as if everything that happens to them is just *so* important, *so* dramatic.

Another popular usage for the term hysterical is to denote some somatic symptom that's not a "real" symptom, but rather the expression of a phony illness, a disease that's "all in the mind." In fact, hysteria is frequently equated, incorrectly, with malingering. But whereas the malingerer can usually be shown to have had a clear conscious intent to deceive (for example, acting sick or wounded to avoid military duty or to pursue a bogus financial claim), the hysteric typically "believes" that he or she* is somatically impaired; the hysteric, as it were, fools herself, if no one else.

The Psychodynamics of Hysteria

Freud's career as a psychotherapist began with hysteria; indeed, clinical work with hysterics formed the backbone of early psychoanalytic theory and practice. According to Freud,[1] hysteria occurs when the ego is confronted by so painful an experience or feeling that no chance of conscious resolution seems possible. Rather than splitting and isolation of emotion, which is the obsessive-compulsive's favorite defense mechanism, for the hysteric, "the incompatible idea is rendered innocuous by its sum of excitation being transferred into something somatic. For this I should like to propose the name of *conversion*."[2]

Thus, Freud coined the term that has come to stand for the transformation of an unacceptable unconscious idea or wish into a bodily symptom. The *psychological* conflict, said Freud, is expressed in the form of a *physical* symptom, thereby banishing it from consciousness. This symptom, moreover, bears a symbolic relationship to the repressed material. For example, fear of retaliating for an act of aggression might express itself as a paralysis of movement. Or the wish to drown out disturbing information might emerge as hysterical deafness. Fear of impulsively giving away some dirty little secret might produce a hysterical loss of speech, and so on.

---

* The diagnosis of hysteria and the hysterical personality is made more frequently in women, and for that reason, I'll use the generic "she" and "her" for descriptive purposes in this chapter, just as I use "he" and "him" to describe the obsessive-compulsive, paranoid, and impulsive cognitive styles. But although there's somewhat of a gender predominance in each of these personalities and cognitive styles, all types can occur in both men and women, so what I have to say in this chapter applies equally to males and females with hysterical personalities and symptoms.

And as with the other character defenses considered so far, subsequent study has shown that individual variations in cognitive style seem to be associated with this particular kind of defensive reaction.

The Hysterical Cognitive Style

According to David Shapiro,[3] the hysterical style is the virtual opposite of the obsessive-compulsive and paranoid styles. Hysterical cognition is global, relatively diffuse and lacking in sharp focus of attention and detail—in other words, highly impressionistic. In contrast to the compulsive's active and prolonged searching for details, the hysteric tends to respond quickly and impulsively, and is highly susceptible to what's immediately striking or merely obvious. Hysterics see only forests, never trees; their perceptions and conclusions are based on immediate, emotionally salient impressions, not on active analysis of the situation. Their lack of intense intellectual concentration and their resulting distractibility and impressionability account for the largely nonfactual world—the "fantasy world"—in which hysterics typically live.

For the hysteric, the hunch or the impression is the guiding cognitive process. This explains why hysterical personalities are typically lacking in intellectual curiosity, even the mundane inquisitiveness about events around them that most people display. Inasmuch as most intellectual pursuits require at least some degree of sustained, focused attention, the hysteric, sorely deficient in this faculty, shows a decided disinclination for cognitively demanding work.

Hysterics are often remarkably lacking in everyday factual knowledge that has no immediate emotional impact or practical use. They may follow intently the lives of soap opera characters or *People* magazine celebrities, but be unable to name the current governor of their state, to explain who fought World War II or why, to tell what paper is made of, or give the correct freezing point of water.

It's not that hysterics as a group are any dumber than the rest of us in the usual sense; they can learn skills or information when necessary for some particular purpose, like a job or card game. Indeed, they often show reasonably good practical intelligence when it comes to dealing with common, everyday situations or things that capture their fancy. But sustained intellectual concentration and a range of interests that transcend the immediate or personal are alien to them.

The hysterical style has a particularly clear connection with the basic defense mechanism of *repression*, and this may occur in two different ways. First, the original thought or plan is not sharply and factually defined in the first place, and is therefore not likely to be mentally coordinated with other facts such as names, dates, places, and so on. Instead, the input itself is highly impressionistic (''Oh, he's wonderful!'' ''That's a terrible idea!'') and highly susceptible to displacement by, or fusion with, other previous or subsequent impressions.

Thus, even at the input stage, there's a failure of analysis, categorization, and cross-referencing of information with other incoming and already-stored data that would provide the necessary context for a stable mental representation. This, after all, is how we ordinarily form coherent personal histories—they evolve and develop as new experience continues to interact with previously formed self-conceptions throughout our lives. But the hysteric's input is amorphous, garbled, unanalyzed, and unarticulated, especially with respect to those forms of input that require any kind of sustained or focused attention.

Second, the problems of inattention, impressionability, and distractibility also affect the recollection of already-stored material. Thus, clear, sharp, factual recall of memories is difficult even under the best of circumstances.

Remembering something normally requires some measure of active, directed attention, a kind of internal search mode. This, in turn, is facilitated by a certain degree of analysis, categorization, and sometimes verbal labeling to enable you to pull from the numberless bits of stored data in your brain just those fragments of fact and experience that are relevant to the situation at hand.

But when such internal scanning is deficient, one memory blends fuzzily with the next. Scenes and events, persons and places, thoughts and reactions are commingled in an undifferentiated mental mishmash. Thus, the hysteric gives one version of a story one minute, another version the next— not out of willful prevarication, but because what's remembered is more dictated by the feeling of the moment than by any concentrated effort to produce a factual recall. Hence, Breuer and Freud's famous comment that "hysterics suffer mainly from reminiscences."[4]

So, for example, last week your hysterical friend had lunch with a coworker who told her something that got her upset, and that friend looks or sounds like an in-law she never got along with, but who also resembles a TV actress whose character she loves. Now you ask her, "How did that lunch go?" The story you get will reflect whatever complex of associations happens to be called up at the time of your query. If she saw the favored TV show last night, the answer might be "Great—we had a swell time. I offered to treat and she was so gracious about accepting and insisting that next time it's on her." Ask the question again tomorrow after she's spoken to the hated in-law and it's "Terrible— what a bitch she is. She even stuck me with the check." And so on.

The oft remarked-on "naiveté" of hysterics is also understandable in light of their cognitive style. We've all known people who live in their own little fantasy lands, blithely unconcerned with the realities of the real world around them. Indeed we may marvel at how these individuals *can* ignore the events and responsibilities that at times press so heavily upon our own lives. Are these people lazy or crazy?

Neither, really. The hysteric's inability to become fully aware of unpleasant thoughts or feelings lying at the periphery of awareness is abetted by her incapacity to clearly and sharply focus attention. This cognitive style also predisposes her to the idealized romantic recollection for which the histrionic Sarah Bernhardts of stage, screen, and literary fiction are so renowned. Typically, the hysteric's recollection is conspicuously lacking in factual detail and, Shapiro notes, one sometimes get the impression that a sober, dispassionate analysis of objective facts would "spoil" the story.

This same quality is evident in the hysteric's idealization of the object of her romantic love. Blindness to a beloved's objective flaws comprises for most of us one of the tender alloys from which Cupid's arrowhead is forged. And this projectile smites the heart of the hysteric especially hard. Conversely, immediate, global impressions of revulsion, disgust, petulant jealousy, and wounded outrage come just as easily and with the same obliviousness to complicating details or extenuating circumstances. The hysterical romantic view thus has its villains as well as its heroes—often the same person at different times or in different moods.

It seems that the hysteric's romantic, fantastical, and nonfactual experience of the world also extends to her experience of her own self. Hysterics often don't *feel* like very substantial beings with real and factual histories, with stable identities. Indeed, they're often barely aware of their own personal histories, except to the extent that these histories exist in the form of what Shapiro refers to as a *romance-history*, a life-story populated by impressionistically perceived romantic or idealized figures.

Regarding the often cited overemotionality of hysterics (as in the phrase "getting hysterical"), the relative absence of complex cognitive integration and the quick impression-istic mode of information processing are frequently paral-leled by the hysteric's abrupt and often explosive emotional displays. Easily triggered or excited, these erupt into con-sciousness as the final emotional product, just as the im-mediate, global impression emerges as the final cognitive product. The emotion undergoes little mental elaboration before being expressed in its raw, elemental form. This ten-dency is in turn aided by the hysteric's global, immediate, and impressionistic style: Feelings are experienced all at once, in an all-or-none fashion, and responses to feelings are correspondingly immediate and intense. ''Hysterical outbursts'' thus complete the picture of the hysterical cog-nitive style.

Hysterical Conversion: The Brain's Role

No discussion of hysteria can omit what has come to be seen as the hallmark of this syndrome: hysterical conversion re-actions. The expression of psychological conflicts in somatic form is a puzzling clinical conundrum that has impressed and baffled doctors from Hippocrates through Freud to the modern classifiers of mental disorders. Additionally, how-ever, it represents a profound philosophical problem that pokes at the very heart of the mind-body problem. How can something in the *mind* be transformed into something of the *body*?

Over half a century ago, in what today might be called a ''sociobiological'' theory of hysteria, Ernst Kretschmer[5] ar-gued that most forms of hysteria represent two instinctive reaction patterns which he believed were prevalent through-out the animal kingdom. Both, he asserted, were mecha-nisms of biological adaptation to dangerous or threatening situations.

The first Kretschmer characterized as the *violent motor reaction*, exemplified by the wild flailing response many animals show when trying to escape injury, capture, or confinement. The counterpart to this in human hysteria could be seen in fugue states, convulsive paroxysms and violent emotional attacks with subsequent amnesia and tremors—just the kinds of wild activity popularly and often pejoratively labeled "hysterical."

The second kind of reaction was the *sham death* or *immobilization reflex*, in which inaction and seemingly stuporous features predominate. Many animals, including humans, "freeze" when confronted with a threat; this immobilization serves to obscure the identity or whereabouts of the threatened party or conveys a message of innocuous nonchallenge that will hopefully deflect the confrontation. Human hysterical analogs to this second pattern, Kretchmer said, might include dreamy hypnoid states, "spells," blindness, deafness, analgesia, paralysis, and speech and movement disorders.

More recently, Kretschmer's formulation has been revived and expanded by Arnold Ludwig.[6] Ludwig posits a natural tendency for animals and humans to react in progressively more primitive ways when confronted with potentially dangerous and inescapable situations. Under such conditions, organisms readily and automatically resort to behaviors appropriate to earlier stages of development, behaviors that appear regressive or "childish." These include urinary incontinence, babbling, rocking, head bobbing, crying, vivid fantasizing, and so on—the kind of reactions often associated with "shell shock" or catastrophic stress reactions, for example.

This type of regressive activity contributes to the posture of helplessness and defenselessness which, like Kretschmer's sham death–immobilization reflex, wards off attack. In addition, the resulting alteration in consciousness blurs reality testing and thereby provides a certain psychological insulation from the dangerous event. In the case of human hysteria, if any of these primitive behaviors are reinforced by their success in actually removing or escaping from the danger or threat, they'll more than likely be resorted to in the future under similar circumstances.

Like Shapiro's theory of the hysterical cognitive style, Ludwig places attentional dysfunction at the pathological core of the hysterical conversion syndrome. In Ludwig's view, the hysteric experiencing, say, a sensory-loss conversion reaction suffers from a dissociation in the brain between systems responsible for mediating the raw sensory data, the "meaning" of the incoming stimulation, and those which deal with the individual's ability to attend to that stimulation in the first place.

Quick—how heavy is this book? Had to think about it for a moment, didn't you? You're also probably not aware of the gentle pressure of your clothing against your skin or your watchband on your wrist until I mention it. Or how many times have you been surprised when a loudly humming air conditioner, which you never "noticed," suddenly turns off? The point is, there's a lot in our sensory environment that we're ordinarily not conscious of, unless it's called to our attention in some way.

Neurophysiological research has shown that the conscious appreciation of a particular sensory impression, whether sight, sound, smell or body sense, depends not just on the sensory pathways conveying that sensation, but also on the participation of a separate, collateral system. Called the *reticular activating system* (Fig. 8, page 174), this chain of neural structures and pathways is responsible for literally "directing attention" to incoming sensory information at different levels of processing.

Damage to this system produces a curious dissociative condition where the sensory areas of the brain process the information normally (as shown, for example, by the EEG), but the person remains subjectively unaware of the stimulus; it simply doesn't "register." Normal sensory perception, then, depends on the coordinated activity of the neural sys-

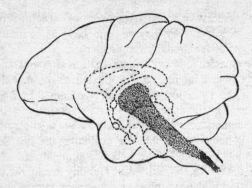

Fig. 8: The *reticular activating system*, represented by the shaded area in this drawing is a complex meshwork of neural structures and pathways that stretches from the spinal cord up into the core of the brain. It plays an important role in helping the brain "take notice" of incoming stimuli and for the ability to focus attention on important events. (From R. F. Thompson, *Introduction to Physiological Psychology*, 2d ed. Copyright © 1975 by R. F. Thompson. Used by permission of Harper & Row Publishers, Inc.)

tems conveying sensory information *and* the reticular mechanisms governing appropriate attention to and registration of this information.

Even intense stimuli like the pain from a serious battlefield wound, which under ordinary circumstances would certainly consume all of our interest, may be relegated to the back burner of consciousness if more pressing concerns—like figuring how to get the hell out of there—supervene. Also, it's frequently difficult to "pay attention" to some trivial external situation when we're preoccupied by some more pressing inner concern. As interested as you are in a particular magazine article, it would almost surely have less appeal and less command of your attention if you were reading it in the doctor's waiting room while awaiting a biopsy report, than if you were relaxing on vacation.

Yet it's clear that in most circumstances we do have a

certain flexibility and volitional control over attentional processes. For example, you can "force" yourself to concentrate on unengaging material if you know you're having a test on it tomorrow. In the same way, you can "force" your attention away from something which you know is exceedingly unpleasant, like a recent disappointment, injustice, humiliation, or obsessive worry. It's as if "one part" of you wants to dwell on the nasty business, while "another part" wants to let it go, not let it eat you up inside. In many cases, this is adaptive: Why torture yourself with anticipatory anxiety or lingering regret if there's nothing further you can do about the situation?

But then there are those people who seem to have no trouble at all turning their attention away from unpleasant things, even when they *can*—or *should*—do something about it. No bad thoughts are tolerated, no matter what the consequences. We call these people "unrealistic," "dreamers," "evaders of responsibility," "cockeyed optimists," or sometimes "hysterics."

According to Ludwig, in hysterical conversions that involve derangements of sensory processing and movement (because normal motor activity depends on adequate sensory feedback from muscles), there occurs a dissociation between attention and certain sources of incoming stimulation. Hysterics, remember, are masters at diverting attention. And attention to a symptom of disability, like anesthesia or paralysis, is usually necessary for there to be any degree of concern over it.

Thus, inhibition of reticular attentional mechanisms may be responsible for the disability itself because there can be no normal function—feeling or movement—without attention. At the same time, it's also responsible for the blithe unconcern that frequently surrounds the disability, *la belle indifférence*[7] that has been noted since the last century to be one of the hallmarks of hysterical conversion.

Moreover, posits Ludwig, there exists in hysterical conversion an ideomotor schism that renders it impossible for the hysteric to adequately mobilize attention toward the symptom. The patient cannot, therefore, willingly remedy the dysfunction. Ludwig proposes that hysterical conversion may be due to the action of attention-inhibiting impulses brought about by particularly intense emotional experiences. The awareness of bodily function is, as it were, shouted down by the emotional cacophony that competes for the reticular attentional mechanism. In line with this, temporary improvement or disappearance of the symptoms would be most likely to occur during periods of relaxed vigilance, or under disinhibitory conditions, such as hypnosis or the use of barbiturate drugs. Such drugs, it's been shown, selectively inhibit the reticular formation.[8]

Several studies have, in fact, confirmed the existence of psychophysiological changes in hysterical conversion reactions, and attempts have been made to demonstrate abnormalities in nervous system arousal and reactivity in patients with these "somatoform disorders," as contemporary clinicians term them.[9]

In one study,[10] conversion patients were characterized as manifesting "physiological negativism" on the basis of their responses to the cold-pressor procedure. In this technique the subject immerses his hand in a bath of ice water, which usually produces a significant rise in blood pressure as peripheral vessels reflexively constrict. But hysterics were observed to show a significantly lessened blood pressure response to this procedure, suggesting that their nervous systems are characteristically underresponsive to physiologically activating stimuli.

Unfortunately, the opposite seemed to hold true in another experiment,[11] which used a different kind of psychophysiological activating procedure. This study found greater than normal physiological activity in the form of higher heart rate, sweat gland activity, and muscle activity in patients with chronically debilitating conversion symptoms, poor interpersonal and occupational coping skills, and long histories of multiple medical complaints.

Thus, these studies hardly confirm any consistent direction in hysterics' physiological reactivity. However, I think what they do suggest is that hysterics may show an unusually greater *lability* of physiological reactivity to certain stressful stimuli. That is, the nervous system of individuals with conversion symptoms may be prone to wider psychophysiological swings back and forth than normal.

Lader[12] has interpreted such findings to mean that patients with conversion symptoms have a consistently high anxiety level. Earlier, Lader and Sartorius[13] had compared hysteria patients with chronic anxiety patients and found that the hysterics actually rated themselves as more anxious than did the anxiety patients. Curiously, however, the ratings of the examining psychiatrists went in the opposite direction: They rated the hysterics as less anxious than the anxiety patients. When recordings were made of the subjects' levels of psychophysiological arousal, the physiological readings agreed with the patients, not the doctors. That is, the hysterics displayed greater physiological signs of arousal than did the anxiety patients.

Could this mean that *la belle indifférence*—the seemingly bland unconcern that characterizes hysterics with conversion reactions—is merely an artifact? Could it in fact be masking a deeper, inner anxiety that's not observable on the surface during a cursory clinical interview? Finally, this study found that conversion symptoms tended to persist longer in those hysteria patients who had both high anxiety self-ratings and greater recorded physiological arousal, supporting the notion that greater lability of arousal mechanisms may be associated with greater susceptibility to hysterical conversion.

We've been talking about the body's reactions, but what about the brain itself? One technique that's been used to study the brain's response to arousing stimuli is the *cortical evoked response*. Here, a stimulus is delivered more or less naturally to one of the senses. This could be a flicker of light, a tone or a touch, depending on which sensory modality is being studied. The activity "evoked" in the brain as it processes this incoming sensory data is picked up by means of recording electrodes. In most experimental human studies, these are generally applied to the scalp (as in a regular EEG recording), whereas in animal research, or in humans where there's a dire clinical question to be answered, the probe might actually be placed within the brain tissue itself. In either case, this enables clinicians or researchers to assess the brain's electrophysiological activity as it processes certain kinds of information. This can yield clues to the overall state of cerebral health, as well as to the way different brain regions handle different types of information.

The first studies of the evoked response, carried out by Hernandez-Peon and colleagues,[14] were with cats. These researchers found that the brain activity of a cat showing strong and reliable evoked responses to an auditory tone would become abruptly silent when the smell of fish or the sight of a live mouse was introduced at the same time as the tone. Fish and mice, being generally more "important" to cats than the electronic buzzes and whines of their human keepers' apparatus, overrode the evoked response to the tone. In essence, the cat's attention was diverted from the tone to the fish or mouse, and this was reflected in the brain's activity.

What this showed is that sensation and perception are not just passive processes. Rather, the cerebral cortex actively regulates the amount and type of incoming information arriving over the different sensory pathways. And it does this by means of the reticular attentional system. Thus, a cat— or anyone else—can only be attending to, aware of, "conscious" of, just so much information at any given moment. Next time you're at a party, try to listen to *two* conversations simultaneously and you'll experience the same kind of phenomenon. You can flip back and forth between the two, but you can't process both dialogues at the very same time.

Could such reticular system influence over incoming sensory information somehow be responsible for the hysteric's seeming out-of-touchness with her own body and its functions?

An early application of the evoked-response technique to the study of hysterical conversion was carried out by the Hernandez-Peon group themselves.[15] The case involved a fifteen-year-old girl with *glove-and-stocking anesthesia* over the left side of her body. This syndrome is so named because the patient typically complains of complete loss of feeling in the hands or feet that abruptly ends at some point mid-arm or mid-leg—exactly as if the zone of sensory loss were defined by the contours of a glove or sock.

Organic brain dysfunction that produces sensory loss virtually never involves such a sharply demarcated zone of impairment. Instead, the sensory loss over a given area tends to have irregular borders and a graded severity. More-anesthetic areas are surrounded by regions of lesser impairment and shade gradually into normal sensibility. Occasionally, damage to peripheral nerves in the limbs themselves can produce a syndrome resembling the glove-and-stocking one, but this is usually accompanied by other symptoms, such as pain and motor disorders that distinguish it from its hysterical counterpart.

Hernandez-Peon's patient showed clear-cut evoked responses from the sensory-processing areas of the brain that handle input from the normal right forearm. However, when the conversion-impaired left forearm was stimulated, no definite evoked response was seen. It was as if this patient were suffering from an impairment of attention related to perception of the hysterically anesthetic limb.

More recently, Levy and Behrman[16] studied a forty-three-year-old woman with right-side hysterical hemi-anesthesia.

This time, two levels of sensory stimulation were used, high
and low. In addition, the experimenters also varied *where*
they delivered the stimuli. In some cases the stimulus was
applied to the skin surface of the forearm, other times directly to the ulnar nerve, one of the peripheral nerves in the
arm that conveys sensory information to the central nervous
system.

They found that high-intensity stimuli applied to the ulnar
nerve on the hysterically anesthetic side of the body produced evoked responses equal to those obtained on stimulation of the normal side. With low-intensity stimulation,
however, the response to stimulation on the affected side
was less than that of the normal side. When the stimuli were
applied to the skin of the forearm, the evoked responses
from the affected side were diminished, compared with the
normal side, and this was true both for high and low levels
of stimulation.

Thus, the hypothesized cortex-to-reticular inhibition could
apparently be overridden when the sensory stimulation was
intense enough *and* if it was applied directly to the sensory
nerve itself, as opposed to having to go through "chan-
nels," that is, as a normal sensation from the skin surface.
These findings have since been replicated with several patients having hysterical anesthesias, showing that this is far
from an isolated phenomenon. Moreover, in cases where
the hysterical conversion disappears or goes into remission,
the differences in evoked responses between the normal and the
merly affected side seem to disappear as well. That is,
the electrophysiological brain activity changes in accord with
the clinical course of the hysterical conversion syndrome.

And so the attentional component of Ludwig's theory of
hysterical conversion seems reasonably supported: The process of conversion apparently takes advantage of cortico-
reticular mechanisms in a way that's foreign to what most
of us consider normal functioning. The hysteric appears to
be able to allocate attention in a special and peculiar way

in which certain types of bodily function, as well as concern over loss of that function, are "canceled out."

What about the cognitive component? Along with Ludwig himself, Bendefeldt and colleagues[17] sought to examine Ludwig's memory-attentional dysfunction hypothesis by administering a battery of psychological tests to a group of hospitalized psychiatric patients with hysterical conversion reactions. The tests were also given to a group of matched nonhysterical control subjects. The test battery included measures of memory, attention, concentration, suggestibility, and field-dependency versus field-independency. This last measure refers to the tendency for people to base perceptual judgments on, respectively, external influences or internal, autonomous decisions.

In comparison to controls, the patients with hysterical conversion disorders were found to be more suggestible, more dependent on outside environmental cues and influences in making perceptual decisions (that is, more field-dependent), to have greater memory impairment, and to show diminished vigilance and attention. The findings, therefore, appear to support Ludwig's cognitive conceptualization of the hysteric. Of equal interest is the similarity between the cognitive profile suggested by their data and Shapiro's delineation of the hysterical cognitive style. That is, the hysteric's approach to experience is one of global, impressionistic, uncritical receptivity. Paradoxically, in contrast to the exquisite—albeit "unconscious"—attentional control that the hysteric exerts over internal bodily states, his or her attention to the external world at large is disturbingly fuzzy. Perhaps in this very lability of neuropsychodynamic information processing lies the clue to the hysterical cognitive style.

Neuropsychology of the Hysterical Cognitive Style

An ambitious study that sought to compare cerebral laterality patterns in hysterical versus obsessive personalities was carried out by Smokler and Shevrin.[18] To understand the rationale of their study, recall the concept of "hemispheric metacontrol"[19] described in the last chapter. According to this idea, different kinds of cognitive tasks are handled differently by the two cerebral hemispheres. It would stand to reason that, given a particular task or situation, a person would apply the most appropriate hemisphere to that job.

Since few tasks are entirely of one kind or another, each hemisphere will normally contribute its talent to those components of the task it's best suited for. The idea is that at some level of processing, the brain makes a "decision" about how to allocate hemispheric responsibility for the solution of different problems or the handling of different kinds of psychological processes. In most cases, according to the theory, people can adaptively direct this sort of metacontrol in their own brains, albeit usually without awareness of anything other than "figuring out" how to solve a problem or get a job done.

However, some people may characteristically use the "wrong," or less proficient, hemisphere to solve cognitive tasks or deal with broader life situations, even though they may end up with a less-than-optimal result. The reason for this could be that the overall cognitive style of the preferred hemisphere may be relied upon for more general features of personality and thereby comes to dominate behavior, resulting in less flexible overall functioning.

Smokler and Shevrin reasoned that a strongly "left-hemisphere" individual would analyze everything in a piecemeal, analytic manner, even in situations where this might be inappropriate—as is the case with obsessive-compulsives. Conversely, a strongly "right-hemisphere" person would deal with all situations in a global, holistic manner, rarely analyzing details in a direct way—the hallmark of the hysteric.

To check out their theory, Smokler and Shevrin recruited a large group of volunteers and gave them all a series of psychological tests to determine which of them had predominantly obsessive-compulsive personality styles, which had mainly hysterical personality styles and which had a predominance of neither style (control subjects). Next, the subjects were given an examination of *conjugate lateral eye movements* (CLEMs, or more commonly, just LEMs—"conjugate" merely meaning they move in the same direction), which are believed to be an index of dominant hemisphericity for problem solving.[20]

To understand how this technique works, the next time you ask someone a question, watch his or her eyes. Studies have shown that a person's gaze typically flits to one side just at the end of hearing the question, prior to giving an answer. The direction of the LEMs may indicate which hemisphere is most activated by the question and by the cognitive work of coming up with an answer. Because of the way the brain controls eye movements, the shift is in the direction opposite to the activated hemisphere.

It would stand to reason, then, that a particular LEM could be influenced either by the type of question asked—for example, verbal or logical questions would result in a rightward shift (left hemisphere), spatial or emotional questions would cause a leftward shift (right hemisphere)—or by the type of processing style the person uses to handle most problems, regardless of question type—for example, an overrational person would show many right shifts (left hemisphere), despite the nature of the question, and an overemotional person would show a left-shift predominance (right hemisphere) under the same circumstances.

To examine the effect of question-type on hemispheric activation, Smokler and Shevrin asked the subjects a series of forty questions, divided into three types: spatial-emotional, spatial-nonemotional, and verbal-nonemotional. An example of the first type might be "Can you imagine a time when you felt particularly happy?" An example of the last type might be "Describe how an electrical battery works."

What the investigators found was that the subjects with hysterical personality styles tended to look to the left during questioning, indicating predominant activation of the right hemisphere. The obsessive-compulsives, on the other hand, looked predominantly to the right, reflecting higher left-hemisphere activity. Further, the type of question had no effect on LEM shifts, suggesting that personality style had a greater effect on hemispheric activation than problem type. An obsessive, it seems, thinks "rationally," under all circumstances, even when the problem demands a more expansive, nonrational approach. Hysterics, for their part, rely on more diffuse, global cognitive processing, even in situations where a more focused and logical approach would clearly be more effective.

And the differences between the hysteric and the obsessive-compulsive cognitive styles—styles that seem so diametrically opposed at the experiential level—appear to have a basis in opposite patterns of hemispheric activation, a rigid fixation of the normally flexible hemispheric metacontrol mechanism in one mode or the other, resulting in two entirely opposite ways of dealing with reality.

A study with a similar premise was carried out by Peter Magaro and colleagues,[21] who began with a commonplace observation of how different people go about looking through their home or workplace for an object. Some people use what may be called a *serial search strategy*, that is, they seem to explore carefully and methodically, considering each alternative hiding place in its turn; although this approach may at times seem slow and labored, they usually end up finding what they're looking for.

Not always so fortunate are those who rely on a *parallel search strategy*. You must have observed some people (and, under frantic enough circumstances, yourself as well) "looking everywhere at once," the search proceeding virtually at random, but sooner or later covering all the possibilities one way or another, sometimes with success, other times resulting only in further exasperation.

In addition to their more everyday applications, search strategies are also important to the solution of certain experimental cognitive tests. Magaro and colleagues reasoned that someone with a compulsive cognitive style would be more likely to demonstrate a serial search strategy on such tasks, while someone with a hysterical cognitive style should characteristically use a parallel search strategy. To test this, groups of compulsive, hysteric and control subjects, as determined by a specially designed personality inventory, were administered a visual search task in which they had to scan arrays of fifty five-letter rows for a predesignated target letter.

Contrary to the investigators' expectation, it was the hysterics, not the compulsives, who were more likely to use a serial processing style. Compulsives seemed to conform more to the actual demands of the task in handling the stimuli; that is, they used both serial and parallel strategies as the situation demanded, and didn't—as the theory would predict—exhibit a dominant personality-based serial processing strategy that overrode task demands. However, although the hysterics relied on a serial processing style, they did worse on the task than the compulsives or controls; that is, they were significantly slower to scan and process the stimuli. What's going on?

The answer seems to be that it's not just what you use, but how you use it. That is, the investigators suggest, hysterics have great difficulty in focusing on specific elements in a stimulus field. So when they gamely attempt a careful serial analysis of stimulus elements, they quickly fall into trouble. What the results of this study suggest is that, contrary to the original hypothesis, hysterics don't necessarily use parallel processing all the time as an exclusive, preferred mode of response. Instead, they often do try to use a serial processing strategy, but use it badly. The hysterics may indeed have had a general, overall preference for a parallel processing strategy but, because they believed that this particular task demanded a serial approach, they used an unaccustomed and unfamiliar serial processing strategy—with dismal results.

Another approach to the neuropsychology of hysteria has been taken by Flor-Henry and colleagues.[22] They gave ten patients who satisfied strict diagnostic criteria for hysteria a lengthy and extensive neuropsychological test battery. Their performance on these measures was compared with that of a larger group of previously tested subjects who had no prior history of neurologic or psychiatric illness. As an added control, ten patients with schizophrenia and ten others with depressive disorders were studied.

The test results showed that, on the one hand, hysterics exhibited bilateral frontal and right fronto-temporal dysfunction when compared to controls. On the other hand, findings suggestive of disturbed left-hemispheric functions were also present. Moreover, the neuropsychological impairment patterns of hysterics resembled to some degree that of schizophrenics.

On the basis of these findings, Flor-Henry suggested that hysteria as a stable clinical syndrome actually stems from left-hemisphere dysfunction. In turn, the observed signs of right-hemisphere involvement relate not to the essential core hysterical syndrome, but to the associated clinical features such as female predominance, emotional instability, dysphoric (sad) mood, and the presence of asymmetrical conversion symptoms—phenomena associated with the right hemisphere.

The investigators further argue that, based on family studies, as well as neuropsychological results, hysteria in the female is the syndromic equivalent of psychopathy, or antisocial personality, in males who, as we'll see in the next chapter, also exhibit predominant left-hemisphere dysfunction. Moreover, the investigators suggest that hysteria represents in the female a relatively benign variant of schizophrenia characterized by imprecise verbal communications, a subtle form of emotional incongruity, as well as the conversion dimension.

Thus, to Flor-Henry, the core deficits in hysteria consist of the impairment in verbal communication, the incongruity of emotional responsivity, and the disturbances in processing signals from internal bodily states. These are the consequences of altered dominant hemispheric functioning which produces, when it occurs in the female, a secondary disorganization of the contralateral right hemisphere. This in turn determines the flamboyant façade of female hysteria—the "hysterical" quality—but which at the same time may mask its fundamental left-hemisphere substrate. Hysteria in women is thus seen as the analog of impulsive antisociality in men—a theme we'll return to in the next chapter.

Hysterical Conversion and the Hysterical Cognitive Style

Can neuropsychology shed light on why the hysterical cognitive style seems to lend itself so readily to the production of conversion symptoms?

As discussed previously, patients with damage to the right cerebral hemisphere frequently show contralateral neglect in which the environment and body areas that lie in the sensory field opposite the side of the lesion are ignored or

otherwise abnormally perceived. In some cases dysfunctional body parts are denied ownership by the patient, or
even attributed to someone else; shallow rationalizations for
these beliefs may contribute to the clinical picture. As we've
also seen, bizarre delusional systems have been known to
develop around the affected body part or area, some even
including paranoid psychotic features. Although neglect and
related disorders can occur with left-hemisphere lesions (affecting perception of right hemi-space), left-sided perceptual syndromes from right-hemisphere damage appear to be
both more common and more clinically striking. In addition, the right hemisphere seems to play a special role in
the processing of emotional aspects of somatic signals coming from the body as a whole.

All this becomes important for understanding hysterical
conversion when we consider that conversion symptoms
themselves tend to show an asymmetrical pattern of distribution. That is, if the pattern of symptoms were randomly
distributed from patient to patient, we'd expect to see the
anesthesias, paralyses, and other symptoms equally on both
sides of the body. Yet this is not the case. Studies have
shown that conversion symptoms occur more frequently on
the left side of the body than on the right, and this is as true
for left-handers as for righties.[23] Moreover, complaints of
pain—and this includes both the hysterical, "psychogenic"
variety, as well as pain due to bona fide organic disease—
appear to be more frequently referred to the left side of the
body.[24] In addition, the right hemisphere may be more important than the left for mediating the ability to endure pain
sensations in general.[25]

Early psychoanalytic writers like Sandor Ferenczi[26] posited that the left side of the body is naturally more accessible to unconscious influences than the right side, which in
turn was believed to be better defended against unconscious
impulses by virtue of its being more active and skillful. And
as we saw in Chapter 4, a number of modern neuropsychol-

ogists have seized on the idea of the nonlinear, holistic, multiply convergent, emotionally predominant and verbally inarticulable right-hemisphere cognitive style as forming the cerebral substrate for unconscious processes in general.

Recall that some writers regard right-hemisphere cognition as congruent with unconscious-style thinking, or compare certain features of isolated right-hemisphere functioning in split-brain patients to certain "pure" aspects of unconscious thought. Similarly, the reinforcement of early emotional reaction patterns at a developmental stage prior to the sufficient maturation of the cortex of the left cerebral hemisphere may preclude adequate verbal-rational mediation of early experience. This, then, could form the basis for repression, which involves an inability to self-communicate and self-comprehend infantile wishes, fears, and immature behavior patterns.

This brings us back to the role of attention in the production and perpetuation of hysterical symptoms. As we've seen, studies of both brain-damaged and normal individuals suggest that the right hemisphere plays a special role in mediating the attention and arousal involved in the processing of stimuli from both sides of the body and in preparing both hemispheres for a response. At the same time, the right hemisphere appears to have greater reciprocal connections with the reticular formation than the left, so that even given bilateral representation of somatic arousal, some degree of contralateral (that is, left-body) predominance exists.

Attention, however, is an active process, and several investigators have stressed the importance of a corticothalamic-reticular arousal loop, whose cortical representation in humans is found in the dorsolateral ("upper-outer") portion of the frontal lobe, the part of the brain most involved in directing and controlling mental processes such as attention. In addition, recalling Part II of this book, reciprocal mediobasal ("inner-lower") frontal-limbic connections are important in handling emotional and motivational aspects of information processing and adaptive behavior, and evidence exists further for a predominant role for the right hemisphere in mediating these emotional aspects of experience and behavior. What we need to look at now is a case where brain dysfunction sheds light on the neuropsychodynamics involved in creating just these kinds of psychical dissociations that lie at the core of the hysterical cognitive style.

A Tale of Two Memories

This patient, reported by Antonio Damasio and colleagues,[27] whom we'll call Don, was a fifty-five-year-old, right-handed man whose education included high school and one year of college. He'd been employed as a newspaper advertising and printing salesman for twenty-seven years and was involved in a variety of professional, recreational, and family activities—like Evan in Chapter 6, another example of a normal, well-adjusted individual soon to be zapped by fate.

Don's ordeal began at the age of forty-eight when he developed herpes simplex encephalitis, a viral infection of the brain that produces confusion, disorientation, seizures, and fever. After a three-day coma, Don gradually regained consciousness and he was discharged from the hospital, awake and alert, one month later. His neurologic condition at that time appeared normal, except for an impaired sense of smell, some changes in behavior, and a peculiar memory disorder.

CT scans showed the infection-induced brain damage to encompass most of the inner surface of the frontal lobes, as well as cortical and deeper subcortical portions of the temporal lobes. This type of damage heavily involves the limbic system, the chief brain network involved in memory, emotion, and the motivational "meaningfulness" of events in general. The problem with smell has to do with the evolutionary origins of the limbic system as a primitive olfactory brain mechanism. That we retain this connection between smell, memory, and emotion is evidenced by the common use of colognes and perfumes to induce lasting allure ("Your Windsong stays on my mind . . ."). Our colloquial speech also reflects this, as when we "sniff out" the solution to a problem, or suspect duplicity when something "smells rotten," and so on.

Back to Don's story. Prior to his illness, Don's family had described him as a "kind and gentle" person. Now these traits seemed to have been exaggerated, to have drifted beyond the point of mere mellowness into the domain of limp placidity. Don was totally unperturbed by daily events, whether distant or close. He showed no concern for practical matters such as where he was, whether or not he had money, where members of his family were or what he would be doing during the next few minutes, hours, or days. The only thing he did seem to show a stable interest in was food or other oral stimuli such as cigarettes or chewing gum. According to his wife he displayed absolutely no interest in sex. Actually, these findings were less surprising, since such hyperorality and hyposexuality not infrequently follow damage to limbic system–temporal lobe structures.

Despite appearing alert, pleasant, and cooperative, as soon as anyone started up a conversation with Don, he invariably confabulated—jumbled and confused people, places, and events. Ask him where he was, what he'd done recently or what he planned to do next, he would produce blatant fabrications that could involve anyone, including the questioner. Often the stories had a certain degree of internal logic and self-consistency, but unfortunately no basis in reality. If you questioned his first story in a politely uncomprehending way, he'd quickly produce another wild tale which he apparently thought would be better received. But if you actually challenged him, showed him that you knew the story was bogus, he'd clam up and offer no more alternatives. "I don't know," he'd sullenly reply.

It seemed as if Don's cognitive modus operandi was to formulate random hypotheses about his experiences and the world around him and then bounce these versions off his interlocutors to assess how close to the truth they actually came. If he got it right, fine. If he was way off base, also fine—unless the questioner kept probing, in which case he'd grow annoyed and withdraw from the conversation.

But what was most striking about Don's problem was the dissociation between what seemed to be separate and different aspects of his memory. He could correctly recall certain important facts about his life and family, such as what kind of jobs he'd held, the companies he'd worked for, the names of his wife, children, and other close relatives, as well as his stint in the military. However, these bits of memory remained as isolated, unconnected elements in his consciousness. No single remembered event seemed to be linked to another as it is for most of us, and it seemed impossible for Don to place such memories in their proper frame of time.

For example, Don could tell you that he was a newspaper advertising salesman, but he couldn't say when he actually began that profession. He had two different bosses during his advertising career and could recite the names of both, but he couldn't recall whom he'd worked for first. With either job, he couldn't state how long he'd held it, and he didn't know if it was before or after World War II or the Korean War, or whether he'd been married or had which of his children at the time. Nor could he get the chronology of his own family life straight. He described his two children as college students when, in fact, they were married and had kids of their own. He usually recognized photos of his family taken during the early 1970s, but referred to current pictures of his wife, who had gray hair, as his mother-in-law.

When Don was shown photos covering his life as an adult, he was able to correctly recognize cars, houses, animals, meals, holiday decorations, and activities flawlessly, but he couldn't connect them to his own recalled experiences, couldn't tell when he'd restored that old car or bought that dream house, how he'd played with that pet or what he did that Christmas. The link between recall of objective events and his personal *involvement* in those events had been shattered.

Don's case illustrates quite poignantly the separate brain mechanisms involved in the memory of isolated events on the one hand, and, on the other hand, the memory of the *relationships* between those events and the personal context that ordinarily makes a memory meaningful. Damasio and colleagues further suggest that memory for separate events may be mediated by deeper subcortical structures, while the personal and time-related aspects that tie it all together are contributed by the frontal lobe–temporal lobe–limbic system network—the brain system destroyed by Don's cerebral herpes infection.

What's this got to do with hysteria?

Just as Don's brain damage forced a wedge between his relatively intact memory of isolated details and his appallingly garbled reconstruction of the *relationship* between those details, so the cognitive style of hysterics predisposes them to characteristically resort to a mix-and-match strategy in processing and recalling life events. Hysterics are notoriously poor historians because, like Don, what they "remember" is dictated more by the whims of the moment than by any systematic search through the memory store. "How it sounds" is the principle that supersedes "how it actually happened." Since memory scanning involves an adequate ability to mobilize attention, the hysteric's further difficulties in this particular area make for particularly poor recall—just the setup for a cognitive style that relies heavily on repression and confabulation.

Conclusions

It's tempting to view the global, inattentive, nonfocused, nonfactual, overemotional, and paramnesic cognitive style of hysterics as having a right-hemisphere neuropsychological substrate. Indeed, many of the above studies support this association. But as a number of the same kind of studies suggest, this relationship is probably more complex than allowed for by a narrow localizationist "syndrome = hemisphere" approach.

For example, does hysterical cognition involve an overreactivity of the right hemisphere or an overreliance on the "wrong" (left) hemisphere to solve inappropriate problems? Also, what components of the hysterical syndrome relate to an overreactive right hemisphere versus a deficient left one? Flor-Henry is probably correct in emphasizing the separateness—syndromically and neuropsychologically—of the cognitive components from the associated conversion and emotional symptomatological manifestations of the syndrome of hysteria.

Don's case suggests that the diffuse attention and memory aspect of the hysterical cognitive style may stem from a functional lability in the temporal lobe and frontolimbic mechanisms that normally link isolated memories together in a sequence and give them meaning and context. The right-hemisphere component probably has more to do with the reticular attentional process itself and with the heightened emotionality and conversion symptoms that hysterics display.

After all, the right hemisphere, which has the greater role in emotion and bodily perception, is also the one with the strongest links to reticular attentional systems that are themselves reciprocally influenced by the frontal lobes and their limbic connections. Thus, the key components of hysteria—conversion symptoms, heightened emotionality, and a global, impressionistic, and impulsive cognitive style—have a common link in the neuropsychodynamic model: a dys-regulation of the processes of volitional attention and self-evaluation that guide and organize thought, feeling, and action. Freed of this neurocognitive guidance, the hysteric's life is dominated by a quirkishly impulsive self-delusion in both body and mind. Not really "crazy," perhaps, but psychologically rudderless—a hole in the self.

But there's one more main cognitive style to consider, one that takes impulsivity to an exaggerated—and often danger-ous—degree.

CHAPTER 9

THE HEEDLESS SELF

The Impulsive Style

They didn't let me go out very often, as each time I returned beaten up by the street urchins. But fighting was my only pleasure and I gave myself up to it body and soul. Mother would flog me with a strap, but the punishment only put me in a worse rage and the next time I fought even more violently, and as a result was punished more severely. And then I warned mother that if she didn't stop beating me I would bite her hand and run away into the fields to freeze. This made her push me from her in amazement, and she walked up and down the room, her breath coming in weary gasps, and said, "Little beast!" That living, throbbing gamut of feelings called love slowly faded in me and in its place there flared up, more and more often, smoldering blue fires of ill will against everyone. Discontent festered in my heart and a feeling of utter isolation in that gray, lifeless and ridiculous world dragged me down.

—MAXIM GORKY

Just as the meaning and the adequate sense of things as a whole are lost with semantic aphasia in the circumscribed field of speech, although the technical mimicry of language remains intact, so in most psychopaths the purposiveness and the significance of all life-striving and of all subjective experience are affected without obvious damage to the outer appearance or superficial reactions of the personality.

—HERVEY CLECKLEY

Boredom is a vital problem of the moralist, since at least half the sins of mankind are caused by the fear of it.

—BERTRAND RUSSELL

Crime! Anarchy! Wildness in the streets! While most of us enjoy the periodic shedding of formal daily restraints, relish a few opportunities to let ourselves go, we also have our limits. True, the line each of us draws may be different from those of our fellows, but for most of us, there exist certain consensual rules of normal conduct, without which we know that life in a civilized society would be impossible.

So what do we make of people who regularly flout those rules, whose unrestrained conduct not only gets them in repeated trouble, but leaves a swath of misery for others in its wake? What are the features of a cognitive style that would predispose an individual to a life of self-serving and seemingly conscienceless abandon?

Psychodynamics of Impulsivity

Freud[1] saw the genesis of impulsivity in the basic intolerance of tension and frustration shown by almost all young infants. The infant tries to discharge tension immediately and experiences any undue excitement as trauma. "Growing up," both in the developmental and colloquial senses of the word, involves the ability to postpone the immediate discharge of tension, to delay gratification, to tolerate frustration. *Impulse neurotics*, as Freud termed them, continue to behave as if any buildup of tension or frustration constitutes a dangerous trauma. They have to act and act *now*, despite the fact that such impulsive actions frequently lead to trouble.

As Otto Fenichel[2] further elaborated, the actions of the impulsive person are directed less toward the positive aim of achieving a goal than toward the negative aim of getting rid of tension. Any tension is felt as a "hunger" just as it's experienced by an infant, that is, as a threat to the individual's very existence. The guiding principle, then, has to be: Action first. However, a continual pattern of action in the absence of thought or reflection leads to perhaps the most ruinous impoverishment of the self we've yet encountered.

The Impulsive Cognitive Style

According to David Shapiro,[3] the distinctive quality of the impulsive style involves an impairment of the normal feelings of deliberateness or intention, a distortion of what for most of us is the normal experience of autonomous motivation for our actions.

All of us are prey to whims and urges of the moment, temptations to forgo a greater long-term goal for a more immediate gratification. But most of us are able to "take hold" of ourselves, consider the trade-offs and behave in a manner roughly in accordance with our larger sense of values and priorities. We may *fantasize* about pulling off the greatest jewel heist in history, trysting with the beach bunny or surf hunk behind our spouse's back, or blowing away a personal rival with make-my-day aplomb. But in most cases we don't actually *do* these things because we know that in "real life" the consequences just aren't worth it.

"Consequences" is a concept for which the impulsive personality has little grasp and even less regard. These people, Shapiro notes, seem to live their lives according to the credo of the "irresistible impulse." Their actions are dictated largely by whim, by abrupt, transient, and partial experiences of wanting, choosing, or deciding —experiences of action that lack the normal sense of active attention and deliberateness. This sense of nondeliberateness is an important element in impulsive characters' apparent self-confidence and freedom from inhibition and anxiety—their casualness, their "coolness."

In fact, there seems to be a parallel between the freedom from restraint that many of us feel after a couple of stiff drinks and the impulsive character's more or less constant experience of disinhibition. In both cases, the person involved may describe the situation (for most of us, usually in rueful retrospect) as "not knowing what I was doing." The difference is, of course, that where you and I experience these lapses of normal restraint in a time-limited and usually situation-specific manner, the impulsive character is like this all the time; with or without actual intoxication, he's the "life of the party" long after the party is over, when most of us have settled down to the more sober responsibilities of normal life.

Each of the qualities of impulsive action—speediness, abruptness, and lack of planning—seems to reflect a short-circuiting of the mental processes that we normally use to translate incipient motives into action. For most people, a whim may be dismissed out of hand, considered provisionally, or, reinforced by some additional information or increasing motivational impetus, transformed into an active, intended, and deliberate want, choice, or decision. It is now no longer just a whim, but a sustained desire. With this develops a basis for planning, and with planning, the sense of deliberateness is further consolidated. But, Shapiro says,

> when a whim cannot accrue affective and associative support from stable and continuous aims and interests, it cannot develop into a sustained, active want, choice or intention. It remains an impulse, lacking in a sense of intention, transient and partial. When the content of a whim or impulse fails to be modified by stable aims or enriched and modulated by associative and affective connections in such an integrative process, that content remains primitive and bare, and failing to be anchored in stable interests, it tends to shift erratically.[4]

Thus, impulsive personalities are lacking in active interests, aims, values, or goals much beyond the immediate concerns of their own lives. Durable emotional involvements, such as deep friendships or stable love relationships, are conspicuously absent from their personal histories. Even family interests and personal career goals are usually not very strong or occupying. While children or teenagers, they may run away from home, or, later, abandon their families for long periods, only to return when resources are exhausted. Schooling and jobs are likewise approached in a desultory manner, their involvement lingering only so long as immediate needs are satisfied. What seem glaringly absent from these life-scripts are any realistic long-range personal plans or ambitions—not to mention more abstract aims, purposes, or values.

Typically, impulsive characters are quite uninterested in cultural, intellectual, ideological, or political issues. Events of general public interest—war and peace, political policies, economic changes, developments in the arts and sciences—characteristically evoke only bored unconcern. As long as *he's* not drafted, as long as a perilous economy or fragile ecology doesn't cut into *his* good times, as long as rising poverty and global starvation don't immediately affect *him*, to hell with it.

As a vicarious expression of the rebel in all of us (most of us, anyway), literature and cinema have immortalized the impulsive character, often elevating him to the popular icon of the "antihero." Whereas originally this cultural prototype typically had some redeeming higher-order philosophical or social agenda to fuel his iconoclasm—much in the tradition of Thoreau, for example—the modern incarnation seems increasingly to tend toward an idealization of heedless and frequently destructive irrationality. Even the "rebels without a cause" of a few years ago made some existential point about the effects of alienation and hypocrisy within modern society. This is being rapidly replaced by a growing battalion of Ramboid hell-raisers whose gratuitous savagery is cheered as an end in itself. But that's another story.

Lack of planning—*planfulness*, really—is only one feature of a cognitive style in which active concentration, capacity to abstract, ability to generalize, and overall reflectiveness are all impaired. This insufficiency of integrative processes also appears in the emotional domain; indeed, Hervey Cleckley,[5] in his now classic treatise on the psychopath, referred to the *semantic aphasia* that typifies impulsive, antisocial character types, the seeming inability to "get the point," even when their impulsive heads have been knocked repeatedly against a punitive reality. This is not a true comprehension disorder, as in the standard aphasias, but more of an inability of the lessons of life to "get through" on any level that has meaning for the psychopath's everyday behavior.

Similar deficiencies, you may recall, also characterize the hysterical mode of cognition, which Shapiro describes as impressionistic. But in the impulsive style, the deficiency of active, searching, critical attention is more severe, his cognition more passive and concrete. The so-called "intelligence" of some impulsive characters is not a planning, abstracting, reflecting intelligence. Rather, these people often have a keen practical cunning-conning type of intelligence, a streetwiseness that's admirably suited to the execution of short-range, immediate aims.

Indeed, they may appear positively ingenious in their mastery of the quick hustle, or in the deftness with which they can worm their way out of some kinds of trouble. Closer examination, however, reveals that such strategies generally work best in familiar and stable environments; when the situation demands a novel and flexible approach, even the ace conman is out of his league and is soon brought down.

In fact, the very model of the impulsive character, says Shapiro, is the psychopath (or sociopath, or delinquent, or antisocial personality, depending on which descriptive classification you follow) who

exhibits in a thorough and pervasive way what for others is only a direction or tendency. He acts on whim, his aim is the quick, concrete gain and his interests and talents are in ways and means. From a long-range point of view, his behavior is usually erratic, but from the short-range point of view, it is often quite competent.[6]

Thus, a good deal of the "antisocial" behavior of psychopaths may be understood not as the direct consequence of some innate deficiency of moral values or conscience—this was the classic "moral idiot" characterization that still appears in some textbooks. Rather, antisociality may follow from the core features that comprise the impulsive cognitive style itself: an egocentric viewpoint, a general lack of aims and values much beyond immediate, tangible gain, and a tendency to pursue quick, nondeliberate modes of action. It's in this respect that the distinction between a "bad" behavior and a "bad" person becomes so complex. Can neuropsychology address such questions of morality, conscience, and social deviance?

The Impulsive Brain

If you want to study impulsivity, go where the impulsive people are. One such place is a facility for delinquents where Berman and Siegal[7] compared the neuropsychological performance of adjudicated adolescent delinquent boys with that of volunteer nondelinquents from a similar socioeconomic background. Compared to the control group, the delinquents were impaired in their ability to comprehend, manipulate, and utilize verbal-conceptual information. Also deficient was their ability to organize nonverbal and spatial perceptions and to operate effectively on the basis of those perceptions. The worst performance was seen when a combination of approaches was required, that is, using verbal-symbolic reasoning to solve spatial and perceptual tasks. In fact, on these measures of cross-modal cognitive processing, the delinquents did so badly that their test results fell well within the "brain damaged" range.

The most profound impairment occurred on a measure

called the Category Test, a concept-formation task that requires the subject to use his prior experience of hits and misses to come up with some abstract rule that will effectively guide further performance. On this measure, the delinquents showed a clear inability to profit from experience and repeatedly used poor judgment—a feature of cognitive-behavioral functioning that also seems to characterize the impulsive delinquent lifestyle as a whole.

But bad boys commit many kinds of impulsive acts, not all of which may be of equivalent "badness." Is the delinquent who shoplifts and forges his parent's signature on checks the same as the one who mugs and rapes? What's the relationship between actual level of violence and neuropsychological functioning?

To answer this question, Frank Spellacy[8] looked at the differences in neuropsychological performance between two groups of delinquent boys from a residential treatment school, carefully classified into violent and nonviolent groups. The findings showed that, first, the violent boys were found to have overall lower IQs than the nonviolent boys. But even controlling for intelligence, the violent boys were more impaired than expected on tests of visual memory, perceptual organization, and language processing.

To see if what's true of bad boys also applies to bad men, Spellacy[9] replicated his original study with adult male violent and nonviolent penitentiary prisoners. In virtually every sphere of cognitive functioning measured, Spellacy found the violent prisoners to be inferior to the nonviolent group. This was especially true on tasks assessing conceptual, perceptual, language, and sensory-motor abilities.

So far, we've been considering performance on neuropsychological tests alone. What would happen if we supplemented such assessments with a somewhat more direct measure of brain activity? This was the approach taken by Krynicki,[10] who combined a series of neuropsychological tests with EEG recordings. As in other studies, Krynicki chose adjudicated delinquents as subjects and, like Spellacy, he divided his subjects into two groups: those with a history of repetitively assaultive behavior and those with "milder" forms of delinquency. But since one object of this study was to see if any of the subjects showed neuropsychological evidence of brain damage, Krynicki took the necessary empirical precaution of including a separate subject group who actually *were* organically brain-damaged.

Not only were the neuropsychological and EEG profiles of the assaultive delinquents impaired relative to the non-assaultive boys, but the brain indices of the assaultives resembled that of the organically brain-damaged group. Both the assaultive delinquents and brain-damaged subjects were found to have a greater number of abnormal EEGs, more poorly established hand dominance, poorer verbal memory, and more perseverative errors on conceptual classification tasks, indicating impaired cognitive flexibility and difficulty switching from unproductive strategies—a classic "frontal lobe" sign.

And, consistent with the neuropsychological test findings, the delinquents' abnormal EEG activity was found to be located mainly in the frontal or frontotemporal regions of the brain. Krynicki also points out that the combination of more poorly established hand dominance and deficits in verbal memory implicates left-hemisphere dysfunction. Further, the perseverative responding seen in the assaultive subjects probably reflects their characteristic impulsivity. In the real world, this impulsivity may be related to a tendency to rely on poorly controlled aggression as a preferred response to frustrating or tension-producing social situations.

Dorothy Lewis and colleagues[11] tested a group of incarcerated adolescent boys with regard to reading level, neurological impairment, and psychiatric status. Severe reading disability was found to be associated with paranoid thinking, visual hallucinations, difficulty in organizing thoughts coherently, impaired short-term memory, violent behaviors, and past experiences of physical abuse.

On the basis of these findings, the investigators hypothesized that the overall "loose-rambling-illogical" thought processes observed in this delinquent group are manifestations of the egocentric language and autistic logic characteristic of young children. They further speculated that in some cases the behaviors of these delinquents reflect a basic neurodevelopmental immaturity that affects impulse control (recall Freud's point), as well as an inability to appreciate the perspective of a victim of aggression and an inability to envision the long-term consequences of an act—reminiscent of the frontal lobe-mediated deficit in time contiguity discussed in Chapter 3.

An extensive intellectual and neuropsychological test battery was used by Lorne Yeudall and colleagues[12] to study a group of delinquents that included both boys and girls. Here, as in previous studies, a high percentage of the delinquents showed neuropsychological deficits in comparison to a control sample. Furthermore, the specific pattern of deficits implicated frontal brain regions. Unlike other studies, however, there was no appreciable difference in performance between violent and nonviolent delinquents, both types doing worse on the neuropsychological measures than nondelinquent controls. Could this have anything to do with having both boys and girls in the sample?

In fact, gender differences did emerge with respect to pattern of laterality. Delinquent girls showed greater evidence of right-hemisphere dysfunction, while left-hemisphere dysfunction seemed to characterize the boys, recalling the neurodevelopmental principles discussed in Chapter 2. Interestingly, reports by the institutional staff, as well as observations by the testers, indicated that a high percentage of the delinquent subjects showed signs and symptoms of depression.

Since depression has been associated with right-hemisphere

dysfunction (see Chapter 5), and since more females than males seem to be affected by this mood disorder, the curious pattern of deficits may have reflected a high prevalence of mood disorders in this coed population—an intriguing example of the neuropsychodynamic role of sex differences in emotion and cognition. This also jibes with Flor-Henry's point from the last chapter on the kinship of hysteria and mood disorders in women with impulsive antisociality in men.[13] Recall that in this model, the basic neuropsychodynamic basis of both cognitive styles lies in the left hemisphere, but the more florid symptoms of hysteria—heightened emotionality and conversion—stem from the right hemisphere.

Finally, the results of Yeudall's study suggested that delinquents in general may have significant problems in planning their actions and, more importantly, in perceiving the consequences of those actions. For example, they may have difficulty in appropriately changing an action once started in order to achieve the original goal—a capacity which, as we've seen, is crucially associated with frontal lobe functioning.

Arthur Brickman and colleagues[14] administered an intellectual, scholastic, and neuropsychological battery to a particularly nasty group of male and female delinquents whose histories were characterized by multiple violent felonies, including murderous assaults. The aggressive and recidivistic delinquents—those who committed more violent acts and did so again and again—showed a distinctly abnormal neuropsychological pattern, extending over a wide range of functions.

Not only was impairment seen in the so-called higher intellectual functions often associated with school performance, but striking abnormalities were seen in time sequencing, the ability to appreciate rhythm, expressive speech functions, and in attention and concentration. Furthermore, a pronounced emotional lability was noted—the subjects could be calm and sedate one moment, wild and emotional the next.

Based on these findings, the investigators speculated that problems in attention and concentration on the one hand, and in emotional stability on the other, could have reciprocal effects and stem from a common cause. That is, it may be that these youths failed to develop the cognitive controls needed to manage their emotions and moods, and the problems in establishing these controls may themselves have served as a source of emotional lability, inattention, and delinquency. On the other hand, difficulties in abstract thinking, time sequencing, and concentration may contribute to a weakness in developing and applying the cognitive controls themselves.

An extensive neuropsychological test battery was used by Ernest Bryant and colleagues[15] to study adult male prison inmates. The men were divided into two groups, a violent-offender group whose crimes included mainly aggressive assaults against persons, and a nonviolent-offender group whose illegal proclivities ran more to property crimes and theft.

The violent offenders showed serious intellectual deficits, scoring within the pathological range with regard to reading, writing, and arithmetic skills. What's more, the violent group was also impaired on neuropsychological tasks requiring complex integration of information from visual, auditory, and other processing systems, as well the ability to create, plan, organize, and execute goal-directed behaviors. The study's investigators stressed that many of these types of behavior disorders have a distinctly frontal lobe quality about them, characterized as they are by lack of foresight and restraint.

One researcher who makes no bones about the relationship between impulsive psychopathy and frontal lobe impairment is Ethan Gorenstein.[16] In a well-known study, Gorenstein examined the neuropsychological test perfor-

mance of adult male patients at two public hospitals where
they were receiving treatment for substance abuse and/or
psychiatric disorders. After excluding all patients who were
frankly psychotic or had organic neurological impairment,
the remainder were divided into psychopathic or nonpsychopathic groups. A control group consisted of normal male
college students matched for age.

A selected battery of neuropsychological measures was
used, including the Wisconsin Card Sorting Test (WCST),[17]
a measure that is reported to be especially sensitive to frontal lobe impairment. In brief, the WCST requires the subject
to match a set of stimuli, one at a time, to a set of cues,
according to prearranged abstract conceptual criteria or
"rules." The catch is that the subject isn't told what these
rules are; he's got to figure them out for himself by whether
the examiner says "right" or "wrong" after each attempted
matching. Furthermore, the rules are subject to change
without notice; again, the only way the subject knows this
is by noting which of his responses, once "right," are now
"wrong." Only a change in matching strategy in response
to this implicit change in matching rule can keep the subject
on a winning streak with regard to "right" responses. The
test thus requires a certain degree of cognitive flexibility,
abstract conceptual reasoning, and the ability to modify
thinking and behavior in an adaptive way.

Most normal people of at least average intelligence can
perform this task adequately. That is, they can eventually
figure out the implicit sorting rule, match stimuli according
to that rule, detect when the rule has changed, and shift
their response pattern in accordance with the new rule. Even
some brain-damaged persons can do all right, although
they're apt to make more errors overall.

What seems to distinguish the performance of many frontal lobe–impaired patients on the WCST, beyond just making a lot of mistakes, is the sheer *inertia* of their responding.
The average person who's having trouble figuring out the

new or current sorting rule may try a variety of unsuccessful strategies: Sort according to this rule; nope, try that rule; uh-uh, what about this other rule; bingo!

But the frontal patient *perseverates*: Even after many successive "wrong" responses, he persists in using the old, no-longer-effective sorting strategy, as though he's stuck in some kind of cognitive rut. This isn't the same as just being wrong. Remember, even an unintelligent or psychotic or brain-damaged person usually knows enough not to keep making the same type of wrong responses. The alternative strategy or matching principle he chooses may still be an incorrect or bizarre one, but at least he tries something new. It's the inertia, the rootedness to the immediate situation, the contextlessness of the cognitive activity that distinguishes the frontally impaired person.

What Gorenstein found was that the psychopaths, in contrast to the nonpsychopathic patients and normal controls, exhibited the performance pattern of frontal-lesioned patients on just those measures known to be especially sensitive to frontal lobe impairment—especially perseveratory errors on the WCST. On other tests of equal difficulty, but unrelated to frontal lobe integrity specifically, the psychopaths did as well as the other subjects.

These results led Gorenstein to hypothesize that, although psychopaths are able to acquire abstract concepts, they're hampered by a peculiar tendency to persist with a previously reinforced, but currently maladaptive response set. This tendency toward perseveration means that a previously rewarded behavior or a behavior that's more clearly favored by immediate circumstances will remain relatively stable, even in the face of new contingencies, new rules of the game. The thinking and behavior of the psychopath, cognitively rooted to the immediate situation, is more than usually refractory to adaptive change. And what applies to sorting tests may also have relevance for the psychopath's legendary failure to learn from experience.

Robert Hare[18] isn't so sure. He challenged Gorenstein's conclusions about psychopaths and frontal lobes, arguing that Gorenstein's results were confounded by problems in subject selection and proper diagnosis. Hare's own diagnostic protocol for psychopathy derives directly from the theoretical model of Hervey Cleckley, introduced earlier in this chapter (this is the same Cleckley, incidentally, who coauthored *The Three Faces of Eve*, about multiple personality, but that's another story). Over more than a decade of research, Hare's research group has adapted Cleckley's theoretical model into a diagnostic instrument called the Hare Psychopathy Index. This was one of the measures used in Hare's neuropsychological study to divide a group of prison inmates at a Canadian medium-security prison into high, medium, and low psychopathy groups. A control group of nonpsychopathic inmates was also studied. In addition, Hare took into account the effects of alcohol and drug use by his subjects. All subjects were administered the tests found by Gorenstein to yield the most pronounced "frontal" findings, including the WCST.

Hare's results showed that the psychopaths didn't differ appreciably from the other inmates on the cognitive variables presumed by Gorenstein to be related to frontal lobe functioning—including WCST perseveratory errors. Moreover, the performance of the inmates in general and the psychopaths in particular was very similar to that of normal, noncriminal individuals, and not at all like that of frontal-lesioned patients.

Why the contrast between the two studies? According to Hare, it's doubtful whether the subjects referred to by Gorenstein as "psychopaths" would satisfy the criteria for psychopathy enumerated by Cleckley, that is, Gorenstein's sample were probably not "true" psychopaths—Cleckleyan psychopaths. Hare concluded that approaches such as Gorenstein's may be too quick to reject psychological factors or other explanations before invoking brain-related explanations to account for psychopathic behavior.

Recently, Patricia Sutker and Albert Allain[19] have attempted to directly address the Hare-Gorenstein debate. The subjects studied were inpatients at a Veterans Administration drug abuse treatment program. A rigorous diagnostic evaluation was used to identify a group of psychopathic subjects and to select a normal control group. In addition to "frontal lobe" measures like the WCST, a standardized intelligence scale was also administered.

Results indicated that the psychopaths did not differ from normal controls with respect to the cognitive dimensions of planning, flexibility, attention, control, and abstraction, a finding more in line with Hare's conclusions than with Gorenstein's. Importantly, however, an analysis of the results revealed that, regardless of which group a subject belonged to, intelligence had a significant effect on performance.

That is, the less intelligent subjects, psychopath or not, did worse on the "frontal lobe" measures than the brighter subjects. Put another way, being generally bright may allow subjects to make up for certain specific cognitive deficits. They may still be lacking in certain select skills and abilities relative to someone else in their IQ bracket, but they've got enough overall brain juice to "wing it" and come out in decent shape on the test. Brighter psychopaths may be able to "psych out" the psych test and come up normal, but may still show maladaptive behavior in their everyday dealings with the world.

Another recent attempt to solve the psychopath–frontal lobe problem was undertaken by Joseph Newman and colleagues.[20] They began by reviewing the various ways in which the psychopathic lifestyle has been conceptualized. As we've seen, psychopathic behavior has been described as callous, egocentric, and lacking in forethought. Furthermore, psychopaths display a near total disregard for the negative consequences of their behavior. Although many psychologists have attempted to explain psychopaths' legendary disdain for the rights and feelings of others by a failure of socialization, this wouldn't necessarily account for their apparent disregard for their *own* well-being. Rather, the psychopath's lack of insight into his self-defeating behavior has suggested to many that he is fundamentally, characterologically, unable to learn from his mistakes, a point stressed by Cleckley.

Why can't the psychopath learn to wise up? Perhaps his failure to inhibit self-defeating actions has to do with his very proneness to response perseveration. That is, once rewarded for a particular pattern of behavior, psychopaths have great difficulty switching the program off when the rules of the game change. Even though the same actions get them clonked on the head over and over again, they persist in acting as though there's still something in it for them.

We've already discussed this concept of perseveration in the context of concept formation and sorting behavior on neuropsychological tests like the WCST. In this case, the hypothesis is that once psychopaths adopt a response set for reward—even the word "right"—they have difficulty attending to competing response contingencies. In addition, evidence suggests that psychopaths appear to have difficulty associating events that are separated in time,[21] recalling the role of the frontal lobes in the time-structuring of experience, discussed in Chapter 3.

To examine this hypothesis, a group of psychopaths and a group of nonpsychopath controls were selected by Newman's research team from among male inmates at a minimum-security prison, using a checklist version of Hare's Psychopathy Index. The measure used to assess neurocognitive functioning was a unique kind of computerized card-playing task,[22] which operated as follows:

The one hundred "cards" in the deck were presented, via computer screen, in a prearranged order of face cards and number cards. At the beginning of each trial, a rectangle appeared on the screen with a large question mark in the center and the words DO YOU WANT TO PLAY? printed over the rectangle. On every trial the player had two options, to play the next card or quit the game. To play, the subject pressed the first of four buttons. After each play, the question mark in the rectangle was replaced with an uppercase letter that represented one of the face cards (J, Q, K, A for Jack, Queen, King, Ace) or a number (2 to 10) and the appearance of the words YOU WIN! or YOU LOSE! above the rectangle. To quit, the player pressed the second button. Each player began the task with ten chips, worth five cents each, and were told to play as many cards as he wished. Subjects won five cents whenever a button press was followed by a face card (J, Q, K, or A) and lost five cents whenever a number card appeared. In reality, the game was rigged so that the probability of losing—that is, getting a number card—increased by 10 percent with every block of ten cards, from 10 percent to 100 percent. In other words, the more you played, the worse you'd do.

There were three experimental conditions. In condition 1, players could respond to the next card as quickly as they wished and always received immediate feedback—the computer-delivered message and the gain or loss of a chip. Condition 2 was identical to the first, except that the player received cumulative as well as immediate feedback. That is, after each play, the letter or number that had appeared inside the rectangle was rewritten at the top of the monitor. These letters and numbers appeared in rows of ten across and remained visible throughout the task. Condition 3 was the same as condition 2, except that the rectangle with the question mark and DO YOU WANT TO PLAY? did not appear until after a five-second delay following the feedback for the prior play.

The results of this study provided unambiguous evidence that psychopaths do indeed perseverate, at least under ordinary circumstances. Whereas control subjects had little difficulty noticing the steady increases in the probability of nonreward and adjusting their responding accordingly, psychopaths failed to alter their dominant response set for reward. In fact, three-quarters of the psychopaths in the immediate feedback condition never quit—they played the entire "deck" of one hundred cards, despite losing money on nineteen of the last twenty trials. This, despite the fact that the psychopaths' response persistence resulted in their earning significantly less money than the controls.

But the investigators found something else: Even a psychopath might be able to learn more adaptive behavior, as long as you set up the right conditions. The results for condition 3 indicated that combining a five-second pause with cumulative feedback significantly reduced the perseverative deficit. In fact, under these conditions both the psychopaths and controls in condition 3 quit the game when monetary penalizations became as frequent as monetary rewards. Thus, longer pauses after negative feedback were associated with a better ability to modify behavior in accordance with response feedback.

It seems, then, that if psychopaths are spoon-fed information about specific patterns of rewards and punishments for specific kinds of behavior, *and* if they are literally forced to take notice of this input by delays that prevent them from impulsively plunging ahead on the task, they can learn to alter their behavior appropriately. Remember, even Luria's organic frontal lobe patients could learn simple tasks if the experimenter made the task components crystal clear and artificially provided external guiding strategies.[23]

The problem is that few situations in real life present such clear-cut guidelines; without them, the impulsive psychopath juggernauts his way through one scrape after another. Unable on his own to bolt himself to the deck of the real world, the impulsive character remains a loose cannon throughout his chaotic life.

The Case of the Born Impulsivist

The following case, reported by S. Spafford Ackerly, [24] illustrates what happens when internal drive mechanisms are abnormally uncoupled from frontal cognitive control. Unlike many of the protagonists of previous chapters who came upon their claims to clinical fame after years of normal living, the present case—we'll call him Robbie—seemed bound for trouble from day one. Born after a difficult labor and forceps delivery, he manifested a lifelong history of behavior problems from early childhood.

Although ordinarily exhibiting a precociously polite, almost courtly demeanor—Ackerly refers to this as "Chesterfieldian manners," after the famous Lord Chesterfield—Robbie appeared thoroughly unable to learn from experience. He was disobedient and truant in school and a poor helper at home, unable to finish even the simplest of household chores without close supervision. He never seemed to learn how to get along with peers, had no real friends of either sex, and was heartily disliked by the neighborhood children. Unlike other boys his age, he was never accepted into any group or club or even gang. Yet, despite this seemingly asocial and autistic-like behavior pattern, Robbie was never known to escape into the fantasy worlds of daydreaming or movies and was always described as a "goer" or "doer," rather than a "sitter" or "thinker."

As a teenager, Robbie seemed to bypass the dependency-independency struggles or individuation issues that usually demarcate adolescent psychological development. He seemed to have little desire to "find himself" and suffered from no "identity crises." Also lacking was any real sign of goal-directed sexual activity or socializing with the opposite sex. On the one date he did go on, he acted aloof (if polite) and ended the encounter by casually stealing money from his escort and wandering away. There was no male adolescent sentimentalizing of women, no great enthusiasms or periods of dejection or discouragement. He seldom if ever cried, even when severely punished.

Psychological testing on two occasions showed Robbie's overall intelligence to be in the normal range. Where he had profound difficulty, however, was with tasks requiring abstract conceptualization and shifting from one mode of response to another—that is, altering response patterns in an adaptive way.

Ackerly describes this patient as "showing a marked unawareness of his total life situation involving yesterdays and tomorrows." Not only did Robbie suffer an attenuation of the ability to perceive and conceive of his total life situation, but his very *drive*, the motivational impetus that gives the normal personality its spark, appears to have been dampened.

He was neither prosocial nor antisocial—just asocial. He protected himself by simple denial, by just brushing aside what was unpleasant or painful, by boasting or by indignant remonstrances. When pinned down by disagreeable facts or closed in by physical restraints, his suffering could be intense, but was quickly relieved as soon as the circumstances changed. Pleasure for Robbie appeared to come only in the relief from painful tension. He never seemed to experience what you'd call joy or happiness, and he was never known to show any feeling that might be considered positive delight.

Ackerly describes Robbie's overall picture as one of arrested social development. Simple social feeling and goodwill were present, but his ability to amplify, integrate, and implement these rudimentary social feelings was severely limited. His basic drive systems in general—sexual, aggressive, mastery, self-preservative—seemed weak and ineffectual. In addition, his abstract intellectual functions were simple and underdeveloped.

What was Robbie's problem? The answer came only years later when as an adult he was subjected to a series of neurological examinations. A pneumoencephalogram (a form of brain X-ray) and a later exploratory neurosurgical procedure revealed that the cortex of Robbie's left frontal lobe was severely compressed by abnormal tissue adhesions. The right frontal area, for its part, consisted of little more than a fluid-filled cavity essentially devoid of normal cortical tissue. The answer to Robbie's lifelong difficulties now seemed apparent: It's hard to act like a normal, socialized human being when you grow up essentially without frontal lobes.

Ackerly's final formulation of Robbie's case reminds us of our discussion in Chapter 3. Recall Dimond's emphasis on the role of the frontal lobes in social behavior,[25] as well as Nauta's notion of the stability-in-time deficit that occurs as a consequence of frontal damage.[26] Predating these formulations, Ackerly comments,

> It would indeed be surprising if a man could carry on a satisfactory social existence without imagination and without a sense of continuity with the past. And it would be equally surprising if a man could successfully be or have a friend or lover without constantly considering what effects his past and present thoughts, feelings and behavior might have on the future of that relationship. A friendship offers more than mere pleasure. It offers a lingering joy, a positive happiness, not only a diversion or a release from disagreeable tension.[27]

Here was a man deprived at birth of the very neuropsychodynamic substrate for impulse control. Was he "bad"? Certain aspects of his behavior certainly were. But much of his difficulty stemmed not from a basic meanness of spirit, but from a pervasive incapacity—recall both Freud and Shapiro—to pursue any goal beyond immediate gratification and the immediate release of tension.

Now, not everyone we label a psychopath fits this description exactly. Many such individuals *are* mean and their meanness comes from other perturbations of emotion and temperament that are beyond the scope of this chapter. But fundamental to such clinical concepts as "conscienceless-ness," "moral idiocy," "inability to learn from mistakes," and so on, is this underlying deficit in impulse control, a deficit that may have its basis in a neuropsychodynamic maldevelopment of frontal evaluation-and-control pro-cesses, combined with a left-hemisphere verbal reasoning deficit that precludes any kind of meaningful reflection or self-evaluation.

Conclusions

Several basic neuropsychodynamic features of cognitive style appear to characterize impulsive delinquents and psycho-paths. These include impaired sequential organization and coordination of isolated elements; poor ability to compre-hend, manipulate, and utilize verbal conceptual material; inability to profit from experience; repeated use of poor judgment; impaired impulse control; and inability to envi-sion the long-term consequences of an act. In addition, we can also frequently observe the following: motoric impul-sivity, less established hand dominance, poorer verbal memory, poorer language functioning, attention and con-centration difficulties, emotional ability, difficulty in ab-stract thinking, and time-sequencing problems.

An important observation is that the impairments seen in impulsive delinquents and psychopaths relate less to the in-dividual cognitive modalities like language and spatial per-ception than they do to the capacity to *integrate* different abilities for the purpose of carrying out the demands of a goal-directed task.

One is struck, in this regard, by the poor performance of delinquents and psychopaths on such measures as the Cat-egory Test, the WCST, and the computer card game, re-quiring sufficient cognitive flexibility to be able to form, maintain, and shift conceptual sets according to implicit rules, to respond adaptively to feedback from the environ-

ment. In addition, in most studies where the distinction between impulsively violent and nonviolent delinquents has
been made, the violent subjects have generally been found
to perform more poorly on these integrative neuropsychological tasks.

The connection with left-hemisphere language dysfunction
is reinforced by the fact that delinquents and psychopaths
characteristically show deficits on measures of verbal intelligence, as well as having histories of dyslexia, learning
disorders, and other school problems.[28] Could the impulsivist be a clear outcome of the kind of neurodevelopmental
anomaly described by the Geschwindian hypothesis[29] we
discussed in Chapter 2?

On this basis, recalling the lessons of Chapters 3, 4, and 5,
the following hypothesis[30] can be offered: The psychopath
or delinquent—the individual with the maladaptively impulsive cognitive style—suffers from a neurodevelopmental
maturational deficit that results in an inability to use inner
speech to modulate attention, emotion, cognition, and behavior.

Neuropsychodynamically, without this left-hemisphere
guidance of frontal lobe control over thought, feeling, and
action, behavior is dictated by transient urges from within and
chance tantalizations from without. Having no recourse to a
stable self-system, the impulsivist cannot structure his behavior by appeal to any internal rule or code. Nor can he easily
"learn from experience," since his neuropsychodynamic impoverishment has led to a shaky and slippery self-
system on which the lessons of life can find no purchase.

Slave to whim, and finding himself frequently knocked
around as a consequence, he may transform his misfortune
into a brutally simple pseudoethic of "get it while you can,"
"do it to them before they do it to you," or some equivalent.
At least in this pathetic sense, the impulsivist strives to extract
some meaning from his chaotic, hostile, and dimly compre-
hended world.

PART IV

ALTERNATIVE NATURES

CHAPTER 10

THE TRANSMUTED SELF

Alcoholism and Addiction

Malt does more than Milton can,
To justify God's ways to man.

—A.E. HOUSMAN

If a man be discreet enough to take to hard drinking in his youth, before his general emptiness is ascertained, his friends invariably credit him with a host of shining qualities which, we are given to understand, lie balked and frustrated by his one unfortunate weakness.

—AGNES REPPLIER

What is dangerous about the tranquilizers is that whatever peace of mind they bring is a packaged peace of mind. Where you buy a pill and buy peace with it, you get conditioned to cheap solutions instead of deep ones.

—MAX LERNER

It seems these days that alcohol and drugs are everywhere. Advertisements for every manner of boozy concoction bombard us constantly, we worry about airline and train crews being stoned on the job, and we break out in icy sweats if our eleven-year-old comes home from school acting a little strange and asking for cash. More to the point, many of us may partake of some of these chemical recreations ourselves, convinced that we're the masters of our indulgences, not the other way around.

But for many people, the desire for mind- or mood-altering substances is more than a recreation—it's a preoccupation, a driving hunger that we call an *addiction*. One person throws two or three back at a party or after-work bar, says when, and lays off it; his friend keeps chugging to the point of slobbering clownishness or belligerence. Some people use drugs and alcohol to "lighten up," help get themselves in a celebratory frame of mind that's appropriate in certain situations; others slavishly devote their whole lives to staying blotto, wrecked, wasted.

Needless to say, there is no dearth of theories to explain addiction, from the biochemical to the political. Can our neuropsychodynamic approach shed some light on why some people seem destined for a career of chemical abuse?

The Psychodynamics of Addiction

Early psychoanalytic writers like Karl Abraham[1] and Sandor Rado[2] characterized the drug and alcohol abuser as narcissistically fixated, weak of ego, and consumed with hateful feelings (albeit largely unconscious) toward people in his early life. Glover[3] hypothesized that drug addiction, especially to opiates like morphine and heroin, constituted a defense against sadistic or aggressive drives. The narcotics were also often used, said Glover, to defend against such unacceptable urges and impulses as sadism and homosexuality.

Somewhat later, Otto Fenichel[4] described the alcoholic or addict as suffering from a diffuse, amorphous, ill-defined state of tension, as someone who treated others in a utilitarian and narcissistic fashion—as "deliverers of supplies," Fenichel put it. The compulsive drug use was an attempt to quell this tension and achieve pharmacologically that feeling of security and self-esteem that the addict lacked in his relationships with others. Both Glover and Fenichel hypothesized that narcotics constituted the psychic bonding elixir that helped hold the addict's fragile ego structure together and prevented a regression into a primitive psychotic mode of thinking and acting.

In the last few decades, theorists in the psychoanalytic

camp have continued to pursue these clinical insights and investigations into the psychodynamics of addiction. The rough consensus[5] seems to center on a conception of the alcoholic/addict as having an extremely fragile ego structure, which is defended against by a certain puffed-up grandiosity. This inner core of ego-weakness is responsible for a marked inability to manage emotions and impulses. The chronic and abusive use of alcohol or drugs is seen as an attempt to artificially shore up primitive defense mechanisms such as denial—a strategy that may become less and less effective as time goes on.

One of the leading modern psychodynamic theorists in this field is Edward Khantzian.[6] Among the many factors associated with addiction, Khantzian is most impressed with the enormous lifelong difficulties addicts have in dealing with aggressive feelings and impulses. The dysphoric feelings associated with anger, rage, and restlessness have a devastatingly disruptive effect on the addict's fragile and unstable ego structure and are relieved in the short term by narcotic drugs, an observation supported by the frequent reduction of aggression and restlessness shown by addicts on methadone maintenance. In fact, it's this sustained anti-aggressive action of methadone that Khantzian views as the basis for the "success" of methadone maintenance programs as a whole.

Another contemporary psychoanalytic theorist of addiction is Leon Wurmser,[7] who conceptualizes alcoholism and drug abuse as forms of artificial emotional defense. The abuser compulsively uses the drug to ward off or bring relief from overwhelming feelings that are potentially disruptive to the unstable structure of the addict's ego. The individual choice of a favorite drug, Wurmser argues, corresponds to whichever particular species of emotion that addict finds especially disturbing.

For example, opiate narcotics like morphine and heroin and sedative-hypnotics like Quaaludes and Valium are deployed against tension-producing feelings such as rage, shame, and jealousy. Stimulants like amphetamines and cocaine are used to outrace depression and fatigue. Psychedelics strobe away boredom and disillusionment, and alcohol drowns guilt, loneliness, and the cold, naked anxiety of isolation. The addict, says Wurmser, suffers from a profound discontinuity in his sense of self, a pervasive instability and unreliability of ego structure—of the self—that's often irritating or infuriating to others, humiliating and depressing for the addict himself.

The psychodynamic view of alcoholism and drug abuse has a certain internal consistency, and seems to jibe with the experience of many practicing clinicians. But how well does this conception hold up against the larger body of research into the psychology of the addictions?

Personality and Psychopathology of Alcoholism and Addiction

This research suggests that three main clinical features seem to characterize the psychological makeup of many alcoholics and drug abusers: 1) antisocial personality, 2) a history of childhood hyperactivity, and 3) depression. Since personality has important implications for a fully fleshed-out neuropsychodynamic theory of the addictions, we'll consider these factors in turn.

Remember the old cinematic stereotype of the charming, even amusing tippler, the colorful town drunk whose only sin is a too-easy temptation by the lure of the bottle, or—in another version—whose inebriated *joie de vivre* may belie a deep, existential sorrow and who, accordingly, needs only the merest assuagement of adversity, the loving caress of an honest woman, or the firm but gentle guidance of his parish priest to trade in his degrading existence for a life of diligence and probity?

Forget it. If we need a stereotype, then the "mean drunk"

is probably closer to the truth. Although a few of the above "sweet-'n'-sour" or "noble sot" types of abuser are occasionally encountered in clinical practice, research suggests that a far more common characterological feature associated with alcoholism and addiction is psychopathy or antisocial personality, which we covered in Chapter 9. Indeed, in his classic study of the psychopath, *The Mask of Sanity*, Hervey Cleckley[8] emphasized in one case history after another how intimately a passion for drink seems to be related to an impulsive, antisocial lifestyle. What's the evidence for a link?

The relationship between impulsive, antisocial behavior and abuse of alcohol and drugs has by now been pretty well documented, especially for men. For example, one study[9] found a strong association between alcoholism and antisocial personality in a sample of medically hospitalized inpatients. In addition to alcoholism, individuals with antisocial personality were also more likely to abuse other drugs and, interestingly, to suffer from hysterical syndromes. Antisocial personality has also been found to be associated with drinking problems at an earlier age, with less control over drinking once it starts, and with more medical complications resulting from alcohol.

Other research[10] has shown that excessive drinking seems to go along with certain specific types of antisocial behaviors and experiences, such as arrests, traffic violations, chronic joblessness, and getting shot, punched, or beaten; evidently, noxious behavior toward others often elicits retaliation in kind. Alternatively, birds of an impulsive, antisocial feather more frequently hang out together, so these kinds of bellicose activities are more likely to occur overall. It's probably some combination of the above that accounts for the fact that antisocial individuals are frequently the victims as well as the perpetrators of violence.

Some researchers[11] have identified hostility as being a common trait in drug abusers that seems to cut across several different personality types. Marvin Zuckerman[12] has described a trait called *sensation seeking*, which includes the need for varied, novel, and thrill-inducing sensations and experiences, as well as a greater than normal willingness to take physical and social risks for the sake of these kicks.

Sensation seeking has been found to be particularly common in impulsive, antisocial psychopaths, suggesting that part of the basis for their "bad" behavior is a perennial need for thrills, chills, and excitement at any cost. Not surprisingly, many studies have found drug addicts to show a greater than average desire for thrills, adventure seeking, and altered states of consciousness.[13] Sensation seeking may also account in part for the strong relationship between drug abuse and violent crime:[14] For some, hurting people is one form of "fun."

If we trace the life history of the impulsive, antisocial alcohol and drug abuser, it's commonly revealed that many have been hyperactive children. *Hyperactivity*, or its more recent diagnostic incarnation, *attention deficit disorder* (ADD), describes children with short attention spans, impulsive behavior, and poor emotional control. A related term, *minimal brain dysfunction* (MBD), refers to the idea that many of these children show deficits in verbal or perceptual skills—learning disabilities or spatial orientation problems, for example—that appear similar in type, if not degree, to those of adults who have acquired brain damage as the result of illness or injury.

This is the kid, usually a boy, who can't seem to sit still, is always "into everything," does lousily in school (dyslexia or math problems frequently compound the picture), has few real friends, and even as a young child seems to have gotten into more than his fair share of trouble in school, at home, or in the playground. *Conduct disorder* is a common (although not necessarily inevitable) concomitant. If big and strong enough, he frequently becomes the class bully, his warped sociability finding expression only in his propensity to pick on other kids. Alternatively, if he's small, weak, and funny-looking, which many are, he may end up as the class clown or the prime butt of the bully's depredations.

A long-range research program at the University of Pittsburgh[15] has been looking at the relationship between neuropsychological, developmental, and personality variables in alcoholism. They've found that those alcoholics with relatively severe drinking problems are more likely to have childhood histories of ADD/MBD. The ADD/MBD group also tend to start drinking and become alcohol-dependent earlier in life than other alcoholics.

Alcoholics rated high in childhood hyperactivity/MBD were compared with low-MBD alcoholics in another study by the University of Pittsburgh group.[16] On personality testing, high-MBD alcoholics showed more overall psychopathology, especially antisocial personality disorder. High-MBD alcoholics were also found to have more interpersonal difficulties, to be less psychologically mature, and to experience more social and emotional problems. They were more likely to use alcohol, as well as other drugs, to alter their mood states, and they were less able to control their drinking once they got started. The investigators suggested that drinking and using other drugs to change moods were the high-MBD alcoholics' way of seeking an optimum level of arousal and emotion, a state they were unable to achieve by their own interpersonal coping skills.

The early lives of individuals addicted to opiate narcotics also seem to be affected by the ADD/MBD/hyperactivity complex. In one study,[17] a higher than normal rate of heroin and methadone addicts seeking help at a drug treatment facility had histories of childhood hyperactivity. Despite roughly average intelligence, the addicts had achieved much lower levels of education and occupational status than their peers who had similar IQs. The addicts also had earlier records of arrests.

Other studies[18] have suggested that the mediating variable between childhood hyperactivity and later substance abuse may be antisocial personality. That is, a history of hyperactivity may not in itself doom a person to lifelong chemical dependence. However, a certain proportion of such children grow up to become delinquents and psychopaths and it is this factor that may play a key role in the development of an impulsive, nonreflective, and thrill-seeking lifestyle that includes getting high on a regular basis.

But some alcoholics and addicts, many with ADD/MBD histories, who *don't* grow up to be adult psychopaths, may develop psychological problems of their own later in life. Few clinical phenomena are as well documented as the occurrence of depression among many men and women with alcoholism.[19] In fact, depressed alcoholics may be more likely to seek treatment for their depression than for the alcohol problem itself. Up to 98 percent of alcoholics admitted to treatment programs show some depressive symptomatology, although after a few weeks many of them may begin to recover. Alcoholics kill themselves fifteen to twenty-five times more often than members of the general population and up to a quarter of all deaths in alcoholics are due to suicide. Interestingly, alcoholics with antisocial personality disorder report many more symptoms of depression and anxiety than other alcoholics, though the symptoms in antisocials tend to be more isolated and fleeting,[20] and may include a self-serving component: "I'm so bad because I'm so sad."

Opiate addicts, for their part, seem especially prone to react to stress with brief episodes of mild-to-moderate depression, according to research carried out by Bruce Rounsaville and colleagues.[21] A smaller but still substantial group have more chronic, pervasive depression. Rounsaville's studies found that a current depressive episode at the beginning of treatment was associated with higher levels of drug use during the subsequent six-month period, supporting the view of Khantzian and Wurmser that addicts may use opiates as a form of self-treatment for intolerable, unpleasant emotions.

Just as depression and antisocial personality are by no means incompatible in alcoholics, so with opiate addicts. Rounsaville's research shows a significant association between depression and antisocial personality disorder in opiate addicts.[22] Moreover, alcoholism may also be part of this syndrome,[23] confirming the observation that many addicts drink heavily when opiates are not available. This leads Rounsaville to speculate that psychopathic character traits may somehow "defend" against underlying depression.

In summary, the alcoholic/addict seems typically to have been a hyperactive, attention-disordered child, to be prone to impulsive feelings and behaviors and to suffer from bouts of depression and despair. Not that all chemical abusers necessarily show all of these traits. In fact, at least for alcoholism, there may actually be two main clusters of predisposing and associated factors, leading to a primarily antisocial type of alcoholic and another primarily depressive type.[24]

But consider the common underlying dynamic: a difficulty dealing with impulses that threaten the stability of the ego, the core of the self. Impulsively dyscontrolled feelings could easily lead to up-and-down mood swings, and since people generally try to do something about downs rather than ups, drinking or drug use would constitute a crude form of "self-medication" for depression.

Where the impulsivity manifests itself in more overt forms of behavior, drinking or drugging may be associated with acts that would be considered psychopathic or antisocial. In such cases, chemicals might be used to induce or enhance the freewheeling, don't-give-a-damn attitude that oils the psychopathic juggernaut. The temporary and mild release from inhibitions that many of us seek from time to time through chemical substances is amplified in the antisocial alcoholic/addict to the point of unrestrained dissipation. In this way does he numb himself to the disturbing urges, impulses, and feelings that threaten to destabilize his fragile self-structure, and at the same time allow for their expression in the grossest form.

The Brain of the Blitzed:
Neuropsychology of Alcoholism and Addiction

One problem in interpreting neuropsychological studies of alcoholism is this: Alcohol is a neurotoxin. So it's not unreasonable to expect that years of heavy drinking would take their toll on the structure and function of the brain, producing impaired performance on neuropsychological measures similar to those seen in individuals with other kinds of brain damage. In fact, many studies support this. A lifetime of serious imbibing does seem to result in a particular pattern of neuropsychological deficits. Whereas routine and overlearned verbal skills appear to be preserved, more novel and abstract visuospatial problem-solving abilities appear to be adversely affected.[25]

But these kinds of studies have generally involved older alcoholics with many decades of boozing under their belts— and sometimes, under those same belts, a diseased liver that can produce metabolic disturbances in brain functioning[26]— making age effects, medical complications, and alcohol-related factors difficult to disentangle.

Another way of looking at the problem is to focus on the kinds of neuropsychological findings that may have little to do with "brain damage" in the usual sense, but may instead reflect characteristic neuropsychodynamic features of the alcoholic's or addict's cognitive style—differences that may antecede or indeed predispose to the abuse of drink or drugs. Many of the studies taking this approach have involved younger subjects without the decades of brain-pickling that typify older alcoholics. In many cases, the "chicken and egg" issue of which comes first, the drinking/drugging or the cognitive dysfunction, is far from clear, but some suggestive findings are beginning to appear.

Ralph Tarter and Oscar Parsons[27] gave the Wisconsin Card Sorting Test (WCST), described in Chapter 9, to a group of chronic alcoholics and found that they had trouble maintaining a stable cognitive set. That is, the alcoholics tended to interrupt a sequence of correct, positively reinforced trials with intrusive errors. The tendency to make such errors was correlated with how many years the subjects had been drinking.

In a subsequent study, Tarter[28] compared the WCST performance of long-term alcoholics, shorter-term alcoholics, and nonalcoholics. Both the long- and short-term alcoholics showed impaired set-maintenance, consistent with the earlier study. The long-term alcoholics took more trials and made more errors than either of the two other groups. The long-term alcoholics also made more perseverative errors, indicating that they had greater difficulty in abandoning a previously formed concept, despite the fact that the old concept was no longer useful in guiding behavior in an adaptive way. Interestingly, Tarter drew an analogy between this performance and similar behavior seen in frontal lobe–damaged patients.

Alcoholics and nonalcoholics were given a battery of cognitive tests by Alfred Heilbrun and colleagues.[29] The results again pointed to a deficiency in the alcoholics' self-control of behavior—a finding that might have profound implications for the self-control of their *drinking* behavior. They were also less proficient in scanning their own internal states of thought and feeling, as well as in using cognitive processes to structure perceptions and control behavior.

Similarly, Oscar Parsons and Stephen Farr[30] concluded that alcoholics show poorer performance on tests of abstracting, problem solving, memory, new learning, and perceptual-motor speed. Moreover, these findings are seen in individuals who for the most part don't have clinically diagnosable organic brain syndromes and who constitute the majority of patients seen in alcoholism treatment centers. And with regard to such treatment, Parsons[31] notes that neuropsychological deficits in alcoholics bode ill for success in rehabilitation and recovery.

Neuropsychological deficits can't be due wholly to the effects of alcohol on the brain, however. Parsons's own research[32] suggests that at least some of the impairment seen in alcoholics may predate heavy drinking. For example, he found that alcoholics and controls differed as much on neuropsychological tests after thirteen months of post treatment sobriety as when they were examined after seven weeks without a drink. If drinking caused the deficits, we'd expect to see some recovery with continuing abstinence.

The now-sober alcoholics in the study were found to do significantly worse than nonalcoholic controls on measures of verbal abstraction and problem solving and on perceptuomotor processing. Patients rated as having made better progress in the treatment program and having a better overall prognosis obtained higher verbal intelligence scores, had better short-term visual memory, did better in complex visuospatial processing and perceptuomotor performance, and made fewer errors on a concept-formation task. Interestingly, the more severe alcoholics in the sample had more than twice as many symptoms (by history) of hyperactivity and MBD, suggesting that it may be this subgroup in particular who show the kind of neurocognitive profile that precedes and predisposes to a lifestyle of impulsive drinking.

Arthur Alterman and colleagues[33] framed their study of alcoholics in terms of the concept of *persistence*, which they defined as the capacity to organize, sequence, and sustain goal-directed behavior within a proper time frame. This capacity, according to the researchers, is related to activity in frontolimbic brain mechanisms and is similar to the concept of time contiguity we discussed in Chapter 3 in connection with the frontal lobes.

They found that relatively young (under forty) male alcoholics were impaired on tasks sensitive to perceptuomotor components of persistence. Moreover, test performance had nothing to do with number of years of heavy drinking. To the investigators, this suggests that the impairments weren't merely the inexorable consequence of slow brain poisoning by alcohol, but rather may reflect a neurocognitive vulnerability to alcohol's adverse effects, one which may have preceded the onset of drinking and which leads in some predisposed tipplers to a rapid decline in cognitive capacity.

What about neuropsychological impairment from drugs other than alcohol? In this regard, one question we might want to ask is: impaired compared to whom? Francis Fields and John Fullerton[34] used an extensive neuropsychological test battery to compare heroin addicts both with nondrug normal controls *and* patients with known brain damage. Results showed that the addicts performed much like normal nonaddicts and that both of these groups did better than brain-damaged subjects. Although only a faint trend, it turned out that the heroin addicts did *better* on some of the measures, especially on the Category Test, a test of abstract reasoning and conceptual classification.

So is heroin addiction good for your neurocognitive health? Not likely. Rather, argue the investigators, it may be a matter of practice and lifestyle. That is, the seemingly higher conceptual ability of heroin addicts may relate to the manner in which many of these individuals are able to skillfully psych out and manipulate their social environments, using a certain cunning/conning type of cognitive skill. Some of the components of that skill—some elements of cognition—may overlap with the task demands of some of the neuropsychologist's tests, and this would account for their good performance.

Hill and colleagues[35] compared heroin addicts, alcoholics, and normal subjects on a variety of neuropsychological test measures. In addition, each subject got a CT scan. On several of the neuropsychological measures the alcoholics came out most impaired, the normals least impaired, and the addicts in between. In addition, the longer the addicts had been using heroin, the worse their neuropsychological performance. Giving up the drug was associated with better performance on some measures and worse performance on others. Overall, there was only a weak correlation between neuropsychological data and CT scan findings.

Rounsaville's research group[36] compared heroin and methadone addicts with matched nonaddict controls and with patients suffering from epilepsy. The addicts were found to have neuropsychological test scores comparable with or superior to the controls, concurring with the main findings of Fields and Fullerton's study. Interestingly, the strongest correlates of neuropsychological functioning had little to do with amount or duration of drug abuse. Instead, addicts with higher educational achievement showed generally superior performance on a number of measures.

This suggests that failure to account for intellectual ability and educational training may have something to do with the reports of the "paradoxically" superior performance of some opiate addicts on certain neuropsychological measures. Like the more intelligent psychopaths in the last chapter, who did all right on the neuropsychological tests that their duller compatriots bombed out on, smarter substance abusers may be able to compensate for specific deficits in complex problem solving by virtue of their overall higher-than-average "smarts."

In sum, while uniformity of results again eludes us (this is the real world of research, after all), the bulk of neuropsychological evidence suggests that alcoholics and addicts have particular difficulty with functions involving planning, conceptualization, integration, and behavioral self-control, particularly where verbal strategies are important. Given the personality data and the histories of childhood hyperactivity in many of these individuals, it's natural to suppose that these neuropsychological findings represent a part of the whole fabric of the addiction-prone personality. How do we go about developing a neuropsychodynamic theory of addiction and the addictive personality out of this mass of data?

Toward a Neuropsychodynamic Model of the Addictions

A good place to start is with the biobehavioral conceptualization offered by Ralph Tarter and colleagues.[37] Their theory was originally intended to cover only alcoholism, but I think it can be expanded to include the other addictions as well.

Tarter begins by citing the evidence linking childhood hyperactivity with a later increased risk for alcoholism. In addition to established drinkers, a high proportion of the as yet nondrinking sons of alcoholic fathers appear to be hyperactive. Other findings indicate that behavioral impersistence is a stable characteristic that predates the onset of heavy drinking. Additional risk factors may include a propensity to become easily distressed, as well as a slowness in returning to a quiescent state after being aroused. An individual with such characteristics would be easily upset and slow to recover. Faced with actual or perceived stresses, he might quickly turn to the bottle, needle, or ampule as a convenient psychological crutch.

What about the stereotype of the merry drunkard, the gregarious slap-on-the-back souse who's the life of every party? Tarter points out that what may pass at first for conviviality is in fact the expression of a highly active, disinhibited labile and impulsive disposition in which true empathy and fellow-feeling are lacking. This is shown even in the prealcoholic personality whose jocoseness seems to neglect any genuine consideration of the feelings of others and who seems strangely unaware of or unconcerned with the loutish impression he frequently makes. And how many charmingly boisterous inebriates have you seen quickly metamorphose into mean drunks when their audience eventually grows tired of the joke?

This kind of egocentric inconsiderateness can be observed early in the interpersonal interactions of some hyperactive children who, as teenagers, are also more likely than their peers to have already begun copping six-packs with phony IDs and sneaking shots from the parental liquor larder. These same adolescent drinkers also show increased aggressiveness, superficial emotional rapport, and general overall difficulties in relating to people.

Tarter goes on to review the biological and neuropsychological substrates of vulnerability to alcoholism, some of which have been discussed above; other data will be summarized here. As we've seen, many alcoholics have histories of childhood hyperactivity and MBD. Children of alcoholics who are themselves at high risk for alcoholism show EEG abnormalities. Families of alcoholics show a high rate of motor disorders such as balance problems and tremors, even in nondrinking members. Young left-handers are more prone to abuse alcohol than righties and more alcoholics seem to be left-handed or ambidextrous than would be expected in the general population, suggesting anomalies in hemispheric lateralization in the high-risk group.

Teenage sons of alcoholic fathers are more neuropsychologically impaired than offspring of nonalcoholics and also show poorer academic achievement. Biological sons of alcoholics, adopted at birth and raised in nonalcoholic foster homes, perform more poorly on verbal but not visuospatial measures of intelligence. About one-third of alcoholics meet diagnostic criteria for residual attention-deficit disorder, the grown-up version of childhood hyperactivity. And as we've also seen, attentional disturbances in childhood are related to risk for later alcoholism.

Nonalcoholic children and siblings of alcoholics perform more poorly on neuropsychological measures of abstracting, problem solving, and perceptuomotor functioning than relatives of nonalcoholics. Prealcoholics often present a behavioral picture of impulsivity, disinhibition, high activity rate, emotional lability, and aggressiveness. And antisocial personality disorder frequently antedates the start of problem drinking. Note that this conceptualization doesn't mean that every hyperactive kid is automatically doomed to a life of bleary-eyed decrepitude. But it *is* the case that without any kind of proper intervention, a higher proportion of hyperactives than other children seem to meet this kind of fate.

Pulling this extensive data base together, Tarter invokes the role of the brain's frontal lobes as the substrate for "executive" functions of behavior. Recall from Chapter 3 the emphasis that Luria[38] gave to the prefrontal cortex's activity in guiding and self-evaluating a person's thoughts, feelings, and actions. Luria further stressed the role of language mediation in facilitating this "executive" control of behavior, a point that Vygotsky[39] had made earlier.

In applying this concept to alcoholism, Tarter cites research[40] on evoked responses in a sample of individuals at high risk for alcoholism. The study found that the normal electrophysiological brain processes involved in language use were disrupted. And evidence from Tarter's own research group[41] indicates that high-risk individuals are deficient on tasks requiring language mediation. In addition, one of the findings from the extensive behavior-genetic studies of Sarnoff Mednick's research team[42] has been that biological sons of alcoholics adopted at birth and raised in nonalcoholic foster homes obtain lower scores than control subjects on verbal, but not visuospatial measures of intelligence. Inasmuch as language processes are instrumental for guiding goal-directed behavior, says Tarter, this deficiency in language processing may be one of the traits that comprise the alcoholism-vulnerable makeup.

Further, Tarter notes, certain of the past and present traits of alcoholics and prealcoholics—hyperactivity, social disinhibition, emotional lability, and impaired attention span—are common sequelae of organic frontal lobe impairment. This may indicate that individuals predisposed to alcoholism are unable to regulate arousal adequately. The neurocognitive setup for developing a drinking problem, therefore, may be this insidious combination of weak autonomous control over mood and arousal states and a deficient self-guiding and self-reflective capacity due to poorly developed language functioning.

Now let's take Tarter's argument a step further. If the "addictive personality" reflects an emptiness of the ego, a hole in the self, and if this deficit in ego autonomy is in turn related to a basic core of impulsivity in thought, feeling, and action, then the outward manifestations might be in the form of substance abuse as well as depression.

In the first case, drugs would be used to mitigate the individual's feelings of being overwhelmed by his own unbridled passions and urges—rage, for example, as posited by the psychodynamic theorists we discussed earlier. Second, depression could result as a consequence of lack of control over emotions; being perennially out of control is no doubt demoralizing. The addictive personality would thus be one expression, one permutation, of the impulsive cognitive style encountered in Chapter 9, and the neuropsychodynamics would be similar.

Thus, the impulsive character, who frequently comes to clinical or judicial or media attention as the psychopath or antisocial personality or drunkard or doper, may suffer from a neurodevelopmental maturational deficit that is responsible for his inability to use inner speech to modulate attention, emotion, thought, and behavior. Under conditions of social frustration or ambiguity, he resorts to regressive or behaviorally immature coping patterns to maintain the integrity of his ego. To the extent that ego integrity requires the development of certain cognitive abilities—what Hartmann, remember, called the ''conflict-free ego sphere''—a lack or distorted development of these capacities may naturally predispose to the use of less effective coping strategies.

And to the degree that the more specialized cognitive skills necessary for intact neuropsychological test performance are intertwined with the more general cognitive style factors involved in overall personality structure, deficits in one may well be associated with distortions in the other. Thus, poor verbal comprehension on an IQ test may also show itself as a deficiency in utilizing inner speech to guide and evaluate behavior: Both capacities rely on the brain's adequate elaboration of a language system, albeit in different ways.

The ''different ways'' aspect also expresses itself in the dissociation we sometimes see between external-manipulative and internal-reflective modes of language. Witness the verbally facile con man who can lay down a smooth rap, charm the bread out of countless pockets or the virtue from equivalent numbers of pants, but whose glibness, in the long run, is no guarantee against repeated bouts of lousy judgment that land him in deep trouble again and again.

Likewise, the alcoholic and addict may be impaired on some measures of conceptual flexibility and reasoning, not because—or at least not *only* because—these substances directly poison the brain, but because poor ability in such tasks is part of a larger preexisting constellation of cognitive personality factors associated with the neuropsychodynamic setup for addiction.

But even this isn't always the case. As we've seen in this chapter, some addicts actually do quite well on this or that test of cognitive ability, while others bomb. Why? As noted above in the case of language and as discussed in Chapter

9, impulsive characters often display a keen practical intelligence for immediate matters and may thus appear quite cognitively competent in the short run. But *only* in the short run. What's missing is the *reflective* component of intelligence, the planning and evaluating of more extended sequences of thought and action that have long-range consequences.

Yet many of the more commonly used neuropsychological tests are clearly of the short-run variety, requiring quick and efficient performance on relatively circumscribed tasks. In the case of the alcoholic/addict with an impulsive cognitive style, but fairly decent immediate cognitive ability, intact performance on such measures could lead to his being assessed as having overall adaptive cognitive competence—a real together dude—until such behavior has to be generalized to more comprehensive and less unambiguous life events: Recall the French frontal lobe cases in Chapter 3, the plight of Evan in Chapter 6, or Robbie's story in Chapter 9. And for those who fail *even* the immediate tasks, the problems in longer-term cognitive flexibility and adaptiveness may be all the more severe.

Indeed, looking over the actual data from many of the studies that found relatively normal performance "on average" in substance abusing groups, one is struck by the wide variability between individual subjects on the various measures used. Some subjects actually do perform "averagely," but others do great on these measures and still others bomb out abysmally. I've used many of these tests for individual assessments of hundreds of alcohol and drug abusers and I've gotten pretty much the same impression: Performance varies across the board.

What *is* different from the "normal" populations used as reference groups is that the intersubject variability among the normals appears somewhat less extreme and seems to correlate better with such related variables as level of education and full-scale IQ. That is, someone who's very bright in general would be expected to do better on a test of any particular cognitive capacity simply because being smarter seems to have a generalized bootstrapping effect on these kinds of cognitive tasks. For most people, that's the case. For many substance abusers, on the other hand, we commonly find "so-smart-yet-so-dumb" patterns of performance on many of these measures of particular cognitive skills.

Indeed, what's particularly striking about the neuropsychological test performance of these alcoholics and addicts is the frequent *dissociation* between overall intellectual ability and performance on measures of conceptual flexibility and complex problem solving. Commonly, even "smart" substance abusers will be stymied by the complex reasoning tasks. Their performance is typically hampered by an inability to grasp a correct principle or, even if verbalized correctly, an inability to use that principle adaptively to solve the problem. Less frequently—but it happens—individuals with low IQs will do fine on the conceptual tests. One thing this shows is that we need a lot more data about how individual cognitive capacities combine to produce what we normally call "intelligence."[43]

The Sober Brain:
Neuropsychodynamics of Abstinence and Recovery

And then there are those individuals, seemingly condemned to a wasted life by genetics or bad upbringing or social blight, who nevertheless rise above their situation and don't get hooked, or if they do, subsequently get their act together and move on. Thus, another important approach to the whole matter of neuropsychodynamic predisposition is to consider why some individuals at high risk for alcoholism or addiction *don't* develop these problems later in life.

One ambitious study[44] followed a group of at-risk children from birth to age eighteen. One of the factors that distinguished the at-risk children who foiled their inebriate destinies was a phlegmatic, easygoing temperament—the kind of personality that elicited positive support from caretakers. Also important was having at least average intelligence, adequate communication skills in reading and writing, a favorable orientation toward achievement, and a responsible, caring attitude. Additional attributes included an overall positive self-concept, a belief in one's own ability to control the events in one's life and confidence that one's own efforts could be effective in solving important problems—traits we've already identified as self-efficacy, ego-autonomy, and personal integrity. In other words, though seemingly damned by their chromosomes to don the family mantle of substance abuse, these individuals were saved by some overriding inherited patterning of the brain that bequeathed a nonimpulsive, more ego-autonomous cognitive style.

Other studies of once well-established, card-carrying alcoholics who have successfully *stopped* drinking[45] point out some intriguing differences between those who seek treatment and maintain sobriety and those who don't. Successful abstainers seem able to maintain a stable conception or mental image of the various negative consequences of drunkenness. This is unlike the frequent relapser whose urge to drink overwhelms the best of his resolutions because his powers of future time extension are no match for his more immediate impulses.

Alcoholics who typically see events as being controlled by random forces outside themselves—recall the concept of internal versus external locus of control—are judged by clinicians to have poorer prospects for recovery. Among abstainers, those who have a better developed sense of their own efficacy and control tend to give credit for their sobriety to their own efforts, while less self-efficacious abstainers attribute their abstinence to external pressure, such as the threat of losing their job or their marriage breaking up, or perhaps the positive (but still largely external) guidance of membership in Alcoholics Anonymous.

In another study,[46] patients in alcoholism treatment programs who were rated by therapists as having a poor prognosis performed significantly worse than good-prognosis patients on neuropsychological tasks measuring visual and perceptuomotor skills, cognitive flexibility, and verbal intelligence. In particular, therapists' judgments of their patients' ability to use analogies and their capacity to generalize from one situation to another were related to performance on the WCST, the test of abstract conceptualization and cognitive flexibility described in previous chapters.

The findings suggest that the cognitive abilities measured by such tests have some relationship to the cognitive abilities required for effective participation in therapy, such as the ability to function in complex interpersonal situations and view things from different perspectives. Indeed, further exploration of the relationship of neuropsychological variables to treatment outcome would be a tremendously productive area of study.

Conclusions

Verbal-conceptual ability, or its impairment, appears to pop up again and again on the list of factors shown to predict the development of, or recovery from, alcoholism and addiction. This highlights the idea developed in earlier chapters that a sense of personal stability—an integrated ego structure—depends on the ability to use internal language codes (Vygotsky's inner speech) to modulate behavior. Lacking this, the sense of self is unsteady and fragile, the ego is vulnerable to disruption by surges of overwhelming impulse and emotion, and substances that temporarily allay these disruptions are favored.

Neuropsychodynamically, this means that frontal lobe modulation of limbic drives and passions may depend on the left-hemisphere inner language system for optimal behavioral adaptation. Without the intact functioning of this system, the ego can be sustained only from moment to fragile moment by the use of a chemical crutch.

In fact, the salient characteristics of alcoholics' and addicts' cognitive styles that we've considered in this chapter—cognitive inflexibility, attenuated time perspective, external locus of control, dependence on external reinforcement, deficient ego strength, and poor object relations—are all features of thought and behavior that have been associated with frontal lobe impairment.

The point here, as throughout this book, is that these deficits need not imply that alcoholics and addicts have neuroanatomic ''lesions'' of the frontal lobes or any other part of the brain. Rather, the typifying features of cognitive style and personality in alcoholics and addicts depend on common neurodevelopmental features of brain organization that resemble in part the picture seen when actual structural left-hemisphere–frontal brain damage occurs. This, of course, is the neuropsychodynamic approach familiar from other chapters.

We know so much more about alcohol than about other substances of abuse because booze has been freely around so much longer and used by so many more people. The message about alcohol we seem to be getting is that while some of the neuropsychological abnormalities seen in heavy drinkers, especially younger ones, probably relate to preexisting variations in personality and cognitive style, long-term alcohol abuse can cause pathological changes in the brain structure itself, leading later in life to still further cognitive and behavioral deterioration—a vicious cycle if ever there was one.

Research interest in other kinds of drug abuse has really only burgeoned in this country since the Vietnam era. This recent crop of smokers, poppers, and shooters has not yet reached the seniority of their dipsophiliac predecessors, but the data starting to come in are not encouraging. We can only wonder if the fifty- and sixty-year-old druggies of the year 2000 will resemble the burnt-out alkies of an earlier generation.

CHAPTER 11

BODY AND SELF:

Personality and Psychosomatics

A bodily disease, which we look upon as whole and entire
within itself, may, after all, be but a symptom of some ailment
in the spiritual part.

—NATHANIEL HAWTHORNE

Use your health, even to the point of wearing it out. That is
what it is for. Spend all you have before you die, and do not
outlive yourself.

—GEORGE BERNARD SHAW

How many times have you been struck down with raging
diarrhea or a scary chest pain just before, during, or after a
particularly stressful situation and been told (or told yourself) "it's psychosomatic"? Or maybe you know someone
who suffers from chronic headaches, stomach cramps, high
blood pressure, or whatever, but no specific physical cause
has been found for what seem to be very real symptoms—
is that "psychosomatic," too?

Colloquially, people sometimes use the term "psychosomatic" as sort of a synonym for "hysterical," that is, to
describe some bodily complaint that's not really real, all in
the mind, psychologically induced, and so on. But clinicians traditionally make a distinction between hysterical
symptoms, for which there's supposedly no organic pathology, and psychosomatic illnesses in which the bodily
changes are real and measurable, but for which the ultimate
cause is presumed to be largely "psychological."

So, for example, a functional paralysis that has none of

the usually associated physical changes such as muscle atrophy, spasticity, or impairment of related muscle groups might be termed hysterical (Chapter 8). Dramatic upshoots in blood pressure that can be measured with a blood pressure cuff, but that don't seem to relate to any pathological physical process such as a hormonal imbalance or dietary excess, may be labeled psychosomatic. The illness is real, but the cause is ambiguous. And since doctors as a group tend to not tolerate ambiguity well, the etiology is ascribed to "psychological" factors. But is it?

Early psychoanalytically oriented psychosomatic theorists, such as Flanders Dunbar,[1] postulated that, in effect, each psychosomatic illness reflects a distinct kind of psychological conflict, which in turn represents a fixation at a particular primitive psychosexual stage of development. Gastrointestinal problems, for example, are an expression of conflicts harking back to infantile oral longings and frustrations. Cardiovascular overreactivity syndromes are manifestations of conflicts over passive dependency versus aggressive hostility, and so on.

Later theorists, such as Franz Alexander,[2] stressed the importance of preexisting somatic vulnerabilities in determining how a particular bodily channel might become the conduit for the expression of a particular kind of psychological conflict. Also, Alexander showed that the kinds of conflict-defense systems that find their way into psychosomatic symptoms are more general and far-reaching than specific oral, anal, or oedipal fixations.

Reflecting the burgeoning knowledge in the neurosciences over the last few decades, more recent writers have emphasized the role of the brain and endocrine system in mediating the interactions between a individual's perception of events, his or her personal history, and the psychological and bodily reactions that ensue.[3] For example, we know that so-called essential hypertension really results from a complex interplay of neural, hormonal, kidney, heart, and blood vessel mechanisms in addition to psychological factors.

But what's been missing from even these more modern accounts is any explanation of the neurocognitive dynamics that may mediate between psyche and soma. That is, there's rarely a direct line between raw perception and bodily reaction—some degree of *interpretation* of events typically precedes a response, whether physiological or behavioral. And the cognitive style factors we've discovered to operate in other aspects of personality are relevant in the somatic sphere as well. In this chapter, we'll apply the neuropsychodynamic model to a few of the more well-known and well-studied psychosomatic illnesses.

The Type-A Behavior Pattern

Your heart pumps the blood needed to nourish every living cell in your body. This blood supply travels from the heart through a system of arteries that branch out ever more finely to suffuse every organ. If blood supply to an organ or body part is cut off, the cells soon die. Most bodily organs can regenerate damaged tissues if blood supply is reestablished. If the blood cutoff is permanent, some organs, such as the liver, can suffer the destruction of a large portion of their bulk and still perform their jobs fairly adequately.

But there are two especially vulnerable organ systems: those composed of nervous tissue and muscle tissue. If blood supply to a part of the brain is interrupted for more than a few minutes, that part of the brain dies and the functions served by that brain area are impaired. We call this a stroke. The heart—which is really a powerful rhythmic muscle—can likewise be permanently damaged by blockage of blood supply that flows through its own unique network of coronary arteries. When this happens we call it a heart attack, which is essentially the cardiac equivalent of the ''brain attack'' that occurs in a stroke.

One of the things that cause arteries to clog and block is *plaque*, a fatty substance that builds up along the walls of arteries and may cause secondary degenerative changes in the blood vessel wall, a condition called *atherosclerosis*. When the blockage reaches a critical point—in some cases, up to 80 percent of a vessel can be clogged without noticeable symptoms—the blood supply is cut off and an *infarction* of the heart tissue occurs. If only a small amount of heart muscle is affected, the remainder may be sufficient to maintain relatively normal blood pumping, and the person recovers. With more extensive damage he may have to live a restricted life in order to minimize stress on the remaining intact heart muscle. Even more damage, and it's goodbye.

Traditionally, it was thought that the main important influences on plaque formation and blood vessel integrity were genetic, hormonal, and dietary. Have long-lived parents and be born with the right body chemistry, don't eat lots of fatty, cholesterol-rich foods, get some exercise, and you'll be all right. Make no mistake—these things are still important (although the exercise link is not without controversy).

But in the 1950s and '60s medical researchers began to notice a connection between the tendency to develop coronary artery disease and certain personality characteristics. They and their followers have since been developing the idea that a certain type of reaction pattern or personality type, called *type-A*, may be associated with a tendency toward cardiovascular overreactivity in many situations, which may predispose to plaque formation, coronary artery disease, and early death.

What are the parameters of the type-A behavior pattern or personality? Type-A researchers Meyer Friedman and Diane Ulmer perhaps sum it up best:

Type-A behavior is above all a continuous struggle, an unremitting attempt to achieve more and more things or participate in more and more events in less and less time, frequently in the face of opposition—real or imagined—from other persons. The type-A personality is dominated by covert insecurity of status or hyperaggressiveness or both.[4]

It's at least one of these two basic components—insecurity or hyperaggressiveness—that generally sets in motion the type-A's lifelong struggle. Eventually, this fosters the emergence of a third personality ingredient, time urgency, the million-things-at-once, get-it-done-yesterday overbusy, frenetic activity pattern that's become a virtual caricature of the compulsive striver. As the struggle continues, the hyperaggressiveness, and also perhaps the status incongruity, usually show themselves in the smoldering, just-below-the-surface anger known as free-floating hostility.

The type-A, incidentally, is commonly contrasted with the *type-B*, who is portrayed as the type-A's diametric opposite: phlegmatic, laid back, quietly confident, and sure of himself. Not lazy or delusionally Pollyannaish—just taking things at a comfortable pace. In actuality, most people fall in between these two extremes of pure type-A and pure type-B. But as in other chapters of this book, it's the extremes we're interested in first.

The type-A's insecurity of status and lack of self-esteem are fueled by the continual invidious comparison of himself to other people and the tendency for his expectations to consistently outdistance his achievements. The hyperaggressiveness of the type-A involves not merely an assertive desire to succeed, to excel, to win, but to *dominate*. To prevail is not enough; the type-A must *crush* his opponents, *cream* his rivals. Friedman and Ulmer quote the author Jess Lair: "Before I had my heart attack, I didn't have any friends. When I played poker, I played to win from the bastards." For the type-A, there are no friendly arguments, board games become fields of mortal combat, opinions are battled over in terms of absolute right or wrong, and so on.

Free-floating hostility is a permanently indwelling anger, a mountainous chip on the shoulder whose unstable terrain can be easily jostled into an avalanche of rancor by the most trivial-seeming words or deeds. But the type-A is very good at justifying the hostility by finding all manner of excuses and rationalizations for his more-or-less permanent state of irritation. In fact, recent research suggests that this factor of hostility, of mistrust, of deep and abiding cynicism may in fact be the most potent of the type-A traits in predisposing to coronary artery disease.[5]

The sense of *time urgency* arises from an insatiable desire to accomplish too much or do too many things in the amount of time available. To deal with this, the type-A resorts to two basic strategies: First, he puts everything into high gear, speeding up all activities. When even that's not enough, he tries to do more than one thing at a time, called *polyphasic activity*. A typical type-A morning routine might include eating breakfast, listening to the radio, making a phone call, and reading the paper—all at the same time.

Some additional aspects of type-A behavior are termed "secondary" by Friedman and Ulmer; we'll soon see, however, that within our present neuropsychodynamic model, they may in fact comprise the very foundations of the type-A's cognitive style. These include a tendency to use numbers and quantities when thinking and speaking, a failure to use metaphors and similes, and a seeming inability or unwillingness to develop various kinds of imagery.

If there's anything the type-A loves, it seems to be numbers, and the type-A tends to employ enumeration increasingly in all phases of his life. A businessman describes success in terms of the number of deals he's made, a surgeon by how many operating hours he schedules, an attorney by the number of cases won, a scientist by the quantity of published papers. And of course, there's the universal, the quintessential, the ultimate measure of worth in our society: *how much money*. In fact, probably one of the main appeals of money to the naturally acquisitive is how deliciously easy it is to count, to measure, to compare from one person to another. Just think of Silas Marner's loving ritual of daily coin counting, how he'd pile the coins one atop the other and experience an almost sensual pleasure as he added each pile to the next to derive his daily sum.

Thus, the type-A calculates the monetary value of a painting without ever stopping to appreciate its beauty, is sensitive only to the bottom line, lives only in the "real world," plays only hardball, and drips with contempt for the suckers and wimps who stop to smell the roses. Silas Marner, Ebenezer Scrooge, Mr. Potter of Bedford Falls—popular culture has iconicized this particular human caricature, just as it has done for the flamboyant hysteric, the impulsive rebel, and the piteous drunkard.

One intriguing theory of the type-A cognitive style—intriguing because it approaches the neuropsychodynamic model of this book—comes from Gregory Garamoni and Robert Schwartz.[6] Their theory is that the type-A behavior pattern is a variation of the compulsive personality and that the type-A pattern is a way of grasping at control of one's impulses through a constellation of compulsive traits.

The type-A pattern is, according to their theory, one of several possible expressions of an underlying compulsive personality organization. To support this, Garomoni and Schwartz cite evidence suggesting that the type-A's overt bravado based on achievement and success may be an unconscious response to unacceptable inner feelings of self-doubt. In some people, such inner unsteadiness might work itself out in the form of a more self-effacing, indecisive, fence-sitting, nebbishy kind of behavior pattern. Alternatively, it could manifest itself in the expansive, overdecisive, aggressively cocksure, ambiguity-intolerant type-A.

Garamoni and Schwartz's conceptualization is a useful beginning, but I'd argue that the type-A pattern is more complex and represents not the expression of a single cognitive style, but rather a blend of styles with a particular outcome. The compulsive cognitive style element is certainly present, as shown by the preoccupation with numbers and the hyperfocus on plans and details necessary to get things done. But there's more. The caustic cynicism and hostility that pervades the type-A's feelings about and interactions with people point to elements of the paranoid cognitive style as well. Still more, the flashpoint reactions of anger and the sudden resolves to destroy and dominate, often followed by depressive crashes, betray a core of impulsivity that keeps the type-A ever off-balance, always unsure of his actions as he barrels his way through life.

What about the neurocognitive dynamics? The type-A seems singularly fixated on the instrumental and utilitarian aspects of things, events and people. No shades of nuance, no dollops of color pollute the stark, line-drawn contours of his consciousness as he cuts his grim swath. Everything is quantities, numbers. It's tempting to speculate that this emphasis on focused calculation stems from an overactivity of the posterior left-hemisphere mechanisms responsible for breaking things down and particularizing them out.

What's missing, of course, is the corollary right-hemisphere skill in perspective and synthesis that cannot be accomplished by pure logic and enumeration alone. Like the compulsive and the paranoid, the type-A relies predominantly on analysis. But like the impulsive, what also seems to be missing is the appropriate left-hemisphere–frontal reflective and autoarticulatory guidance that would help the type-A place his activities within a larger personal perspective.

Indeed, the type-A's ego autonomy receives a triple whammy. To begin with, he's too focused on external numeration and acquisitiveness to be able to employ the capacity of perspective. Second, his self-explicatory skills are too stunted to be of use in adaptively guiding his behavior, so that even his plans and grand schemes have a short-term, impulsive quality to them. Third, and worse still, he's unable to let his guard down even for a moment to permit simple human feeling to dilute his misanthropic bile, or to allow humor or imagery to help place things in their proper context. No wonder the type-A's prime dynamic is that of basic insecurity and self-doubt—much as is the case with the impulsive personality. But at least the impulsivist occasionally has a little fun.

As we saw in Chapter 10, one expression of the impulsive cognitive style is in the form of alcoholism and addiction. Two studies relating the type-A to alcohol abuse bear on this issue. Garamoni and Schwartz cite a study by Glass[7] which found that hospitalized alcoholics scored as high on type-A measures as did hospitalized coronary patients, which are the "usual" type-A group. Glass reasoned that alcoholism and coronary heart disease may be alternative outcomes of the type-A pattern, and Garamoni and Schwartz further hypothesize that the alcoholic can be seen as a "failed" compulsive—an oral personality, to use the idiom of psychoanalysis—fixated at an even more primitive level than the compulsive.

Another study by Folsom and colleagues[8] found that type-As drank up to 30 percent more than type-Bs. This type-A "drinkupmanship" seemed to be due to more frequent imbibing, rather than to more alcohol consumed per occasion. That is, the type-As were not the now-and-then bingers, but more the frequent nip-and-goers who use booze to "fortify" themselves on a fairly regular basis. The authors suggested that since type-As have greater difficulty relaxing than type-Bs, especially away from work, they may drink more often to help them unwind. Also, since type-As are for the most part more outgoing than type-Bs, they may have more opportunities to drink and therefore do so more often. Still another possibility is that since heavy imbibing can increase hostility and social aggression, drinking may promote some of the more bumptious aspects of type-A behavior, rather than the other way around.

It seems, then, that the impulsive side of the type-A personality pattern may lead him to shore up his fragile ego defenses with chemicals, much in the manner of the alcoholic/addict we discussed in Chapter 10. But the neurocognitive compulsive/paranoid component to the type-A picture allows another kind of defense as well, that of frenzied immersion in "productive" activities and the concomitant squeezing out of disturbing feelings and thoughts. The type-A is just too busy and too angry to face himself—until, perhaps, a heart attack stops him cold in his tracks and, if he survives, wrenches around the nape of his perception to stare into his now unavoidable psychic mirror.

Sudden Death

Maybe something like this has happened to you. You're driving home from the supermarket in the rain with your two kids in the back seat when suddenly another car cuts you off. You slam on the brake and your car starts going into a skid. You use all your driving skill to turn the wheel this way and that, apply just enough but not too much pressure on the brake to get you out of the skid, narrowly avoid getting swiped by a passing truck and end up bounced around on the shoulder of the road with a few dents, a flat, maybe a minor bruise on the knee, but otherwise unscathed. You turn around to check your kids: They're okay. Some of the groceries are splattered around the seat, but in general, all seems to be pretty much all right. Only then does your heart start to race and pound, your limbs quiver, and the cold sweat begin to flow, as you realize what just happened—and what *might* have happened.

For some people, such an experience might be the end of them.

Being in a car accident, getting mugged, finding yourself trapped in a smoking building or even in a stuck elevator—such experiences are dangerous enough in themselves for the bodily injuries that can and often do result. But these events, even if leaving the victim physically unhurt, can kill hours later. He or she may literally die of stress.

This is the *sudden death syndrome*, the virtual dead stop of the heart's normal electrical rhythm that seems in some people to follow certain overwhelmingly traumatic situations and is almost invariably fatal. The "suddenness" aspect of the sudden death syndrome relates not only to the speed and abruptness of demise, but also to the fact that the affected individuals frequently have been in relatively good health, heartwise, up to the time of their first—and usually only—attack.

David Monagan[9] has described the basic features of the sudden cardiac death syndrome. He points out that there are actually two kinds of cardiac death, one of which is really not all that sudden, but often heralds itself months or years in advance with bouts of chest pain and breathlessness, and is due to the development of coronary atherosclerosis similar to the kind we've just encountered in talking about the type-A. Although it can seem to strike out of the blue, the actual heart attack occurs after years of heart abuse by bad diet, lack of exercise, smoking, stress, and perhaps just plain unlucky genetics.

Sudden cardiac death, the sudden death syndrome, is different. In most cases it results from an abrupt disruption of the normal electrical rhythm of the heart, leading to a state of ventricular fibrillation—rapid, weak, twitchy contractions of the heart muscle that are useless for propelling blood through body and brain. And without blood you die— quickly.

Mysteriously, up to one-fifth of sudden death victims have no detectable coronary atherosclerosis, and half have no history of smoking, hypertension, high cholesterol or obesity, the standard menu of "risk factors" for heart disease. As many as three-fourths have no evidence of previous heart attacks or heart problems. Still, the kiss of sudden death appears not to favor the young and vigorously healthy, so perhaps some underlying susceptibility exists among those most commonly affected.

About one-fifth of sudden death victims (or occasional survivors) have experienced some acute psychological stress in the preceding twenty-four hours. Recently bereaved widowers (but not widows, apparently) are 40 percent more likely to drop dead than married men the same age, and cardiac deaths (again, in men) take a dramatic upswing in the first year after retirement. Maybe this has to do with the associated finding that social isolation by itself can quadruple the rate of cardiac death. A common emotion preceding sudden cardiac death is anger, and cardiac rhythms can swing dangerously in the face of such socially confrontative stresses as public speaking or driving in heavy traffic.

High-pressure, repetitive jobs that offer little control and little room for advancement seem to be perfect setups for sudden death. And since job status tends to correlate with academic achievement, it's of interest that individuals who have eight years of education or less have three times the sudden death rate as their better-schooled neighbors.

The heart self-regulates its beating through a system of natural electrical "pacemakers" and nerve bundles that are situated at different points in the heart muscle. In addition, the responsiveness of the heart to inner and outer states—changes in rate and force of contraction due to temperature, exercise, emotional factors, and so on—are mediated by branches of the *autonomic nervous system*, which controls many so-called involuntary activities of the body, such as breathing, digestion, and circulation (Fig. 9).

The input to these nerves in turn comes from a complex network of cardiovascular control systems in the central nervous system, from the lowest portions of the brainstem through the rich meshwork of the limbic system to the uppermost reaches of the cerebral cortex. This is why your heart may pound either out of actual physical stress, or the

A. Sympathetic   **B. Parasympathetic**

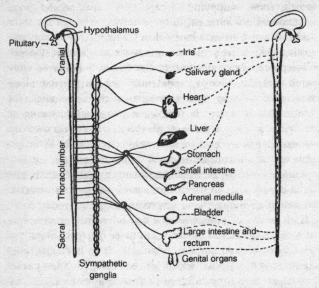

Fig. 9: The *autonomic nervous system* consists of a *sympathetic* branch, which has an activating, "fight-or-flight" effect on the body, and a *parasympathetic* branch, which acts to tone down physiological reactions. Together, the two branches of the autonomic nervous system control the functioning of all the important organ systems in the body. (From R. F. Thompson, *Introduction to Physiological Psychology*, 2d ed. Copyright © 1975 by R. F. Thomspon. Used by permission of Harper & Row Publishers, Inc.)

mere threat of stress, or even the remote anticipation of stress.[10]

An intriguing theory from our present neuropsychodynamic standpoint is one recently proposed by Richard Lane and Gary Schwartz.[11] Their specific hypothesis is that individuals who manifest more lateralized frontal lobe activity during emotional arousal may at the same time generate more activating autonomic input to the heart and be at increased risk for *arrhythmias*—fatal disturbances in the heart's electrical rhythm.

Lane and Schwartz begin by reviewing some of the same material we've already covered in Chapter 5, evidence suggesting that there's greater relative activation of the left hemisphere during positive or "approach" emotions compared to the negative or "avoidance" emotions that are handled mainly by the right hemisphere. In EEG studies, the asymmetries are usually noted over the frontal regions of the brain, and while these trends reflect the average findings for groups of subjects, there's still considerable heterogeneity across individuals.

Lane and Schwartz hypothesize that those individuals who show more lateralized brain activity during emotional arousal may concomitantly generate more activating autonomic input to the heart. The predominant role of the frontal lobes is supported by the experiments of James Skinner,[12] who, using pigs as subjects, bilaterally severed the pathways connecting the frontal lobes to a subcortical brain region known as the *posterior hypothalamus*.

Skinner is a man who knows how to get a pig's goat: He next stressed the animals while at the same time experimentally occluding their coronary arteries, thereby cutting off blood supply to the heart muscle. The idea was to produce a porcine model of the stressed human with a compromised coronary vascular supply. Stressed pigs with surgically interrupted frontal-hypothalamic pathways continued to display relatively normal heart rhythms; those with their brains left intact fibrillated and died. Something about the intact connection between frontal lobe and posterior hypothalamus, then, was important in mediating the stress-arrhythmia relationship.

Experimental evidence indicates that the frontal lobe pathway to the hypothalamus is primarily inhibitory, whereas the hypothalamic-autonomic pathway to the heart is mainly excitatory. So "turning on" the frontal lobe, so to speak, would "turn off" the hypothalamus's excitation of the heart via the autonomic nervous system, as the net effect of increased frontal lobe activation is to slow down the heart. Alternatively, "turning off" the frontal lobe, as it were, would release or "turn on" the hypothalamic-autonomic arousal of the heart, causing it to beat faster and more strongly.

In humans, moreover, the pathways from brain to heart appear to be uncrossed, and an imbalance in autonomic input to the left side of the heart is more likely to generate an arrhythmia than to the right. According to Lane and Schwartz's model, activation on one side of the brain would generate an imbalance in autonomic input to the heart favoring the opposite side.

Here's how it works: Activation of the right hemisphere would inhibit the hypothalamus's excitation of the right side of the heart through the right autonomic nerve branch. Now, remember the principle of cross-hemispheric inhibition. The activated right hemisphere has a dampening effect, via the corpus callosum, on the homologous area of the left hemisphere. The left frontal–hypothalamic inhibitory mechanism is thus attenuated and less able to calm down the excitatory hypothalamic-autonomic effect on the left side of the heart. The more arrhythmia-vulnerable left side then starts to fibrillate—and you're history. And since the right hemisphere is typically activated in the context of negative or avoidance emotions, the whole deadly business of sudden death may stem in large part from a hemispheric imbalance reaction to states of stress or depression.

The neuropsychological evidence seems to support this lateralized interaction between heart and brain. For example, studies have found a correlation between heart rate and amplitude of visual evoked responses in the right hemisphere, but not the left hemisphere.[13] When visual stimuli are presented to the right hemisphere, there occurs an anticipatory increase in heart rate, but no such change takes place when the left hemisphere receives the stimuli.[14] Individuals who have suffered strokes that cause bleeding into or around the brain sometimes show disturbances in heart rhythm—but only if the pathology affects the left frontal lobe.[15]

If right-hemisphere overactivation disrupts the left frontal lobe's inhibitory influence over fatal arrhythmias, could those individuals starting out with a constitutionally, neuropsychodynamically weaker left-frontal system be more vulnerable to stress-induced sudden death? Or might sudden death occur when the frontal lobe–mediated hypervigilance that's maintained throughout the traumatic experience is suddenly relaxed after the ordeal is over? Is an overly labile, or unstable cognitive style too much for some hearts to bear?

Again, here's an example of a pathological outcome—this time a physiological one—being the result not of a lesion or deficit in neuropsychologial functioning, but of a maladaptive variation in the neuropsychodynamic response pattern to the events in our lives, a variation that in some cases may be the death of us yet.

Hemisphericity, Personality, and Psychosomatics

Now that we've had a chance to consider the neuropsychodynamic aspects of a number of individual "psychosomatic" syndromes, we might want to ask: Is there anything like a "psychosomatic personality" and, if so, what might be its neuropsychodynamic basis?

Recall the studies on lateral eye movements (LEMs) showing that the direction in which a person's eyes move in response to a question may indicate which hemisphere is preferentially involved in processing the information. Typically, the eyes move in the opposite direction (the person "looks away") from the activated hemisphere. Using this technique, Ruben and Raquel Gur[16] classified subjects as left-movers, right movers, or bidirectionals. They also assessed the kinds of defense mechanisms typically used by the subjects to ward off unacceptable thoughts, feelings, or impulses, and they took careful account of the number of psychosomatic complaints the subjects reported.

According to psychodynamic theory, psychosomatic symptoms represent a bodily expression of repressed conflicts and anxieties that have to do with unacceptable thoughts, feelings, and wishes. If this is true, subjects who show more of these symptoms should also display more repressive coping styles and thus be more prone to use defense mechanisms. But what about the *type* of defense mechanism?

The Gurs found that eye directionality of LEMs was a powerful predictor of defensive style and associated psychosomatic symptomatology. Left-movers (right-hemisphere activation) tended to employ a defense mechanism called *reversal*, involving a denial of reality, repression of emotions evoked by external stress, and reaction formation—the tendency to behave oppositely from what one actually feels, as when you find yourself fawning and doting over someone you really detest.

Right-movers (left-hemisphere activation) tended to rely more on *projection*, attributing our own bad feelings or bad behavior to someone else, as when we accuse another person of being lazy when it's our own slothfulness we really wish to repudiate. Right-movers also tended to turn against others, which shares with projection an externalizing of the conflict, an acting against the environment, as opposed to taking a more internal, subjective defensive tactic. Projection also involves a certain degree of cognitive elaboration, which may account for why the left hemisphere seems more involved.

In terms of psychosomatic symptoms, left-movers reported significantly more of these than right-movers, suggesting that there's something about the more emotional right hemisphere that ties it to psychosomatic symptomatology—perhaps much in the same way as it is linked to hysterical conversion phenomena, as we saw in Chapter 8.

How does this tie in with the notion of a "psychosomatic personality"? Consider the following clinical vignette.

Mr. Bland has just been fired from his job. He appears for his weekly psychotherapy session and reports this ostensibly disturbing event matter-of-factly to Dr. Swift, who—being a shrink—naturally asks Mr. Bland what *he* makes of this event.

"So how do you feel about being fired?"

"Well, I guess I won't be getting up so early for a while."

"Yes, but how do you *feel* about your getting canned so abruptly?"

"They should have looked at all the facts. I had a good reason for going against the boss's orders. He got real mad, but I figured if I just ignored it, it would blow over."

"What would you like to say to your boss now?"

"I'd like my job back because he shouldn't have fired me."

"How do you *feel* about your boss?"

"I wonder why he didn't see things from my point of view."

"Any dreams lately?"

"Yeah, last night I had a dream where I was standing next to a man on the street."

"What else happened?"

"I think the man spoke to me. Or I spoke to him. I think we had an argument or something."

"Remind you of anything?"

"I think I had a dream like that once when I was a kid. Or maybe not. I don't remember."

"What else happened in the dream?"

"The man walked away and I woke up."

"Anything else bothering you lately?

"Well, I have these cramps most of the time and my hives are a lot worse."

This kind of pulling-teeth exchange is one of the nightmares of the typical psychotherapist. Psychoanalytically oriented therapists, especially, are apt to feel frustrated by the patient who doesn't seem to *do* anything in therapy. He doesn't get particularly sad or angry or happy, he talks about emotionally explosive situations with bland reserve, reports few or no dreams or dreams that are dry and colorless, has no fantasy life to speak of, and remains frustratingly noninsightful despite the therapist's most earnest ministrations. And to top it off, the patient is a veritable museum of psychosomatic symptoms, such as ulcers, headaches, and rashes.

When clinicians find something particularly irritating, they usually give it a name. In the early 1970s, Peter Sifneos[17] coined the term *alexithymia*—meaning "no words for mood"—to describe the kind of literal, concrete, present-oriented, and nonsymbolic mode of thought typically displayed by patients of this type. Men seem to show this disorder more often than women and alexithymia seems to pop up frequently among the ranks of psychosomatic patients, drug abusers, and persons suffering from severe posttraumatic syndromes.[18]

Psychoanalytic theorists[19] speculate that for the alexithymic, the normal experience and expression of emotion has become choked off from conscious awareness. With no other *psychological* outlet, this emotional life—including primitive fantasy and dream life—becomes channeled into *physical* symptoms. Can alexithymia be explained by our neuropsychodynamic model?

Recall from Chapters 4 and 5 that individuals who've suffered right-hemisphere damage often show a bland unconcern for their disability and the distressing circumstances surrounding it. And people who have undergone cerebral commissurotomy ("split-brain" surgery), which separates the main connections between the left and right hemispheres, often display a striking psychological dissociation. When the right brain is shown an emotionally arousing picture, the person may report feeling excited, embarrassed, disgusted, or whatever. But, asked *why* he's titillated or upset, he'll reply that he doesn't know. Without the pathway connecting the emotional-imagery side of the brain to the verbal-analytic side, the source and meaning of the emotional reactions remain beyond rational awareness—they're essentially "unconscious."

Klaus Hoppe,[20] whose work we encountered in Chapter 4, believes that in patients with alexithymia-based psychosomatic disorders the left and right hemispheres behave as if they were actually separated from each other. In his view, alexithymics may have some inborn deficit in the system that processes signals between the hemispheres—a "functional commissurotomy," Hoppe calls it—so that the right hemisphere's passions are inaccessible to the left hemisphere's verbal-conscious consolidation. Emotional life therefore remains out of awareness, that is, "repressed." And since, as we've seen, one of the right hemisphere's specializations is processing body image and somatic awareness, this wayward emotional life is channeled into bodily symptoms.

But if alexithymics have a functional commissurotomy, are patients with *real* commissurotomies alexithymic? Hoppe and neurosurgeon Joseph Bogen[21] studied a group of split-brain patients, using a special Psychosomatic Questionnaire. They found that the scores of these commissurotomy patients were similar to those of a group of diagnosed alexithymics from a psychoanalytic psychotherapy practice. Moreover, from the time of the split-brain operation, the patients' dreams lacked richness, their fantasies were unimaginative, and their style of thinking concrete and rigid—a typically alexithymic profile.

Further evidence comes from the case[22] of a man born without a corpus callosum, but with an otherwise intact brain. This fellow had experienced a lifelong inability to communicate his true feelings to others or to comprehend the subtle motivations of those around him. Not surprisingly, this contributed to a certain distinct social ineptitude. The problems seemed to stem from his inability to verbally label and differentiate different states or changes in emotion. He was therefore unable to self-communicate—autoarticulate— these feelings, and thus remained painfully dense in interpersonal situations. Unfortunately, others saw this as an obnoxious lack of maturity and self-insight. And, interestingly enough, this patient scored high on the alexithymia-sensitive Psychosomatic Questionnaire used by Hoppe and Bogen.

This neuropsychodynamic profile may also explain some of the other characteristics of alexithymics.[23] As proposed by a number of neuropsychological theories discussed in Chapter 2, males generally tend to have weaker left-hemisphere verbal skills than females. If there really is a male predominance in this syndrome, the already lesser ability or inclination of men to verbalize feelings may predispose more of them to fall at the extreme end of the no-words-for-mood continuum.

The neuropsychodynamic model can also explain the higher incidence of alexithymia among drug abusers. As we've seen, many chronic abusers tend to be impulsive, sometimes antisocial types. And this group has been found in study after study to do especially poorly on verbal reasoning and language measures. So it's especially intriguing that Finnish researchers[24] found violent penitentiary prisoners to have particularly high rates of alexithymia, as measured by projective personality tests. Also, recall that a high proportion of drug abusers have multiple somatic complaints. Alexithymia, drug abuse, hysteria, and somatization: All seem to be separate but connected expressions of an impulsive cognitive style, which in turn relates to an inability to self-communicate, to reflect, to steer oneself wisely through the shoals of life.

Conclusions

The predisposition to develop psychosomatic symptoms shares with many of the other syndromes discussed in this book an association with impaired ego autonomy and the way this deficit works itself out via the variations in cognitive style shaped by brain organization. Certain clusters of personality traits are associated with certain patterns of physical symptoms, not by any mystical psychodynamic transformation, but because they both stem from a particular pattern of neuropsychological organization and development.

The pattern of brain lateralization that shapes the type-A's or alexithymic's personality and cognitive style also may determine the ratio of input to the heart—and, as we'll no doubt eventually find, to other organs of the body as well—from left and right, frontal and posterior, cortical and subcortical systems of the brain. Here again, there appears to be a certain unity among brain organization, cognition, personality, and observable symptomatology. The brain is the great integrator not only of the mind, but of the body as well, so that our health—and our very lives, in some cases—depend upon the intimate and intricate relationships between psyche and soma.

CHAPTER 12

BETTER SELVES:

Creativity, Morality, and the "Healthy Personality"

The creative person is both more primitive and more cultivated, more destructive, a lot madder and a lot saner than the average person.

—FRANK BARRON

The remarkable thing is that we really love our neighbor as ourselves; we do unto others as we do unto ourselves. We hate others when we hate ourselves. We are tolerant toward others when we tolerate ourselves. We forgive others when we forgive ourselves. It is not love of self but hatred of self which is at the root of the troubles that afflict our world.

—ERIC HOFFER

We could be in trouble here.

One problem with trying to conceptualize "good" aspects of personality within the neuropsychodynamic model is that there's precious little data to go on. The models of personality types and personality disorders discussed so far in this book—and by clinicians generally—have had at least some neuropsychological analogs in the literature of pathology. This is appropriate, since people usually come to clinical attention, and thereby find themselves as part of studies, by reason of one or another kind of "bad" or "sick" behavior. They drink themselves into ruin, become paralyzed by depression or compulsiveness, somaticize themselves from doctor to doctor, shoplift or embezzle or mug unwisely and get caught, alienate their friends and families with crazy plans and actions and thereby eventually get channeled through the system to become part of some research project in which personality and neuropsychological variables are a component.

But when people are out there being creative, helping their fellow man, leading happy and productive lives and feeling generally okay about themselves—people with ego autonomy, in other words—they tend to stay out of the shrink's office, mental health clinic, hospital, or lab. Further, this book has used many examples of disorders of the self that resulted from direct injury to the brain, and we've seen how brain damage can render a person more concrete, more obsessional, more paranoid, less flexible, less insightful, less in control, and so on. But it's hard to imagine how acquired brain damage could make a person psychologically *healthier*.

Still, remember the basic message of the neuropsychodynamic model: The psychological phenomena we see in their starkest form following actual physical damage to the brain are only extreme examples of the more common variations in brain development and organization that produce the subtle shadings of the personalities of all of us. Thus, although this must necessarily be a more speculative chapter than those preceding, the neuropsychodynamic model can begin to be applied to those aspects of personality and behavior we so commonly admire, envy, and try to emulate.

The Creative Mind

The word "genius" derives from the Latin word for spirit. And indeed, the people we regard as true creative geniuses often seem driven by their muse to create a unique vision of reality and share it with the world. It's this passion for truth, or at least symmetry, and the resolve to pursue it, that distinguish the men and women we call "creative."

John Briggs has made creativity the object of intense and

serious study.[1] He points out that the creative genius is not just someone with superior ability in a given area—math whizzes, musical prodigies, photographic memorizers, and the like. These individuals possess specialized *talents*, and talents contribute to the instrumentation of creativity, but are not its essence. "Prodigies commit themselves intensely to their talent," Briggs tells us; "geniuses commit their talents intensely to their vision."

To be a creative genius, however, it helps to have a few kinds of talent in particular, and certain commonalities seem to pop up again and again in the mental structure of creative people. For one thing, such individuals have a tremendous capacity for concentration and absorption. They can spend hours or days on end, unmindful of bodily needs and totally fixed on the task at hand, be it a sculpture, a chapter of a novel, or a unique scientific theorem.

In addition, creative people seem to be unusually flexible in their thinking and reasoning and are able to tolerate—indeed, may embrace—an inordinate degree of ambiguity and ambivalence. This temporary suspension of normal rationality and the reversion to more loose and primitive modes of thinking was termed "regression in the service of the ego" by psychoanalytic writers such as Ernst Kris.[2] The phrase denotes an ability to violate conceptual boundaries, much as a child does, in order to glimpse aspects of a situation that can't be fully apprehended by normal modes of thinking. This is the regression part.

The ego-serving part stems from the fact that the insights derived from this temporary state are then productively integrated with more "adult" forms of rational thinking. The net result is a higher conceptual synthesis than possible with either kind of thought mode alone. This is probably close to what Briggs calls *omnivalence*, the ability of creative geniuses to appreciate multiple—even contradictory—facets of a problem and ultimately strive to produce a transcending synthesis.

And creative people do produce. They're typically among the most prolific in their respective fields, whether science, music, art, or literature. But they don't operate in a vacuum: The cultural-historical context is a powerful determiner of how the creative work expresses itself. After all, Einstein's theory of relativity could hardly have been formulated without the existing Newtonian physics to serve as scaffolding and foil. Modern art or literature would be meaningless except against the backdrop of more traditional forms, and so on.

Also, creative geniuses don't coast. The "Great Work" may be sparked by flashes of unique insight, but such kindlings would amount to little without the steady flow of labor's fuel. Briggs quotes van Gogh, in turn quoting Whistler (whose portrait of his mother is perhaps the most popularly recognizable painting next to the *Mona Lisa*) as saying that "It took me two hours to do the painting, but forty years to learn how to do it in two hours."

It may also be the particular mental qualities of creative geniuses that historically have gotten them into trouble, that have caused them to be suspected of being a different, iconoclastic, even dangerously nutsy breed. Psychoanalytic observers, especially, have long spoken of a relationship between psychological instability—"madness"—and creative genius.[3] The stereotypes of the eccentric scientist or temperamental musician or melancholy poet are well entrenched in the popular mind. But is it possible to conceptualize creativity in terms of our neuropsychodynamic model, to view true creativity as predicated on a certain degree of brain-based ego autonomy that lies beneath the often unusual surface veneer?

Revenge of the NERDs

You know the type. He stalks the halls of a thousand schools, pens and automatic pencils peeking up from his plastic shirt-pocket protector, briefcase bulging with books, papers, and floppy disks, eyes squinting behind thick lenses. Embarrassingly inept on the ball field or in social banter, he has no peer at the computer keyboard or technical work station.

Sound familiar? This is the NERD—which, according to David Forrest,[4] stands for *NeuroEvolutionary Rostral Developer*. In Forrest's theory, NERDs represent a specialized subtype of human being, a variation most adapted to our expandingly technological, information-age civilization.

The key distinguishing feature of the NERD is a brain more highly developed in its rostral (frontal) region. By comparison, the more caudal (rearward) parts of the brain involved with basic perception, movement, and emotional functions are correspondingly less developed. This unique neuropsychological pattern accounts for many of the NERDlike traits we're familiar with.

For example, NERDs are notoriously clumsy at athletics, which ordinarily requires skills mediated by the brain's more primitive perceptual-motor systems. Similarly, social adroitness may require a well-developed limbic system, the phylogenetically old brain network involved in emotion. By contrast, skills that involve conceptualization, abstraction, verbalization, calculation, and integration rely heavily on the brain's more advanced frontal lobes and perhaps the left hemisphere, accounting for the overall ''braininess'' of NERDs.

NERDs are typically uninterested in the everyday preoccupations of hot looks, fast cars, and high bucks; rather, according to Forrest, they have an almost ''libidinal investment in or sexualization of'' mental processes for their own sake. NERDs, in other words, get off on ideas.

NERDs are also more likely than average to be nearsighted. NERDs' characteristic myopia, says Forrest, may lead to ''an intense interest in minute irregularities of the close, touchable, topographically explorable'' environment—a tendency to prefer looking at the world ''up close.''

Myopic or not, NERDs tend to be extraordinarily visually oriented, as judged by their preoccupation with the printed word, the computer screen, and all those homemade slides you had to sit through in high school classroom presentations.

In fact, recent studies suggest that nearsightedness and heightened intellect may go together as naturally associated traits. In one study, Israeli researchers Mordechai Rosner and Michael Belkin[5] analyzed the incidence of myopia in over 150,000 male military recruits and compared this with IQ and amount of schooling. They found that more intelligent and better educated groups of subjects also contained greater numbers of myopes.

In a subsequent study, behavior geneticists Sanford and Catherine Cohn and Arthur Jensen[6] compared myopia rates of gifted American college students and their more intellectually ordinary siblings. Sure enough, the brainier sibs turned out to have a higher rate of nearsightedness. The researchers point out that there's no direct evidence that myopia is *caused* by excessive reading or other close-up work, so it's not just that compulsive studiers who cram themselves bleary are more likely to accumulate the smarts needed to ace school exams and IQ tests. Accordingly, aspiring scholars needn't necessarily worry about "ruining their eyes" by cracking the books. Myopia appears to be a genuine innate trait that more naturally intelligent and studious people seem to have.

Which brings us back to NERDs. Forrest suggests that some ethnic groups may produce more of these neurodevelopmental variants than others, for example, European Jewish and East Asian populations—who also seem to wear glasses more commonly than members of other groups. Ethnic associations or not, what could account for the appearance of NERDs in the general population? Where do NERDs come from?

One clue is from the work of Norman Geschwind, whose

theory of brain lateralization and development we first encountered in Chapter 2. Recall that Geschwind hypothesized a predominant role for the male sex hormone testosterone in the womb in determining the lateralization and anatomic organization of the brain during gestational development. High levels of fetal testosterone can produce anomalies in brain development by slowing the growth of certain areas. This can lead to higher rates of left-handedness, learning disabilities, immunologic disorders, and other disturbances.

By the same token, isolated areas of deficit may be accompanied by isolated areas of *enhanced* ability, as certain other brain areas mature more quickly and efficiently to fill the neurodevelopmental gap created by the slowed regions. This would produce what Geschwind called a "pathology of superiority." Could it be that the uneven development of abilities seen in Forrest's NERDs represents one expression of this hormonally induced variation? Left-frontal development may burgeon at the expense of other brain regions, and NERDs' weaknesses in athletics and social panache is compensated for by their intellectual precocity and technical skill.

This, in fact, may be the pattern most applicable to the emerging postcybernetic world. "A new character type," says Forrest, "for which anatomical or functional correlates could be sought, might derive its inspiration from our new age, that of scientific man." Forrest argues that as the tools of international power continue to depend more and more on computerized technology, "NERDs at the consoles" of sophisticated weapons systems, as well as in the seats of political and economic power generally, may become the reality the rest of us will have to accommodate to.

Insofar as cultural progress has become applied scientific progress, Forrest argues, "NERDs are our national hope and source of international security." If that's so, then

NERDs may ultimately impart to us not their vengeance, but a more rational way of life.

Morose Geniuses: Mood Swings and Creative Cycles

Although living an accomplished life has its rewards, being productive or creative doesn't necessarily mean being happy or stable. For the most part, we haven't dealt with severe psychopathology, such as schizophrenia and the more serious emotional disorders, because the emphasis of this book has been on the more common expressions of personality and cognitive style—expressions we find bits and pieces of in ourselves and may observe extreme forms of in some of the people we commonly deal with. But, as in a few other places in this book (such as the chapter on paranoia), the more serious forms of mental disorder are useful for illustrating certain important points about the neuropsychodynamic foundations of personality.

Recently, the connection between ego autonomy, creativity, and vulnerability-versus-resilience to psychopathology has attracted the interest of a few psychodynamically oriented psychologists. For example, E. James Anthony[7] argues that the development of an extraordinary creative capacity can be regarded as a superior level of what he calls *competence*. This competence, in turn, is one manifestation of the autonomous capacity of the ego.

A disproportionate number of creative individuals who have made indisputable cultural contributions, says Anthony, appear to be highly vulnerable to the risk of mental disorder. From the beginning, they seem to lack that certain internal buffering system that insulates most of us psychologically from the world around. This overly developed sensitivity, which permits many creative people such a free exchange between outer experience and the psychic interior, may lead to a "breakdown" when the primitive content takes over and allows the milieu of irrationality and unrealism to prevail without constraint.

A second and valued outcome is, of course, an upsurge of creative productivity, delicately controlled by the ego. However, this regression "in the service of the ego" is accompanied by some relinquishing of defenses, which imperils the ego. The weakening of the primary buffering system can therefore be compensated for by an enhanced ego creativity that rehabilitates the battered psyche and brings it back into meaningful contact with the outside environment. However, when the creative energy is expended, the person may lapse into hypervulnerability and ego disintegration. This, says Anthony, explains why many creative artists and writers "manifest cycles of vulnerability and resilience determined by the ebb and flow of the creative urge."

This "ebb and flow" may also manifest itself in an oscillatory overlability of thought and emotion, the kind seen in bipolar, or manic-depressive, illness. Indeed, bouts of black melancholy alternating with paroxysms of exhilarating verve figure prominently in the life histories of many productively creative people.

To study this more directly, Nancy Andreasen[8] examined the incidence of mental illness in thirty creative writers, thirty matched control subjects, and the first-degree relatives (parents, sibs, children) of both groups. The writers had a substantially higher rate of mental illness, particularly manic-depressive disorder, and there was also more emotional disorder—and more creativity—in the writers' relatives. Interestingly, the relatives' creativity was not confined to the literary domain, but included such areas as art, music, dance, and mathematics. Also, the verbal IQ of the writers was equivalent to that of the other groups, except that the writers had a somewhat better working vocabulary—no surprise, considering their daily preoccupation with words and wordplay.

Overall, the results of this study suggested that whatever heritable trait is popping up in the families of creative and emotionaly labile people is a factor that predisposes to creativity in general, not a specific giftedness or specialized talent in verbal areas.

Could it be that creativity draws more on the right hemisphere for its nonrational, emotional, intuitive, and synthetic capacities than on the left? Indeed, several conceptualizations have viewed the right hemisphere as being "more creative" and the left as less so. However, from the lessons learned in this book, it should be apparent that if we adhere to the typical, traditional neuropsychological partialization of verbal functions to the left hemisphere and nonverbal to the right, Andreasen's findings with the writers are difficult to conceptualize neuropsychodynamically.

Remember that the brain of the ego-autonomous and neuropsychologically intact person does not operate like that of a split-brain patient. Rather, fluid and flexible interhemispheric communication is likely to be the rule.[9] This, then, would account for the lyrical and evocative prose of the writer and the soaring harmonies of the composer, as well as for the discipline and precision with which each translates his or her muse into the symbolic representations of written word and musical note that will ensure their communicability and posterity.

But this very fluidity of interhemispheric communication may carry with it the danger of a loosening of the normal interhemispheric reciprocal control of thought and emotion that gives normal mental life its stability and balance. Thus, the phenomenological affinity between creativity and mood swings may have its neuropsychodynamic root in a too-easy communicability between the cerebral hemispheres, the kind of functional *hyper*connectivity that is the opposite of Hoppe's "functional commissurotomy" discussed in Chapters 4 and 11. It may be this very functional hyperconnectivity that accounts for the manic-depressive syndrome itself, determining the slippery neuropsychodynamic balance between mania and depression, as conceptualized by Pierre Flor-Henry.[10]

Flor-Henry argues that the fundamental locus of both depressive and manic components of the affective psychoses is in the nondominant (usually right) hemisphere system. But whereas depression is related more or less directly to right-hemisphere neural structures, euphoria and mania depend on the principle of reciprocal interhemispheric control and release we talked about in Chapters 4 and 5. Thus the "high" emotional states are determined by a contralateral loss of neural inhibition that originates in the right hemisphere but evokes abnormal activation of the left across the corpus callosum. This is what determines the racing verbal thoughts and speech that are the hallmarks of the manic state. At the same time, the left hemisphere regulates certain, but different, aspects of emotion in the right, notably mood stability and probably the whole range of "low" emotions.

But if emotions and creativity are under this exquisite interhemispheric control, what of sanity itself? Are geniuses really all a little crazy?

Genius and Madness: Separate or Equal?

Schizophrenia has been viewed by some as a model or prototype of creativity, a lifelong sabbatical into an alternative world of exceptional vision.[11] This view gained popularity during the 1960s through the writings of R. D. Laing[12] and others. At first glance, the analogy is a tempting one. There does seem to be a surface similarity between the type of regression that characterizes schizophrenic thought and the periodic excursions into "primitive" thinking that many creative people describe. However, a closer look at the cognitive styles of the schizophrenic versus the truly creative man or woman shows that they are not by any means equivalent.

Arnold Rothenberg[12] has described a type of cognition he calls *janusian thinking* (from the two-faced Roman god Janus), which contributes to the creative process in literature, the visual arts, music, and the sciences. Janusian thinking involves actively conceiving of two or more opposites or antitheses simultaneously—recall Briggs's "omnivalence."

In the janusian process, opposite or antithetical words, ideas, or images are clarified, defined, and conceptualized side by side and/or as coexisting simultaneously. They're then usually modified or transformed or otherwise used to produce tangible creative products. The janusian process is a conscious, highly adaptive form of cognition that's not regressive or primitive in the usual sense and is not itself a product of mental illness.

To assess janusian thinking, Rothenberg[14] gave timed word-association tests to 12 creative Nobel laureate scientists, 18 hospitalized schizophrenic patients, and 113 college students divided into high and low creative groups. He found that the Nobel laureates gave the highest proportion of opposite responses; what's more, they did it at the fastest rates. The schizophrenics, for their part, not only gave the fewest opposite responses, they were the slowest of all the groups. And both the Nobel laureates and the highly creative students came up with opposite responses a lot quicker than more conventional nonopposite responses. Overall, the results supported a connection between janusian thinking and creativity, but also demonstrated that this is certainly *not* the same thing as a pathological, schizophrenic cognitive mode.

The big difference, says Rothenberg, is this: The creative thinker is fully aware of the conflict between the opposites and antitheses, but he also knows that such formulations may reveal new truths and lead to new discoveries. One of the functions of the janusian process is to break away from traditional modes of belief and understanding and to structure new and deeper truths, truths that are almost invariably experienced as surprising and unexpected because they contain an affirmation of the opposite of what was formerly or conventionally believed.

Because of a consistent tendency to formulate opposites very rapidly and to conceptualize them simultaneously, therefore, the creative thinker goes beyond ordinary logic into the realms of the unexpected and unknown. Instead of being an illogical mode of thought involving self-contradictory propositions, janusian thinking transcends ordinary reason in what Rothenberg has called a "translogical" process. In contrast, the schizophrenic seems to believe literally in his fundamentally opposite and contradictory assertions. Although the intellectual ambivalence of the schizophrenic may seem superficially similar to janusian thinking, it's not a knowing formulation of simultaneous antitheses that can lead directly to new discoveries and truths.

Nancy Andreasen and Pauline Powers[15] studied the cognitive performance of creative writers, schizophrenics, *and* manic patients by means of the Goldstein-Scheerer Object Sorting Test, a measure of conceptual classification and abstract reasoning ability. Presented with a large set of ordinary items, the subject is asked to group the objects according to which of them "belong" together. Writers and manics tended to be more inclusive in their categorizations, matching up objects you might not expect to go together, except in a unique and offbeat way. For example, they might put a spoon and pencil together because they can both be used to drum out a tune.

But that's where the similarities ended. The writers showed substantially more richness in their classifications, and the manics more idiosyncratic thinking: A manic subject might pair a pot with a belt because both were used to punish him as a child. Schizophrenics tended to be under-inclusive rather than overinclusive and showed much less richness and even less bizarreness than either the writers or manics—a book and an envelope might be put together because they're both made of paper. Again, more evidence against an affinity between schizophrenia and creativity. Can the neuropsychodynamic model explain this?

A number of neuropsychological studies with schizophrenics have implicated dysfunction in frontal regions and/or the left hemisphere.[16] Indeed, thought disorders and verbal weirdness are two of the paramount diagnostic features of schizophrenia.

Based on this kind of data, Muller[17] has attempted more explicitly to explain psychotic symptomatology in terms of disordered frontal lobe functioning. In normal consciousness and thought, Muller notes, the time-delay aspect of prefrontal function is required for a certain remoteness of output from input, that is, of behavior from perception. This is a concept we've already encountered in Chapter 3. This time-delay process enables the output to become more deliberate and more determined by constructed models of reality. These interim representational models can undergo internal modifications even while not in immediate contact with either input or output—which is another way of saying that thought can mediate and determine perception and behavior. In humans, language and language-derived concepts add a new dimension of control (recall Chapter 4), in effect giving the prefrontal areas still more "steering" power over our activities.

According to this view, psychosis is a mental state characterized by gross impairment of reality testing, that is, by a particular difficulty in approximating internal models of the world to real-life exigencies. Dysfunction of prefrontal cortex impairs reality testing by preventing comparison of inputs with their corresponding perceptual models stored in memory. Even though the individual may be sensitive to certain environmental cues and clues—and some paranoid schizophrenics show almost preternatural skill on the receptive end of interpersonal communication—he is unable to steward these perceptions in a useful, adaptive way. In psychosis, says Muller,

> there is a deficiency of the guiding function, a malfunction of the superordinated structures in the psychological sense; this has been summarized in different concepts such as disturbance of identity and loss of ego boundaries, inability to maintain a mental set, difficulty in control and maintenance of a selective processing strategy, etc.; or quite generally, problems in reality testing, the central feature of psychosis.[18]

Thus, we can conclude that schizophrenic regression is hardly "in the service of" the ego. Rather, it represents a fundamental lack of cohesion of the ego, a deficit in ego autonomy that prevents disparate perceptions, thoughts, feelings, and actions from achieving the degree of integration necessary for their subsequent resynthesis in creative modes of expression. The basis for this probably lies not in enhanced efficiency of interhemispheric communication, but in a kind of cross-callosal party line with many voices talking in parallel, independently and simultaneously, without sufficient left-hemisphere autoarticulatory consolidation and/ or frontal lobe reflective evaluation and guidance to provide ego-autonomous structure and support.

The manic-depressive, on the other hand, may possess an overly agile interhemispheric line of communication, but the interchange still retains a degree of neuropsychodynamic regulation—of ego autonomy—that allows for a more reality-based reconstitution and resynthesis of primitive psychological material. This often expresses itself in creative ways. The manic-depressive can dip into the sea of paralogical thought, tethered to the deck of reality by a relatively intact frontal-interhemispheric guyline; the schizophrenic, without this crucial link, becomes submerged.

Indeed, the kinds of sorting and classification tasks that schizophrenics characteristically do so poorly in—like the Goldstein-Scheerer Object Sorting Test or the Wisconsin Card Sorting Test—are the same kinds of tasks that comprise the classic "frontal lobe tests" of neuropsychology.[19]

Of course, a person needn't suffer from manic-depression or any other kind of psychological disorder in order to be creative; many creative individuals lug around no such excess clinical baggage. Instead, they seem to be able to reap the benefits of a particular type of neuropsychodynamic organization without any of the drawbacks. By the same token, possessing the degree of ego autonomy necessary for true creativity hardly guarantees optimum psychological stability or happiness; many creative persons have led less than blissful lives. All that seems to be required is sufficient cognitive flexibility and reflectivity to be able—at least on occasion—to reintegrate, resynthesize, and reconceptualize diverse and unusual observations and experiences and to express them in forms that are unique and progressive.

Two of the cognitive styles introduced in Part II of this book might at first seem to be prime candidates for producing creative works of special quality. The obsessive-compulsive can work tirelessly on projects requiring precise attention to detail. Shouldn't such sheer doggedness and devotion to the task be enough to produce works of originality and lasting value? Or the impulsive, shooting from the hip, acting on pure spontaneity—shouldn't the flint of his free-wheeling cognitive style, rasping against the cold hard steel of everyday reality, regularly send off showers of sparks, any one of which is capable of blazing into an all-consuming creative flame?

No. What the seemingly opposite compulsive and impulsive cognitive styles share is a fundamental deficit in the capacity for *reflectivity*, a trait that has been well-studied by Stanley Messer and colleagues.[20] When given a problem to solve that involves some uncertainty over which of several alternatives is the most appropriate, reflective people generally take a more deliberate and structured approach, considering all aspects of each step of the problem before proceeding.

In reviewing their own and others' studies, many with children, Messer and colleagues found that reflectives verbalize more, use more mature, self-guiding speech, and show more verbal control over their behavior in the form of covert speech. Reflectives also have a more internal locus of control, are more field independent, and manifest a more overall advanced stage of moral judgment.

Neuropsychodynamically, then, what might distinguish the impulsive and the compulsive from the reflective? Our neuropsychodynamic model hypothesizes that the impulsive suffers a weakness in the left-hemisphere substrate for verbal processes, including self-communication, or what Vygotsky[21] called inner speech. Consequently, when the frontally mediated behavioral regulation system fails, behavior becomes stimulus-bound, erratic, and without self-direction. Urges and whims predominate in the absence of any articulable psychological reference point, any coherent self-system.

The compulsive, under similar circumstances of frontally mediated behavioral release, falls prey to his now-intrahemispherically disinhibited hyperverbal and superrationalistic bias, an intensification of the already exaggerated tendency toward analysis, particularization, and overfocus of attention that's part and parcel of the compulsive cognitive style. But while this sustained focus may be present, compulsive cognition contributes not to true reflectivity, but to a *pseudo*reflectivity. The obsessive's agonizing over the "right" decision, choice, or course of action is not a sign of mature ego autonomy; it's resorting to an artificially constrained cognitive processing mode to deal with adaptive challenges that really require a multimodal neurocognitive approach, that necessitate a broadening of perspective, not a narrowing of focus.

Thus, the cognition of the impulsive character is too diffuse, too broad in apperceptive beam to allow the kind of concerted resynthesis of experience necessary for true creativity. The beam of compulsive cognition, by contrast, is so narrowly concentrated that it misses the sensorial, emotional, nuance-laden material that provides the intuitive hues and shadings and the transconceptual leaps that true creativity also relies on.

Reflectivity, the capacity to pull relevant experience from the inner and outer worlds and rework it in unique and creative ways, is precluded by both the impulsive and compulsive extremes of cognition, and ego autonomy and creativity consequently suffer. Two personality traits that ordinarily contribute to the process of true creativity—the ability to focus concentration on details and particulars and the capacity to let go with flights of whim and fancy—in fact doom creativity when either predominates to an abnormal degree. Creativity depends for its existence on a certain measure of personal integrity and ego autonomy, and it may be some optimal state of functioning in the frontal-interhemispheric axis that provides the neuropsychodynamic substrate for this.

But creativity may in fact be only one of the possible "good" manifestations of ego autonomy. What of the personality as a whole?

The Healthy Personality

Throughout this book we've been talking about ego autonomy from the perspective of Heinz Hartmann's pioneering work in the psychology of individual differences.[22] More recently, psychologists have turned to similar concepts to help explain why some personalities seem conducive to successful and satisfying living and others to ruinous maladaptation. Is there such a thing as a "healthy personality"?

Does it contain certain traits that are identifiable, that we can even try to emulate?

Rebecca Behrends[23] has adapted Julius Seeman's theory of personality integration[24] in a way that comes quite close to our current neuropsychodynamic conceptualization of ego autonomy. Seeman concluded that one of the hallmarks of the healthy, or *integrated*, personality is the ability to maximize the available amount of information needed to make adaptive decisions about behavior. As the present book does, Seeman regarded personality as being comprised of multiple components, including perceptual, cognitive, emotional, and interpersonal subsystems. Personality integration would entail the degree to which the individual has an effective internal communication network between the various subsystems. The psychologically healthy or emotionally mature or well-integrated person, then, is the one who can avail him or herself of the maximum amount of inner and outer information and who can also synthesize this information effectively, a process we've discussed in terms of the neuropsychodynamic frontal-interhemispheric axis.

In her extension of Seeman's theory, Behrends has defined the main ingredients of what we ordinarily regard as healthy or integrated personalities. To begin with, high-integration men and women have broad interests that involve them in significantly more activities than their less well-integrated peers. They also show greater *cognitive complexity*, the capacity to conceptualize social behavior in a multidimensional way. The highly integrated person flexibly uses different ways of thinking about and relating to other people, is less stereotypic in his attitudes and more flexible in his judgments and perceptions of others—which naturally increases his ability to respond to different social environments appropriately.

The integrated person defines him or herself in terms of self-perceived competence and high personal regard. As is implicit in the very term "integration," the highly integrated person is better able to organize his or her experiences to form an internally consistent, stable concept of self. Better-integrated men and women show more ambiguity-tolerance, are more field-independent, and they're better able to retain a focused mental image—a clear goal or perspective—in the face of competing or irrelevant information.

A person's *intellectual efficiency* refers to how well his or her actual performance or accomplishments measure up to their aptitude. High-integration individuals have been found to show superior academic achievement compared to non-highs, despite having equivalent academic aptitude as assessed by college entrance examination scores. Importantly, it's not intellectual capacity—the absolute amount of sheer "brainpower"—that accounts for the effective mastery shown by the highly integrated individual. Instead, high-integration persons make maximal use of those capacities they *do* possess and they actively seek out situations where their intellectual endowments—at whatever natural level—can be actualized.

High-integration individuals show greater degrees of communicative richness, using language that's fertile with both nuance and descriptive power. Indeed, as Wexler[25] has argued, since the input of the high-integration person comes from a variety of sources, it would be reasonable to expect that the optimal use of that information should be reflected in the person's language. Interestingly, communicative richness seems not to depend on particularly high verbal intelligence scores. Again, it's the efficiency with which the integrated person *uses* what he or she *has* that counts, not the absolute raw level of ability.

Wexler has also proposed that the optimally functioning person is the one who allocates his or her attention not to what's the most routine, the most familiar, the most easily organized, but rather to the unique and novel aspects of the available information. And, as we've seen, flexible and adaptive attention to novelty makes it more likely that the person will be able to meet the demands of a complex and rapidly changing environment.

The high-integration person, then, is the one who is better able to process novelty, deal with uncertainty, and tolerate ambiguity. All of these are important aspects of ego autonomy and all, according to our neuropsychodynamic model, are dependent on the optimally adaptive functioning of the frontal-interhemispheric axis.

High-integration individuals also seem to be able to scan their own short-term memory stores more quickly and efficiently, thus giving them greater overall access to their own internal repositories of data and inner states of feeling and responding. Interestingly, rapid scanning of short-term memory has been found to be associated with high verbal ability.[26] This is no doubt related to the communicative richness shown by these individuals, and highlights the role of internal verbal coding strategies discussed in Chapter 4. High-integration individuals also show a greater tendency to conceptually elaborate their own feelings and experiences, which has been associated with the ability to process more overall information in tasks that demand selective attention.[27]

High-integration individuals are also good self-monitors.[28] That is, they're acutely sensitive to the appropriateness of their actions in particular situations and quickly learn the correct rules for new and novel situations. They seem to be able to "fit in" almost anywhere and they consistently make a "good impression" on almost anyone they're with.

Unlike the transient social slickness of the psychopath, whose dissembling works only for the short run, the interpersonal adroitness of the high-integration man or woman is related to his or her ability to conceptualize people and social situations in multidimensional ways, a sign of cognitive flexibility and a fundamental prerequisite for true empathy. Also unlike the guarded aloofness of the paranoid, the high-integration person is free in expressing his own views and feelings, and demonstrates flexibility of rapport and response because his social interrelatedness comes from within; it's not a tacked-on con job or a form of strategic politicking.

It should come as little surprise, then, that high-integration individuals have more stable, yet flexible, self-concepts and greater ego autonomy; at the same time they're more amenable to self-change. Only a personality with some room to maneuver, so to speak, can effectively profit from any genuine method of therapy, education, or self-improvement. Without even a smidgen of cognitive flexibility or ego autonomy to grab hold of, the psychotherapeutic or self-change process slips away like a climber's pylon on sheer frozen rock.

Goodness and Morality

But do healthy personalities naturally lead to "good" personalities, or at least to good works? Put another way, does the tendency to act in moral and altruistic ways debouch naturally from a neuropsychodynamically based ego autonomy of the kind we've been dealing with?

Nancy McWilliams[29] conducted an intensive study of individuals who've devoted their lives to humanitarian concerns. Out of twenty candidates, she chose five exceptional people based on certain special criteria. These included repeated acts of helping which were in some way nonconforming and costly to the doer in monetary or social terms; which were nonreciprocal, with no specific "payback" expected; and which did not stem from psychopathology or emotional disturbance—rather, the doer was perceived by self and others as functioning well and psychologically stable. The five "altruists" who were finally selected for this study (called by McWilliams's fictionalized names for them) were:

Frank Butler, age twenty, a college student and aspiring doctor who, since childhood, had distinguished himself by undertaking humanitarian projects, especially medical ones—for example, organizing a blood bank.

Beatrice Lopez, age thirty-four, a psychotherapist with a reputation for unusual effectiveness and devotion to helping "difficult" psychotic, sociopathic, or poverty-stricken patients.

Paul Anders, age forty-four, the organizer of many projects to arrange for the adoption of war-traumatized, physically handicapped, mentally retarded, racially stigmatized, or otherwise "undesirable" orphaned children, and who personally adopted several such youngsters into his own family.

Ruth Frankl, age forty-six, the mainstay of an international movement to provide more humane approaches to the difficulties of victims of leprosy and their children.

Vivian Bentley, age seventy-nine, a crusader in a long series of humanitarian projects and social movements, from her work as a medic in World War I, through a major role in the civil rights movement (Martin Luther King, Jr., used her Florida home as a regional headquarters in the early 1960s), to her current dedication to court and prison reform.

In exhaustive observations and interviews with her subjects over several years, McWilliams discovered certain traits in common that seemed to characterize these altruists. To begin with, they were a sociable lot. They enjoyed company, sought out companionship, placed great value on intimacy and loyalty, and were themselves attractive, appealing people. They were also happy. They found their activities rewarding and their lives satisfying, hardly considering themselves to be "self-sacrificing" individuals. They possessed a wry, somewhat self-deprecatory sense of humor, and even seemed a little embarrassed at being singled out for a "study of altruism."

These altruists were not godlike paragons of psychological perfection, either. McWilliams was able to pick up a certain defensive drivenness around her subjects' activities. All of them had a compulsive bent—they maintained their self-esteem by *doing*. They themselves saw their humanitarianism as fulfilling a strong inner need. Paul commented, "I don't see myself as altruistic—I do what I have to do." If circumstances even temporarily prevented these activities, they became depressed.

Not the least of the consequences of trying to juggle their humanitarian activities with more everyday personal concerns was a pervasive fatigue. Burning the candle at both ends also sometimes led to narrow brushes with larger failures. Paul flunked one year of college because of his altruistic extracurricular activities. Frank risked rejection from medical school because his blood-drive work cut into his study time. What seemed to maintain their emotional balance was their very immersion in doing good, combined with overall good judgment in limiting other obligations to a minimum.

A large part of the impetus behind their altruistic behavior seemed to come from an unconscious identification with the people they aided. By placing themselves in the role of helper or rescuer, they seemed to work through their own inner needs for nurturance and support. They also relied heavily on a defense mechanism which McWilliams calls *reversal* and which earlier psychoanalytic writers have termed *undoing*. Paul's adoption-promotion efforts, for example, seemed to be psychologically reversing or undoing his own position as an orphan whom someone else had saved at age two when his mother died. In general, these altruists were always counting their blessings and reminding themselves of how worse off others were.

All of the altruists took great pains to suppress feelings

of anger and hostility, although righteous indignation on someone else's behalf was acceptable. When McWilliams probed to find out whether they felt they had any personal problems or failings, Frank complained of a tendency to get "snappish"; Beatrice deplored her "fast temper"; Paul apologized for finding his teenage children's problems irritating; Ruth commented that she harbored anger "and it comes out at inopportune moments"; and Vivian spoke of working for years to develop an even-tempered attitude. All seemed to measure themselves against some superhuman standard of equanimity and benevolence, and McWilliams suggests that one function of altruism may be to act as a foil against unconscious hostility.

In terms of their own development, the altruists all seem to have had adequate nurturance in the first few years of life, but each had suffered some kind of major loss or deprivation between the ages of two and three. Yet each had had the benefit of a strong role model at around that same time, who was him- or herself an exemplar of altruism. All of McWilliams's subjects had, in effect, been "rescued" at a critical point in their early lives, when separation and loss might otherwise have been catastrophic. The rescuer was subsequently regarded with enduring gratitude and idealization, and served as an object of identification.

All of the altruists were strongly religious, but their devotion consisted not of rote ritualization, but rather was actualized through their humanitarian good works. Although deeply attached to their individual religious heritages, none regarded his or hers as the only "true faith." Their religion seemed to be a way of reinforcing their adherence to clear, consistent, moral principles—to give themselves what McWilliams describes as a psychological, even spiritual "center of gravity," close to what we have referred to in this book as personal integrity, ego autonomy.

Commenting on these five extraordinary altruists, McWilliams notes:

Dynamically, self-esteem and altruism may be seen as related in two ways: Self-esteem produces altruism, in that a person who develops a positive self-representation in early life feels that he or she has something to give; and altruism produces self-esteem, in that it compensates for narcissistic vulnerabilities. By meeting the standards of an internal critic, altruistic behavior may unconsciously reassure one of the continued presence of the internalized good object. A kind of "virtuous cycle" could thus be in motion in the altruistic personality.[30]

Thus, despite childhood experiences that would have conduced to significant psychopathology in many people, these individuals avoided that fate, indeed, turned their adversity around into something of inestimable social value, thanks to their inner core of personal integrity, of ego autonomy. Recall also, in this regard, the "high-risk" alcoholism-prone subjects in Chapter 10, whose ego autonomy appears to have played a role in protecting them from a drunkard's life.

A similar finding emerged from a study of J. Kirk Felsman and George Vaillant,[31] who followed a group of men for forty years, from childhood through middle age. Despite often horrendous circumstances while growing up, many of these individuals prevailed psychologically and went on to lead successful and productive lives: the researchers characterized them as "resilient."

And what was the basis for this resilience? Not a repressive blotting out of the past, but rather the ability to experience the pains and sorrows, utilize the lessons to be learned therefrom, and draw on the past as a source of strength, not bitterness. The resilient men possessed a certain mature perspective on their own situations and could take appropriate satisfaction in what they'd managed to secure for themselves and their families. A critically important factor, the researchers point out, was these men's genuine capacity for empathy, which seemed to be related to an overall quality of ego strength. As with McWilliams's altruists, this ego strength seemed to stem from some "innate factor" that the researchers were unable to identify.

The Fates of Self: Determinism, Freedom, and Self-Change

But maybe we can try. The qualities that make up ego autonomy, ego strength, personal integrity, high integration, resilience, the healthy personality—call it what you will— all revolve around the capacity to reflect, to self-communicate motives and actions, to direct those actions in a volitional manner, and to use internal and external feedback to appraise and change oneself—one's *self*.

Can you change your self? Many try through therapies, self-help programs, or their own earnest efforts. But if there's an important lesson in this book, it's that the processes of neuropsychodynamic development endow each of us with a different inner potential to affect our destinies, bequeath to us different personalities. Unfortunately, today's psychiatrists and psychologists are too quick to automatically regard variations of personality as *personality disorders*, as if any deviation from some Socratic ideal of self-organization constituted ipso facto a pathology, a disease of the psyche.

Of course, some of this is purely self-serving: Clinicians get paid for *treating* things. And the things that get treated (and that insurance companies reimburse for) are *disorders*, *diseases*, not natural variations in cognitive style. Helping a person with an obsessive-compulsive style learn to reframe his thinking and alter his actions in progressively adaptive ways doesn't have the same doctorly ring to it as prescribing a pill or embarking on a course of hospital "treatment." So since clinicians, particularly medical clinicians, make their living treating specific disorders, the more kinds of such clinically sanctioned disorders there are . . . well, you get the idea.

This is not to deny that chemical therapies are appropriate in treating some of the manifestations of certain psychiatric disorders, such as the disabling mood swings of manic-depression or the disruptive psychotic thinking in schizophrenia. But the view of personality that the evidence of this book supports is that variations in personality traits and personality types depend on differences in underlying cognitive style and neuropsychodynamic organization that may be but expressions of extreme points along the natural continuum of self.

People who commit atrocious acts, who hamstring themselves with obsessive behavior, who alienate others with lurid histrionic displays, or drive themselves to the brink of cardiovascular or chemically dependent doom are not necessarily "sick" in the mind. As shown throughout this book, their personalities are the combined product of early brain development, cognitive style, life experience, and phylogenetic heritage. These factors have, in turn, all contributed to their own unique final version of ego autonomy and adaptiveness of self.

This is not a narrow determinism, and the neuropsychodynamic approach does not imply the immutability of behavior. Other than in the case of extreme atrophy or strangulation of the will, as with some forms of organic brain damage or severe psychosis, most people retain the capacity to alter their thinking, feeling, and acting in more productive and self-satisfying ways. Some may need more help than others. And some may even occasionally have to be hit over the head with the proverbial frying pan to see the necessity or desirability of seeking paths to self-change. Further, we retain a certain responsibility for our actions: No "blaming the brain" or "my-frontal-lobes-made-me-do-it" excuses tolerated here.

It's probably true that some people can undergo a greater degree of change than others by virtue of the way they're neuropsychodynamically put together. This is a fact of life, like differences in height, intelligence, physical strength, musical talent, or susceptibility to colds. Even Abraham Maslow[32] recognized that true self-actualization could probably be attained by only a few, but that fact, to his mind, did not diminish the nobility of the struggle.

You may not be able to radically alter your basic personality and cognitive style, to rearrange your particular endowment of talents and deficiencies. But you have some say in what you do with them, how you use them for either adaptation or maladjustment, for good or ill. To a greater or lesser degree, at least some portion of your ultimate state of ego autonomy is still in your hands. *Predisposition* is not *predestination*. To deny this is to illegitimately twist the neuropsychodynamic model into a neophrenological counsel of despair.

The neuropsychodynamic approach, in recognizing that different people have different abilities with regard to self-determination, and different needs with regard to self-change, will best be able to meet the current challenge of designing more effective and individually targeted therapies and treatment approaches for the common travails of daily life. This may ultimately apply also to those conditions that *can* be legitimately termed "disorders."

For many people—most people, really—change *is* possible, even necessary. Although we must recognize that the degree of potential change will vary from individual to individual, in a few cases even seemingly miraculous transformations of the self may occur. We won't know unless we try. It is the continuing and enduring task of the brain and behavioral sciences to foster the understanding of people's behaviors, their limits and potentialities, and the delicate fortunes of the human spirit.

REFERENCE NOTES

CHAPTER 1: NEUROPSYCHOLOGY AND PERSONALITY

1. Pervin, L. A. (1985). Personality: Current controversies, issues and directions. *Annual Review of Psychology, 36*, 83–114.
2. Baumeister, R. F. (1987). How the self became a problem: A psychological review of historical research. *Journal of Personality and Social Psychology, 52*, 163–176.

    Holt, R. R. (1965). Ego autonomy reevaluated. International *Journal of Psychoanalysis, 46*, 151–167.
3. Markus, H. (1983). Self-knowledge: An expanded view. *Journal of Personality, 51*, 543–565.
4. Bandura, A. (1977a). Self-efficacy: Towards a unifying theory of behavioral change. *Psychological Review, 84*, 191–215.

    Bandura, A. (1977b). *Social Learning Theory.* Englewood Cliffs: Prentice-Hall.

    Bandura, A. (1982). Self-efficacy mechanism in human agency. *American Psychologist, 37*, 122–144.

299

5. Hartmann, H. (1939/1958). *Ego Psychology and the Problem of Adaptation.* New York: International Universities Press.

6. Goldstein, K. (1938). *The Organism.* New York: American Books. Maslow, A. H. (1968). *Toward a Psychology of Being.* New York: Van Nostrand Reinhold.

7. Freud, S. (1915/1957). The unconscious. Standard *Edition of the Complete Psychological Works of Sigmund Freud,* Vol. 14, pp. 161–215.

8. Carver, C. S. & Scheier, M. F. (1982). Control theory: A useful conceptual framework for personality, social, clinical and health psychology. *Psychological Review, 92,* 111–135.

9. Klein, G. S. (1954). Need and regulation. In M. R. Jones (Ed.), Nebraska Symposium on Motivation. Lincoln: University of Nebraska Press.
   Klein, G. S. (1958). Cognitive control and motivation. In G. Lindzey (Ed.), *Assessment of Human Motives.* New York: Rinehart.

10. Gardner, R. W., Holzman, P. S., Klein, G. S., Linton, H. B. & Spence, D. P. (1959). Cognitive control: A study of individual consistencies in cognitive behavior. *Psychological Issues, 1,* 1–185.

11. Shapiro, D. (1965). *Neurotic Styles.* New York: Basic Books.

12. Shapiro, 1965, p. 1.

CHAPTER 2: THE ORIGINS OF SELF

1. Wells, S. R. (1872). *How to Read Character: A New Illustrated Handbook of Phrenology and Physiognomy for Students and Examiners, with a Descriptive Chart.* New York: Wells.

2. Boring, E. G. (1951). *A History of Experimental Psychology* (2nd ed.). New York: Appleton-Century-Crofts.
   Clarke, E. & O'Malley, C. D. (1968). *The Human Brain and Spinal Cord: A Historical Study Illustrated by Writings from Antiquity to the Twentieth Century.* Los Angeles: University of California Press.

3. Dimond, S. J. (1980). *Neuropsychology: A Textbook of*

Systems and Psychological Functions of the Human Brain. London: Butterworth.

4. Levy, J. (1978). The mammalian brain and the adaptive advantage of cerebral asymmetry. *Annals of the New York Academy of Sciences, 299*, 264–272.

5. Geschwind, N. & Galaburda, A. M. (1985). Cerebral lateralization. Biological mechanisms, associations and pathology. A hypothesis and a program for research. *Archives of Neurology, 42*, 428–459, 521–552, 634–654.

6. Geschwind, N. & Behan, P. (1982). Left-handedness: Association with immune disease, migraine and developmental learning disorder. *Proceedings of the National Academy of Sciences, 79*, 5097–5100.

   Geschwind, N. & Behan, P. (1985). Laterality, hormones and immunity. In N. Geschwind & A. M. Galaburda (Eds.), *Cerebral Dominance: The Biological Foundations*. Cambridge: Harvard University Press.

7. Carlson, N. R. (1977). *Physiology of Behavior*. Boston: Allyn & Bacon.

8. Beatty, W. W. (1979). Gonadal hormones and sex differences in nonreproductive behavior in rodents: Organizational and activational influences. *Hormones and Behavior, 12*, 112–163.

   Money, J. (1977). Human hermaphrodism. In F. A. Beach (Ed.), *Human Sexuality in Four Perspectives*. Baltimore: Johns Hopkins University Press.

9. Diamond, M. (1977). Human sexual development: Biological foundations for development. In F. A. Beach (Ed.), *Human Sexuality in Four Perspectives*. Baltimore: Johns Hopkins University Press.

   Ehrhardt, A. A. & Meyer-Bahlburg, H. F. L. (1981). Effects of prenatal sex hormones on gender-related behavior. *Science, 211*, 1312–1318.

10. Malatesta, C. Z. & Izard, C. E. (1984). The ontogenesis of human social signals: From biological imperative to symbol utilization. In N. A. Fox & R. J. Davidson (Eds.), *The Psychobiology of Affective Development*. Hillsdale: Erlbaum.

11. Durfee, K. E. (1974). Crooked ears and the bad boy syndrome: Asymmetry as an indicator of minimal brain dysfunction. *Bulletin of the Menninger Clinic, 38*, 305–316.

Wilson, J. Q. & Herrenstein, R. J. (1985). *Crime and Human Nature*. New York: Simon & Schuster.

12. Kretschmer, E. (1939). *Medizinische Psychologie* (5th ed.). Stuttgart: Georg Thieme Verlag.

CHAPTER 3: THE IMPETUS OF SELF

1. Teuber, H. (1964). The riddle of the frontal lobe in man. In J. M. Warren & K. Akert (Eds.), *The Frontal Granular Cortex and Behavior*. New York: McGraw-Hill.

2. Nauta, W. J. (1971). The problem of the frontal lobe: A reinterpretation. *Journal of Psychiatric Research, 8,* 167–187.

3. Blumer, D. & Benson, D. F. (1975). Personality changes with frontal and temporal lobe lesions. In D. F. Benson & D. Blumer (Eds.), *Psychiatric Aspects of Neurologic Disease*. New York: Grune & Stratton.

   Damasio, A. (1979). The frontal lobes. In K. M. Heilman & E. Valenstein (Eds.), *Clinical Neuropsychology*. New York: Oxford University Press.

   Stuss, D. T. & Benson, D. F. (1984). Neuropsychological studies of the frontal lobes. *Psychological Bulletin, 95,* 3–28.

4. Luria, A. R. (1980). *Higher Cortical Functions in Man* (2nd ed.). New York: Basic Books. P. 248.

5. Fuster, J. M. (1985). The frontal lobes, mediator of cross-temporal contingencies. *Human Neurobiology, 4,* 169–179.

6. Dimond, S. J. (1980). *Neuropsychology: A Textbook of Systems and Psychological Functions of the Human Brain*. London: Butterworth.

7. Franzen, E. A. & Myers, R. E. (1973). Neural control of social behavior: Prefrontal and anterior temporal cortex. *Neuropsychologia, 11,* 141–153.

8. Lhermitte, F. (1986). Human autonomy and the frontal lobes. Part II: Patient behavior in complex social situations: The "environmental dependency syndrome." *Annals of Neurology, 19,* 335–343.

9. Lhermitte, 1986, p. 342.

CHAPTER 4: THE AWARENESS OF SELF

1. Wonder, J. & Donovan, P. (1984). *Whole-Brain Thinking: Working from Both Sides of the Brain to Achieve Peak Job Performance*. New York: Morrow.

2. Miller, L. Neurobabble. (1986). *Psychology Today*, April, pp. 70–72.

3. Dimond, S. J. & Blizard, D. A. (Eds.), *Evolution and Lateralization of the Brain*. New York: New York Academy of Sciences.
   Springer, S. P. & Deutsch, G. (1985). *Left Brain, Right Brain* (rev. ed.). New York: Freeman.
   Walsh, K. W. (1978). *Neuropsychology: A Clinical Approach*. New York: Churchill Livingstone.

4. Delis, D. C., Wapner, W., Gardner, H. & Moses, J. A. (1983). The contribution of the right hemisphere to the organization of paragraphs. *Cortex, 19*, 43–50.

5. Bradshaw, J. L. & Sherlock, D. (1982). Bugs and faces in the two visual fields: The analytic/holistic processing dichotomy and task sequencing. *Cortex, 18*, 211–226.

6. Wyler, A. R. & Ray, M. W. (1986). Aphasia for Morse code. *Brain and Language, 27*, 195–198.

7. Freud, S. (1894/1966). The neuro-psychoses of defense. *Standard Edition of the Complete Psychological Works of Sigmund Freud*, Vol. 1, pp. 45–65.

8. Freud, S. (1915/1957). The unconscious. *Standard Edition*, Vol. 14, pp. 161–215.

9. Galin, D. (1974). Implications for psychiatry of left and right cerebral specialization: A neurophysiological context for unconscious processes. *Archives of General Psychiatry, 31*, 572–583.
   Galin, D. (1977). Lateral specialization and psychiatric issues: Speculations of the evolution and development of consciousness. *Annals of the New York Academy of Sciences, 299*, 397–411.

10. Tucker, D. M. (1981). Lateral brain function, emotion and conceptualization. *Psychological Bulletin, 89*, 19–43.

11. Joseph, R. (1982). The neuropsychology of development: Hemispheric laterality, limbic language and the origin of thought. *Journal of Clinical Psychology, 38*, 4–33.

12. Dimond, S. J. (1980). *Neuropsychology: A Textbook of*

Systems and Psychological Functions of the Human Brain.
London: Butterworth.

13. Salazar, A. M., Grasman, J. H., Vance, S. C., Weingart-
ner, H., Dillon, J. D. & Ludlow, C. (1986). "Consciousness and Amnesia After Penetrating Head Injury:
Neurology and Anatomy" *Neurology, 36,* 178–187.

14. Puca, F. M., Antonaci, F., Savarese, M., Covelli, V.,
Tarascio, G., Bellizzi, M., Lamorgese, C., Musmeci, G.
M. & Sorrento, G. (1985). Memory impairment and painful side: Neuropsychological and electrophysiological study
of 21 classic migraine sufferers. In C. Rose (Ed.), *Migraine: Proceedings of the Fifth International Migraine
Symposium.* Basel: Karger.

15. Luria, A. R. (1980). *Higher Cortical Functions in Man*
(2nd ed.). New York: Basic Books.

16. Gazzaniga, M. S. (1970). *The Bisected Brain.* New York:
Appleton-Century-Crofts.

17. Gazzaniga, M. S. (1985). *The Social Brain: Discovering the
Networks of the Mind.* New York: Basic Books.

18. Gazzaniga, 1985, p. 73.

19. Hoppe, K. D. (1977). Split brains and psychoanalysis.
Psychoanalytic Quarterly, 46, 220–244.

20. Freud, 1915.

21. Vygotsky, L. S. (1962). *Thought and Language.* Cambridge: MIT Press.

22. Joseph, 1982, p. 24.

CHAPTER 5: THE PASSIONS OF SELF

1. Hurwitz, T. A., Wada, J. A., Kosaka, B. D. & Strauss,
E. H. (1985). Cerebral organization of affect suggested by
temporal lobe seizures. *Neurology, 35, 1335–1337.*

2. *Critchley, M. (1953). The Parietal Lobes.* New York: Haf-
ner.

3. Gainotti, G. (1973). Emotional behavior and hemispheric
side of lesion. *Cortex, 8,* 41–55.

4. Robinson, R. G. (1986). Post-stroke mood disorders. *Hospital Practice, 21,* 83–89.

   Robinson, R. G., Kubos, K. L., Starr, L. B., Rao, K. &
Price, T. R. (1984). Mood disorders in stroke patients:
Importance of location of lesion. *Brain,* 107, 81–93.

Robinson, R. G., Lipsey, J. R. & Price, T. R. (1985). Diagnosis and clinical management of post-stroke depression. *Psychosomatics, 26,* 769–778.

5. Ross, E. D. (1981). The aprosodias: Functional-anatomic organization of language in the right hemisphere. *Archives of Neurology, 38,* 561–569.

   Ross, E. D. & Rush, A. J. (1981). Diagnosis and neuroanatomical correlates of depression in brain-damaged patients: Implications for a neurology of depression. *Archives of General Psychiatry, 38,* 1344–1354.

   Ross, E. D. & Stewart, R. S. (1987). Pathological display of affect in patients with depression and right frontal brain damage: An alternative mechanism. *Journal of Nervous and Mental Disease, 175,* 165–172.

6. Sacks, O. (1985). *The Man Who Mistook His Wife for a Hat and Other Clinical Tales.* New York: Summit.

7. Ahern, G. L. & Schwartz, G. E. (1985). Differential lateralization for positive and negative emotion in the human brain: EEG spectral analysis. *Neuropsychologia, 23,* 745–755.

8. Schaffer, C. E., Davidson, R. J. & Saron, C. (1983). Frontal and parietal electroencephalogram asymmetry in depressed and nondepressed subjects. *Biological Psychiatry, 18,* 753–762.

9. Beck, A. T. (1976). *Cognitive Therapy and the Emotional Disorders.* New York: International Universities Press.

   Beck, A. T., Rush, A. J., Shaw, B. F. & Emery, G. (1979). *Cognitive Therapy of Depression. New York: Guilford.*

10. Kovacs, M., Beck, A. T. & Hollon, S. D. (1981). Depressed outpatients treated with cognitive therapy or pharmacotherapy: A one-year followup. *Archives of General Psychiatry, 38,* 33–39.

    Murphy, G. E., Simons, A. D., Wetzel, R. D. & Lustman, P. J. (1984). Cognitive therapy and pharmacotherapy: Singly and together in the treatment of depression. *Archives of General Psychiatry, 41,* 33–41.

11. Sackeim, H. A., Greenberg, M. S., Weiman, A. L., Gur, R. C., Hungerbuhler, J. P. & Geschwind, N. (1982). Hemispheric asymmetry in the expression of positive and

negative emotions: Neurologic evidence. *Archives of Neurology, 39*, 210–218.

12. Robert G. Robertson, M. D., personal communication.

13. Tucker, D. M. (1981). Lateral brain function, emotion and conceptualization. *Psychological Bulletin, 89*, 19–43.

   Tucker, D. M. (1986). Neural control and emotional communication. In Blanck, Bush & Rosenthal (Eds.), *Nonverbal Communication in the Clinical Context*. University Park: Pennsylvania State University Press.

   Tucker, D. M. & Williamson, P. A. (1984). Asymmetric neural control systems in human self-regulation. *Psychological Review, 91*, 185–215.

14. Don M. Tucker, Ph. D., personal communication.

CHAPTER 6: THE CONTROLLING SELF

1. Freud, S. (1894/1966). The neuro-psychoses of defense. *Standard Edition of the Complete Psychological Works of Sigmund Freud*, Vol. 1, pp. 45–68.

2. Freud, S. (1896/1966). Further remarks on the neuro-psychoses of defense. *Standard Edition*, Vol. 1, pp. 159–185.

3. Shapiro, D. (1965). *Neurotic Styles*. New York: Basic Books.

4. Shapiro, 1965, pp. 27–28.

5. von Economo, C. (1931). *Encephalitis Lethargica: Its Sequelae and Treatment*. Oxford: Oxford University Press.

6. Brill, H. (1975). Postencephalitic states or conditions. In M. F. Reiser (Ed.), *American Handbook of Psychiatry* (2nd ed.). *Vol. 4: Organic Disorders and Psychosomatic Medicine*. New York: Basic Books.

7. Schilder, P. (1938). The organic background of obsessions and compulsions. *American Journal of Psychiatry, 94*, 1397–1413.

8. Grimshaw, L. (1964). Obsessional disorder and neurological illness. *Journal of Neurology, Neurosurgery and Psychiatry, 27*, 229–231.

9. McKeon, J., McGuffin, P. & Robinson, P. (1984). Obsessive-compulsive neurosis following head injury: A report of four cases. *British Journal of Psychiatry, 144*, 190–192.

10. Gibson, J. G. & Kennedy, W. A. (1960). A clinical-EEG

study in a case of obsessional neurosis. *Electroencephalography and Clinical Neurophysiology*, 12, 198–201.

11. Flor-Henry, P., Yeudall, L. T., Koles, Z. T. & Howarth, B. G. (1979). Neuropsychological and power spectral EEG investigations of the obsessive-compulsive syndrome. *Biological Psychiatry*, 14, 119–129.

12. Insel, T. R., Donnelly, E. F., Lalakea, M. L., Alterman, I. S. & Murphy, D. L. (1983). Neurological and neuropsychological studies of patients with obsessive-compulsive disorder. *Biological Psychiatry*, 18, 741–751.

13. Behar, D., Rapoport, J. L., Berg, C. J., Denckla, M. B., Mann, L., Cox, C., Fedio, P., Zahn, T. & Wolfman, M. G. (1984). Computerized tomography and neuropsychological test measures in adolescents with obsessive-compulsive disorder. *American Journal of Psychiatry*, 141, 363–369.

14. Baxter, L. R., Phelps. M. E., Mazziotta, J. C., Guze, B. H., Schwartz, J. M. & Selin, C. E. (1987). Local cerebral metabolic glucose rates in obsessive-compulsive disorder: A comparison with rates in unipolar depression and normal controls. *Archives of General Psychiatry*, 44, 211–218.

15. Phillips, A. G. & Carr, G. D. (1987). Cognition and the basal ganglia: A possible substrate for procedural knowledge. *Canadian Journal of Neurological Science*, 14, 381–385.

16. Eslinger, P. J. & Damasio, A. R. (1985). Severe disturbance of higher cognition after bilateral frontal lobe ablation: Patient EVR. *Neurology*, 35, 1731–1741.

17. Eslinger & Damasio, 1985, p. 1732.

18. Nauta, W. J. (1971). The problem of the frontal lobe: A reinterpretation. *Journal of Psychiatric Research*, 8, 167–187.

19. Carey, G. & Gottesman, I. I. (1981). Twin and family studies of anxiety, phobic and obsessive disorders. In D. F. Klein & J. G. Rabkin (Eds.), *Anxiety: New Research and Changing Concepts*. New York: Raven Press.

20. Eysenck, H. J. (1979). The conditioning model of neurosis. *Behavioral and Brain Sciences*, 2, 155–199.

21. Turner, S. M., Beidel, D. C. & Nathan, R. S. (1985). Biological factors in obsessive-compulsive disorders. *Psychological Bulletin*, 97, 430–450.

CHAPTER 7: THE GUARDED SELF

1. Freud, S. (1896/1966). Further remarks on the neuro-psychoses of defense. *Standard Edition of the Complete Psychological Works of Sigmund Freud*, Vol. 1, pp. 159–185.

2. Freud, S. (1911/1958). Psycho-analytic notes on an autobiographical account of a case of paranoia. *Standard Edition*, Vol. 12, pp. 3–84.

3. Fenichel, O. (1945). *The Psychoanalytic Theory of Neurosis*. New York: Norton.

4. Shapiro, D. (1965). *Neurotic Styles*. New York: Basic Books.

5. Shapiro, 1965, p. 80.

6. Insel, T. R. & Akiskal, H. S. (1986). Obsessive-compulsive disorder with psychotic features: A phenomenological analysis. *American Journal of Psychiatry, 143*, 1527–1533.

7. MacLean, P. D. (1969). The paranoid streak in man. In A. Koestler & J. R. Smythies (Eds.), *Beyond Reductionism*. Boston: Beacon Press.

8. Gruzelier, J. (1981). Hemispheric imbalances masquerading as paranoid and nonparanoid syndromes? *Schizophrenia Bulletin, 7*, 662–673.

9. Marin, R. S. & Tucker, G. J. (1981). Psychopathology and hemisphere dysfunction: A review. *Journal of Nervous and Mental Disease, 169*, 546–555.

   Merrin, E. L. (1981). Schizophrenia and brain asymmetry: An evaluation of evidence for dominant lobe dysfunction. *Journal of Nervous and Mental Disease, 169*, 405–413.

   Miller, L. (1984). Hemispheric asymmetry of cognitive processing in schizophrenia. *Psychological Reports, 55*, 932–934.

10. Magaro, P. A. & Chamrad, D. L. (1983). Hemispheric preference of paranoid and nonparanoid schizophrenics. *Biological Psychiatry, 18*, 1269–1285.

11. Levy, J. & Trevarthen, C. (1976). Metacontrol of hemispheric function in human split-brain patients. *Journal of Experimental Psychology: Human Perception and Performance, 2*, 299–312.

12. Leftoff, S. (1983). Psychopathology in light of brain in-

jury: A case study. *Journal of Clinical Neuropsychology*, 5, 51–63.

13. Nightingale, S. (1982). Somatoparaphrenia: A case report. *Cortex*, *18*, 463–467.

14. Goldstein, K. (1938). *The Organism*. New York: American Books.

CHAPTER 8: THE AMORPHOUS SELF

1. Freud, S. (1894/1966). The neuro-psychoses of defense. *Standard Edition of the Complete Psychological Works of Sigmund Freud*, Vol. 1, pp. 45–68.

2. Freud, 1894/1966, p. 49.

3. Shapiro, D. (1965). *Neurotic Styles*. New York: Basic Books.

4. Breuer, J. & Freud, S. (1895/1982). *Studies on Hysteria*. New York: Basic Books.

5. Kretschmer, E. (1926). *Hysteria*. New York: Basic Books.

6. Ludwig, A.M. (1972). Hysteria: A neurobiological theory. *Archives of General Psychiatry*, *27*, 771–777.

7. Janet, P. (1920). *The Major Symptoms of Hysteria* (2nd ed.). New York: Macmillan.

8. Bradley, P. B. (1958). The central action of certain drugs in relation to the reticular formation of the brain. In H. H. Jasper (Ed.), *Reticular Formation of the Brain*. Boston: Little, Brown.

9. Miller, L. (1984). Neuropsychological concepts of somatoform disorders. *International Journal of Psychiatry in Medicine*, *14*, 31–46.

10. Rosen, S. R. (1951). Vasomotor responses in hysteria. *Journal of the Mount Sinai Hospital*, *18*, 179–190.

11. Meares, R. & Horvath, T. (1972). "Acute" and "chronic" hysteria. *British Journal of Psychiatry*, *121*, 653–657.

12. Lader, M. (1973). The psychophysiology of hysterics. *Journal of Psychosomatic Research*, *17*, 255–269.

13. Lader, M. & Sartorius, N. (1968). Anxiety in patients with conversion symptoms. *Journal of Neurology, Neurosurgery and Psychiatry*, *31*, 490–495.

14. Hernandez-Peon, R., Scherrer, H. & Jouvet, M. (1956). Modification of electrical activity in cochlear nucleus during attention in unanesthetized cats. *Science*, 123, 331.

15. Hernandez-Peon, R., Chavez-Iberra, G. & Aguilar-
    Figuera, E. (1963). Somatic evoked potentials in one case
    of hysterical anesthesia. *Electroencephalography and
    Clinical Neurophysiology, 15,* 889–896.

16. Levy, R. & Behrman, J. (1970). Cortical evoked poten-
    tials in hysterical hemianesthesia. *Electroencephalography
    and Clinical Neurophysiology, 29,* 400–404.

17. Bendefeldt, F., Miller, L. L. & Ludwig, A. M. (1976).
    Cognitive performance in conversion hysteria. *Archives of
    General Psychiatry, 33,* 1250–1254.

18. Smokler, I. A. & Shevrin, H. (1979). Cerebral lateraliza-
    tion and personality style. *Archives of General Psychiatry,
    36,* 949–954.

19. Levy, J. & Trevarthen, C. (1976). Metacontrol of hemi-
    spheric function in human split-brain patients. *Journal of
    Experimental Psychology: Human Perception and Perfor-
    mance, 2,* 299–312.

20. Gur, R. E. & Gur, R. C. (1977). Correlates of conjugate
    lateral eye movements in man. In S. Harnad, R. W. Doty
    & L. Goldstein (Eds.), *Lateralization in the Nervous Sys-
    tem.* New York: Academic Press.
        Gur, R. E., Gur, R. C. & Harris, L. (1975). Hemi-
    spheric activation, as measured by subjects' conjugate lat-
    eral eye movements, is influenced by experimenter
    location. *Neuropsychologia, 13,* 35–44.

21. Magaro, P. A., Smith, P. & Ashbrook, R. M. (1983).
    Personality style differences in visual search performance.
    Psychiatry Research, 10, 131–138.

22. Flor-Henry, P., Fromm-Auch, D., Tapper, M. & Shop-
    flocher, M. (1981). A neuropsychological study of the
    stable syndrome of hysteria. *Biological Psychiatry, 16,*
    601–626.

23. Axelrod, S., Noonan, M. & Atanacio, B. (1980). On the
    laterality of psychogenic somatic symptoms. *Journal of
    Nervous and Mental Disease, 168,* 517–525.
        Galin, D., Diamond, R. & Braff, D. (1977). Laterali-
    zation of conversion symptoms: More frequent on the left.
    American Journal of Psychiatry, 134, 578–580.
        Stern, D. B. (1977). Handedness and the lateralization
    of conversion reactions. *Journal of Nervous and Mental
    Disease, 164,* 122–128.

24. Mersky, H. & Watson, G. D. (1979). The lateralisation of pain. *Pain*, 7, 271–280.

25. Cubelli, R., Caselli, M. & Neri, M. (1984). Pain endurance in unilateral cerebral lesions. *Cortex*, 20, 369–375.

26. Ferenczi, S. (1926). *Further Contributions to the Theory and Technique of Psychoanalysis*. London: Hogarth.

27. Damasio, A. R., Eslinger, P. J., Damasio, H., Van Hoesen, G. W. & Cornell, S. (1985). Multimodal amnesic syndrome following bilateral temporal and basal forebrain damage. *Archives of Neurology*, 42, 252–259.

CHAPTER 9: THE HEEDLESS SELF

1. Freud, S. (1911/1958). Formulations on the two principles of mental functioning. *Standard Edition of the Complete Psychological Works of Sigmund Freud*, Vol. 12, pp. 213–226.

2. Fenichel, O. (1945). *The Psychoanalytic Theory of Neurosis*. New York: Norton.

3. Shapiro, D. (1965). *Neurotic Styles*. New York: Basic Books.

4. Shapiro, 1965, p. 142.

5. Cleckley, H. (1976). *The Mask of Sanity* (5th ed.). St. Louis: Mosby.

6. Shapiro, 1965, p. 157.

7. Berman, A. & Siegal, A. M. (1976). Adaptive and learning skills in juvenile delinquents: A neuropsychological analysis. *Journal of Learning Disabilities*, 9, 583–590.

8. Spellacy, F. (1977). Neuropsychological differences between violent and nonviolent adolescents. *Journal of Clinical Psychology*, 33, 966–969.

9. Spellacy, F. (1978). Neuropsychological discrimination between violent and nonviolent men. *Journal of Clinical Psychology*, 34, 49–52.

10. Krynicki, V. E. (1978). Cerebral dysfunction in repetitively assaultive adolescents. *Journal of Nervous and Mental Disease*, 166, 59–67.

11. Lewis, D. O., Shanok, S. S., Balla, D. A. & Bond, B. (1980). Psychiatric correlates of severe reading disabilities in an incarcerated delinquent population. *Journal of the American Academy of Child Psychiatry*, 19, 611–622.

12. Yeudall, L. T., Fromm-Auch, D. & Davies, P. (1982). Neuropsychological impairment in persistent delinquency. *Journal of Nervous and Mental Disease*, *170*, 257–265.

13. Flor-Henry, P., Fromm-Auch, D., Tapper, M. & Shopflocher, M. (1981). A neuropsychological study of the stable syndrome of hysteria. *Biological Psychiatry*, *16*, 601–626.

14. Brickman, A. S., McManus, M., Grapentine, W. L. & Alessi, N. (1984). Neuropsychological assessment of seriously delinquent adolescents. *Journal of the American Academy of Child Psychiatry*, *23*, 453–457.

15. Bryant, E. T., Scott, M. L., Golden, C. J. & Tori, C. D. (1984). Neuropsychological deficits, learning disability and violent behavior. *Journal of Consulting and Clinical Psychology*, *52*, 323–324.

16. Gorenstein, E. E. (1982). Frontal lobe functions in psychopaths. *Journal of Abnormal Psychology*, *91*, 368–379.

17. Drewe, E. A. (1974). The effect of type and area of brain lesion on Wisconsin Card Sorting Test Performance. *Cortex*, *10*, 159–170.
    Heaton, R. K. (1981). *A Manual for the Wisconsin Card Sorting Test*. Odessa: Psychological Assessment Resources.
    Milner, B. (1963). Effects of different brain lesions on card sorting. *Archives of Neurology*, *9*, 90–100.

18. Hare, R. D. (1984). Performance of psychopaths on cognitive tasks related to frontal lobe function. *Journal of Abnormal Psychology*, *93*, 133–140.

19. Sutker, P. B. & Allain, A. N. (1987). Cognitive abstraction, shifting and control: Clinical sample comparisons of psychopaths and nonpsychopaths. *Journal of Abnormal Psychology*, *96*, 73–75.

20. Newman, J. P., Patterson, C. M. & Kosson, D. S. (1987). Response perseveration in psychopaths. *Journal of Abnormal Psychology*, *96*, 145–148.

21. Gullick, E. L., Sutker, P. B. & Adams, H. E. (1976). Delay of information in paired-associate learning among incarcerated groups of sociopaths and heroin addicts. *Psychological Reports*, *38*, 143–151.
    Painting, D. H. (1961). The performance of psychopathic individuals under conditions of positive and nega-

tive reinforcement. *Journal of Abnormal and Social Psychology*, 62, 352–355.

22. Siegal, R. A. (1978). Probability of punishment and suppression of behavior in psychopathic and nonpsychopathic offenders. *Journal of Abnormal Psychology*, 87, 512–514.

23. Luria, A. R. (1980). *Higher Cortical Functions in Man* (2nd ed.). New York: Basic Books.

24. Ackerly, S. S. (1964). A case of paranatal bilateral frontal lobe defect observed for 30 years. In J. M. Warren & K. Akert (Eds.), *The Frontal Granular Cortex and Behavior*. New York: McGraw-Hill.

25. Dimond, S. J. (1980). *Neuropsychology: A Textbook of Systems and Psychological Functions of the Human Brain*. London: Butterworth.

26. Nauta, W. J. (1971). The problem of the frontal lobe: A reinterpretation. *Journal of Psychiatric Research*, 8, 167–187.

27. Ackerly, 1964, p. 204.

28. Eaker, H. A., Allen, S. S. & Gray, J. (1983). A factor analytic study of personality and intellectual variables in incarcerated delinquent males and females. *Journal of Clinical Psychology*, 39, 614–616.

    Graham, E. E. & Kamano, D. (1958). Reading failure as a factor in the WAIS subtest patterns of youthful offenders. *Journal of Clinical Psychology*, 14, 302–305.

    Heilbrun, A. B. (1979). Psychopathy and violent crime. *Journal of Consulting and Clinical Psychology*, 47, 509–516.

    Heilbrun, A. B. (1982). Cognitive models of criminal violence based on intelligence and psychopathy levels. *Journal of Consulting and Clinical Psychology*, 50, 546–557.

    Holland, T. R., Beckett, G. E. & Levi, M. (1981). Intelligence, personality and criminal violence: A multivariate analysis. *Journal of Consulting and Clinical Psychology*, 49, 106–111.

    Hurwitz, I., Bibace, R. M. A., Wolff, P. H. & Rowbotham, B. M. (1972). Neuropsychological function of normal boys, delinquent boys and boys with learning problems. *Perceptual and Motor Skills*, 35, 387–394.

    Prentice, N. M. & Kelly, F. J. (1963). Intelligence and

delinquency: A reconsideration. *Journal of Social Psychology*, *60*, 327–337.

Robbins. D. M., Beck, J. C., Pries, R., Cage, D. J. & Smith, C. (1983). Learning disability and neuropsychological impairment in adjudicated, unincarcerated male delinquents. *Journal of the American Academy of Child Psychiatry*, *22*, 40–46.

Spreen, O. (1981). The relationship between learning disability, neurological impairment and delinquency: Results of a follow-up study. *Journal of Nervous and Mental Disease*, *169*, 791–799.

Wiens, A. N., Matarazzo, J. D. & Gaver, K. D. (1959). Performance and Verbal IQ in a group of sociopaths. *Journal of Clinical Psychology*, *15*, 191–193.

29. Geschwind, N. & Galaburda, A. M. (1985). Cerebral lateralization. Biological mechanisms, associations and pathology. A hypothesis and a program for research. *Archives of Neurology*, *42*, 428–459, 521–552, 634–654.

30. Miller, L. (1987). Neuropsychology of the aggressive psychopath: An integrative review. *Aggressive Behavior*, *13*, 119–140.

Miller, L. (1988). Neuropsychological perspectives on delinquency. *Behavioral Sciences and the Law*, *6*, 409–428.

CHAPTER 10: THE TRANSMUTED SELF

1. Abraham, K. (1908/1973). The psychological relations between sexuality and alcoholism. In J. E. London (Ed.), *Selected Papers on Psychoanalysis*. London: Hogarth.

2. Rado, S. (1933). The psychoanalysis of pharmacothymia. *Psychoanalytic Quarterly*, *2*, 1–23.

3. Glover, E. G. (1932). On the etiology of drug addiction. *International Journal of Psychoanalysis*, *13*, 298–328.

4. Fenichel, O. (1945). *The Psychoanalytic Theory of Neurosis*. New York: Norton.

5. Donovan, J. M. (1986). An etiological model of alcoholism. *American Journal of Psychiatry*, *143*, 1–11.

6. Khantzian, E. J. (1978). The ego, the self and opiate addiction: Theoretical and treatment considerations. *International Journal of Psychoanalysis*, *5*, 189–198.

Khantzian, E. J. (1980). The ego/self theory of substance dependence: A contemporary psychoanalytic perspective. In D. J. Lettieri, M. Sayers & H. W. Wallenstein (Eds.), *Theories of Addiction*. Rockville: National Institute on Drug Abuse.

Treece, C. & Khantzian, E. J. (1986). Psychodynamic factors in the development of drug dependence. *Psychiatric Clinics of North America*, *9*, 399–412.

7. Wurmser, L. (1974). Psychoanalytic considerations of the etiology of compulsive drug use. *Journal of the American Psychoanalytic Association*, *22*, 820–843.

Wurmser, L. (1978). *The Hidden Dimension: Psychodynamics in Compulsive Drug Use*. New York: Jason Aronson.

Wurmser, L. (1982). The question of specific psychopathology in compulsive drug use. *Annals of the New York Academy of Sciences*, *398*, 33–43.

8. Cleckley, H. (1976). *The Mask of Sanity* (5th ed.). St. Louis: Mosby.

9. Lewis, C. E., Rice, R. & Helzer, J. E. (1983). Diagnostic interactions: Alcoholism and antisocial personality. *Journal of Nervous and Mental Disease*, *71*, 105–113.

10. Stabenau, J. R. (1984). Implications of family history of alcoholism, antisocial personality and sex differences in alcohol dependence. *American Journal of Psychiatry*, *141*, 1178–1182.

11. Craig, R. J. (1982). Personality characteristics of heroin addicts: Review of empirical research 1976–1978. *International Journal of the Addictions*, *17*, 227–248.

12. Zuckerman, M. (1984). Sensation seeking: A comparative approach to a human trait. *Behavioral and Brain Sciences*, *7*, 413–471.

13. Kohn, P. (1979). Experience-seeking characteristics of methadone clients. *Journal of Consulting and Clinical Psychology*, *47*, 980–981.

Platt, J. & Scurra, W. (1974). Peer judgments of parole success in institutionalized heroin addicts: Personality correlates and validity. *Journal of Counseling Psychology*, *21*, 511–515.

Skolnick, N. & Zuckerman, M. (1979). Personality change in drug abusers: A comparison of therapeutic community and prison groups. *Journal of Consulting and Clinical Psychology*, *47*, 768–770.

14. Nurco, D. N., Ball, J. C., Shaffer, J. W. & Hanlon, T. E. (1985). The criminality of narcotic addicts. *Journal of Nervous and Mental Disease*, *173*, 94–102.

15. Tarter, R. E. (1982). Psychosocial history, minimal brain dysfunction and differential drinking patterns of male alcoholics. *Journal of Clinical Psychology*, *38*, 867–873.
      Tarter, R. E., McBride, H., Buonepane, N. & Schneider, D. U. (1977). Differentiation of alcoholics: Childhood history of minimal brain dysfunction, family history and drinking pattern. *Archives of General Psychiatry*, *34*, 761–768.

16. Alterman, A. I., Tarter, R. E., Baughman, T. G., Bober, B. A. & Fabian, S. A. (1985). Differentiation of alcoholics high and low in childhood hyperactivity. *Drug and Alcohol Dependence*, *15*, 111–121.

17. Eyre, S. I., Rounsaville, B. J. & Kleber, H. D. (1982). History of childhood hyperactivity in a clinic population of opiate addicts. *Journal of Nervous and Mental Disease*, *170*, 522–529.

18. Loney, J. (1980). The Iowa theory of substance abuse among hyperactive adolescents. In D. J. Lettieri, M. Sayers & H. W. Person (Eds.), *Theories of Drug Abuse*. Washington, D.C.: Department of Health and Human Services.

19. Jaffee, J. H. & Ciraulo, D. A. (1986). Alcoholism and depression. In R. E. Meyer (Ed.), *Psychopathology and Addictive Disorders*. New York: Guilford.

20. Cadoret, R., Troughton, E. & Widmer, R. (1984). Clinical differences between antisocial and primary alcoholics. *Comprehensive Psychiatry*, *25*, 1–8.

21. Rounsaville, B. J., Weissman, M. M., Crits-Christoph, K., Wilber, C. & Kleber, H. (1982). Diagnosis and symptoms of depression in opiate addicts. *Archives of General Psychiatry*, *39*, 151–156.

22. Rounsaville, B. J., Weissman, M. M., Kleber, H. & Wilber, C. (1982). Heterogeneity of psychiatric diagnosis in treated opiate addicts. *Archives of General Psychiatry*, *39*, 161–166.

23. Kosten, T. R. & Rounsaville, B. J. (1986). Psycho-

pathology in opiate addicts. *Psychiatric Clinics of North America*, *9*, 515–532.

24. Cloninger, C. R. (1987). Neurogenetic adaptive mechanisms in alcoholism. *Science*, *236*, 410–416.

25. Miller, L. (1985). Neuropsychological assessment of substance abusers: Review and recommendations. *Journal of Substance Abuse Treatment*, *2*, 5–17.

    Parsons, O. A. & Farr, S. P. (1981). The neuropsychology of alcohol and drug abuse. In S. B. Filskov & T. J. Boll (Eds.), *Handbook of Clinical Neuropsychology*. New York: Wiley.

26. Tarter, R. E., Edwards, K. L. & Van Thiel, D. H. (1988). Neuropsychological dysfunction due to liver disease. In R. E. Tarter, D. H. Van Thiel & K. L. Edwards (Eds.), *Medical Neuropsychology: The Impact of Disease on Behavior*. New York: Plenum.

27. Tarter, R. E. & Parsons, O. A. (1971). Conceptual shifting in chronic alcoholics. *Journal of Abnormal Psychology*, *77*, 71–75.

28. Tarter, R. E. (1973). An analysis of cognitive deficits in chronic alcoholics. *Journal of Nervous and Mental Disease*, *157*, 138–147.

29. Heilbrun, A. B., Tarbox, A. R. & Madison, J. K. (1979). Cognitive structure and behavioral regulation in alcoholics. *Journal of Studies on Alcohol*, *40*, 387–400.

30. Parsons & Farr, 1981.

31. Parsons, O. A. (1983). Cognitive dysfunction and recovery in alcoholics. *Substance and Alcohol Actions/Misuse*, *4*, 175–190.

32. Parsons, O. A. (1987). Do neuropsychological deficits predict alcoholics' treatment course and posttreatment recovery? In O. A. Parsons, N. Butters & P. E. Nathan (Eds.), *Neuropsychology of Alcoholism: Implications for Diagnosis and Treatment*. New York: Guilford.

33. Alterman, A. I., Tarter, R. E., Petrarulo, E. W. & Baughman, T. G. (1984). Evidence for impersistence in young male alcoholics. *Alcoholism: Clinical and Experimental Research*, *8*, 448–451.

34. Fields, S. & Fullerton, J. (1975). Influence of heroin addiction on neuropsychological functioning. *Journal of Consulting and Clinical Psychology*, *43*, 114.

35. Hill, S. Y., Reyes, R. B., Mikhael, M. & Ayre, F. (1979).
    A comparison of alcoholics and heroin abusers: Comput-
    erized transaxial tomography and neuropsychological func-
    tioning. *Currents in Alcoholism*, *5*, 187–205.

36. Rounsaville, B. J., Jones, C., Novelly, R. A. & Kleber,
    H. (1982). Neuropsychological functioning in opiate ad-
    dicts. *Journal of Nervous and Mental Disease*, *170*, 209–
    216.

37. Tarter, R. E., Alterman, A. I. & Edwards, K. L. (1985).
    Vulnerability to alcoholism in men: A behavior-genetic
    perspective. *Journal of Studies on Alcohol*, *46*, 329–356.

38. Luria, A. R. (1980). *Higher Cortical Functions in Man*
    (2nd ed.). New York: Basic Books.

39. Vygotsky, L. S. (1962). *Thought and Language*. Cam-
    bridge: MIT Press.

40. Schmidt, A. L. & Neville, H. J. (1984). Event-related
    brain potentials in sons of alcoholic fathers. *Alcoholism:
    Clinical and Experimental Research*, *8*, 117.

41. Tarter, R. E., Hegedus, A. M., Goldstein, G., Shelly, C.
    & Alterman, A. I. (1984). Adolescent sons of alcoholics:
    Neuropsychological and personality characteristics. *Alco-
    holism: Clinical and Experimental Research*, *8*, 216–222.

42. Gabrielli, W. F. & Mednick, S. A. (1983). Intellectual
    performance in children of alcoholics. *Journal of Nervous
    and Mental Disease*, *171*, 444–447.

43. Miller, L. (1986). "Narrow localizationism" in psychiat-
    ric neuropsychology. *Psychological Medicine*, *16*, 729–
    734.
      Sternberg, R. J. (1988). *The Triarchic Mind: A New
    Theory of Human Intelligence*. New York: Viking.

44. Werner, E. E. (1986). Resilient offspring of alcoholics: A
    longitudinal study from birth to age 18. *Journal of Studies
    on Alcohol*, *47*, 34–40.

45. Ludwig, A. M. (1985). Cognitive processes associated
    with "spontaneous" recovery from alcoholism. *Journal of
    Studies on Alcohol*, *46*, 53–58.

46. Parsons, O. A. (1987), pp. 273–290.

CHAPTER 11: BODY AND SELF

1. Dunbar, F. (1938). *Emotions and Bodily Changes*. New York: Columbia University Press.
2. Alexander, F. (1950). *Psychosomatic Medicine: Its Principles and Applications*. New York: Norton.
3. Reiser, M. F. (1975). Changing theoretical concepts in psychosomatic medicine. In M. F. Reiser (Ed.), *American Handbook of Psychiatry (2nd ed.). Vol. 4: Organic Disorders and Psychosomatic Medicine*. New York: Basic Books.

   Weiner, H. (1977). *Psychobiology and Human Disease*. New York: Elsevier.
4. Friedman, M. & Ulmer, D. (1984). *Treating Type A Behavior and Your Heart*. New York: Fawcett Crest. p. 33.
5. Booth-Kewley, S. & Friedman, H. S. (1987). Psychological predictors of heart disease: A quantitative review. *Psychological Bulletin, 101*, 343–362.

   Williams, R. B. (1984). An untrusting heart: Cynicism lies at the core of the type A personality. *The Sciences*, September/October, pp. 31–36.

   Wright, L. (1988). The type A behavior pattern and coronary artery disease: Quest for the active ingredients and the elusive mechanisms. *American Psychologist, 43*, 2–14.
6. Garamoni, G. L. & Schwartz, R. M. (1986). Type A behavior pattern and compulsive personality: Toward a psychodynamic-behavioral integration. *Clinical Psychology Review, 6*, 311–336.
7. Glass, D. C. (1977). *Behavior Patterns, Stress and Coronary Disease*. Hillsdale: Erlbaum.
8. Folsom, A. R., Hughes, J. R., Buehler, J. F., Mittelmark, M. B., Jacobs, D. R. & Grimm, R. H. (1985). Do type A men drink more frequently than type B men? Findings in the Multiple Risk Factor Intervention Trial (MRFIT). *Journal of Behavioral Medicine, 8*, 227–235.
9. Monagan, D. (1986). Sudden death. *Discover*, January, pp. 64–71.
10. Natelson, B. H. (1985). Neurocardiology: An interdisciplinary area for the '80's. *Archives of Neurology, 42*, 178–184.
11. Lane, R. D. & Schwartz, G. E. (1987). Induction of

lateralized sympathetic input to the heart by the CNS during emotional arousal: A possible neurophysiologic trigger of sudden cardiac death. *Psychosomatic Medicine*, *49*, 274–284.

12. Skinner, J. & Reed, J. (1981). Blockage of frontocortical-brainstem pathway prevents ventricular fibrillation of ischemic heart. *American Journal of Physiology*, *240 (Heart and Circulatory Physiology, 9)*, H156–H163.

13. Walker, B. & Sandman, C. (1979). Human visual evoked responses are related to heart rate. *Journal of Comparative and Physiological Psychology*, *93*, 717–729.

    Walker, B. & Sandman, C. (1982). Visual evoked potentials change as heart rate and carotid pressure change. *Psychophysiology*, *19*, 520–527.

14. Hugdahl, K., Franzon, M., Anderson, B. & Walldebo, G. (1983). Heart-rate responses (HRR) to lateralized visual stimuli. *Pavlovian Journal of Biological Science*, *18*, 186–198.

15. Strober, T. & Kunze, K. (1982). Electrocardiographic alterations in subarachnoid hemorrhage. *Journal of Neurology*, *227*, 99–113.

    Yamour, B., Sridharan, M., Rice, J. & Flower, N. (1980). Electrocardiographic changes in cerebrovascular hemorrhage. *American Heart Journal*, *99*, 294–300.

16. Gur, R. E. & Gur, R. C. (1975). Defense mechanisms, psychosomatic symptomatology and conjugate lateral eye movements. *Journal of Consulting and Clinical Psychology*, *43*, 416–420.

17. Apfel, R. J. & Sifneos, P. E. (1979). Alexithymia: Concept and measurement. *Psychotherapy and Psychosomatics*, *33*, 180–190.

    Sifneos, P. E. (1972). *Short-Term Psychotherapy and Emotional Crisis*. Cambridge: Harvard University Press.

    Sifneos, P. E. (1973). The prevalence of alexithymic characteristics in psychosomatic patients. *Psychotherapy and Psychosomatics*, *22*, 255–262.

18. Lesser, I. M. (1981). A review of the alexithymia concept. *Psychosomatic Medicine*, *43*, 531–543.

    Lesser, I. M. & Lesser, B. Z. (1983). Alexithymia: Examining the development of a psychological concept. *American Journal of Psychiatry*, *140*, 1305–1308.

Taylor, G. J. (1984). Alexithymia: Concept, measurement and implications for treatment. *American Journal of Psychiatry*, *141*, 725–732.

19. deM'Uzan, M. (1974). Psychodynamic mechanisms in psychosomatic symptom formation. *Psychotherapy and Psychosomatics*, *23*, 103–110.

Krystal, H. (1979). Alexithymia and psychotherapy. *American Journal of Psychotherapy*, *33*, 17–31.

Krystal, H. (1982). Alexithymia and the effectiveness of psychoanalytic treatment. *International Journal of Psychoanalytic Psychotherapy*, *9*, 353–378.

Marty, M. & deM'Uzan, M. (1963). *L'investigation Psychosomatique*. Paris: Presses Universitaires.

Nemiah, J.C. (1977). Alexithymia: Theoretical considerations. *Psychotherapy and Psychosomatics*, *28*, 199–206.

20. Hoppe, K. D. (1977). Split brain and psychoanalysis. *Psychoanalytic Quarterly*, *46*, 220–244.

21. Hoppe, K. D. & Bogen, J. E. (1977). Alexithymia in twelve commissurotomized patients. *Psychotherapy and Psychosomatics*, *28*, 148–155.

22. Buchanan, E. T., Waterhouse, G. J. & West, S. C. (1980). A proposed neurophysiological basis of alexithymia. *Psychotherapy and Psychosomatics*, *34*, 191–220.

23. Miller, L. (1986–87). Is alexithymia a disconnection syndrome? A neuropsychological perspective. *International Journal of Psychiatry in Medicine*, *16*, 199–209.

24. Keltikangas-Jarvinen, L. (1982). Alexithymia in violent offenders. *Journal of Personality Assessment*, *46*, 462–467.

CHAPTER 12: BETTER SELVES.

1. Briggs, J. (1988). *Fire in the Crucible: The Alchemy of Creative Genius*. New York: St. Martin's Press.

2. Kris, E. (1952). *Psychoanalytic Explorations in Art*. New York: International Universities Press.

3. Ellis, H. A. (1926). *A Study of British Genius*. Boston: Houghton Mifflin.

Freud, S. (1910/1957). Leonardo da Vinci and a memory of his childhood. *Standard Edition of the Complete Psychological Works of Sigmund Freud*, Vol. 11, pp. 59–138.

Kubie, L. S. (1958). *Neurotic Distortion of the Creative Process*. Lawrence: University of Kansas Press.

McNeil, T. F. (1971). Prebirth and postbirth influence on the relationship between creative ability and recorded mental illness. *Journal of Personality*, *39*, 391–406.

4. Forrest, D. V. (1988). NERDs, or Neuroevolutionary Rostral Developers: A contribution to the future of characterology. *Journal of the American Academy of Psychoanalysis*, *16*, 491–511.

5. Rossner, M. & Belkin, M. (1987). Intelligence, education and myopia in males. *Archives of Ophthalmology*, *105*, 1508–1511.

6. Cohn, S. J., Cohn, C. M. G. & Jensen, A. R. (1988). Myopia and intelligence: A pleiotropic relationship? *Human Genetics*, *80*, 53–58.

7. Anthony, E. J. (1987). Risk, vulnerability and resilience: An overview. In E. J. Anthony & B. J. Cohler (Eds.), *The Invulnerable Child*. New York: Guilford.

8. Andreasen, J. C. (1987). Creativity and mental illness: Prevalence rates in writers and their first degree offspring. *American Journal of Psychiatry*, *144*, 1288–1292.

9. Miller, L. (1988). Ego autonomy, creativity and cognitive style: A neuropsychodynamic approach. *Psychiatric Clinics of North America*, *11*, 383–397.

10. Flor-Henry, P. (1979). On certain aspects of the localization of cerebral systems regulating and determining emotion. *Biological Psychiatry*, *14*, 677–698; p. 682.

11. Heston, L. L. (1966). Psychiatric disorders in foster home-reared children of schizophrenic mothers. *British Journal of Psychiatry*, *112*, 819–825.

Karlsson, J. L. (1970). Genetic association of giftedness and creativity in schizophrenia. *Hereditas*, *66*, 177–182.

Walder, R. (1965). Schizophrenic and creative thinking. In H. M. Ruitenbeek (Ed.), *The Creative Imagination*. Chicago: Quadrangle.

12. Laing, R. D. (1968). *The Politics of Experience*. New York: Ballantine.

13. Rothenberg, A. (1979). *The Emerging Goddess: The Creative Process in Art, Science and Other Fields*. Chicago: University of Chicago Press.

14. Rothenberg, A. (1983). Psychopathology and creative

cognition: A comparison of hospitalized patients, Nobel laureates and controls. *Archives of General Psychiatry, 40,* 937–942.

15. Andreasen, J. C. & Powers, P. S. (1975). Creativity and psychosis: An examination of conceptual style. *Archives of General Psychiatry, 32,* 70–73.

16. Flor-Henry, P. (1985). Psychiatric aspects of cerebral lateralization. *Psychiatric Annals, 15,* 429–434.

   Goldberg, E. (1985). Akinesia, tardive dysmentia and frontal lobe disorder in schizophrenia. *Schizophrenia Bulletin, 11,* 255–263.

   Goldberg, T. E., Weinberger, D. R. & Berman, K. F. (1987). Further evidence for dementia of the prefrontal type in schizophrenia? *Archives of General Psychiatry, 44,* 1008–1014.

   Marin, R. S. & Tucker, G. J. (1981). Psychopathology and hemisphere dysfunction: A review. *Journal of Nervous and Mental Disease, 169,* 546–555.

   Miller, L. (1984). Hemispheric asymmetry of cognitive processes in schizophrenics. *Psychological Reports, 55,* 932–934.

   Miller, L. (1985). The subcortex, frontal lobes and psychosis. *Schizophrenia Bulletin, 12,* 340–341.

   Seidman, L. J. (1983). Schizophrenia and brain dysfunction: An integration of recent diagnostic findings. *Psychological Bulletin, 93,* 195–238.

17. Muller, H. F. (1985). Prefrontal cortex dysfunction as a common factor in psychosis. *Acta Psychiatrica Scandinavica, 71,* 431–440.

18. Muller, 1985, p. 437.

19. Drewe, E. A. (1974). The effect of type and area of brain lesion on Wisconsin Card Sorting Test performance. *Cortex, 10,* 159–170.

   Milner, B. (1963). Effects of different brain lesions on card sorting. *Archives of Neurology, 9,* 90–100.

   Stuss, D. T. & Benson, D. F. (1984). Neuropsychological studies of the frontal lobes. *Psychological Bulletin, 95,* 3–28.

20. Messer, S. B. (1976). Reflection-impulsivity: A review. *Psychological Bulletin, 83,* 1026–1052.

   Messer, S. B. & Schacht, T. E. (1986). A cognitive-dynamic theory of reflection-impulsivity. In J. Masling (Ed.), *Empirical Studies of Psychoanalytic Theory*. Hillsdale: Erlbaum.

21. Vygotsky, L. S. (1962). *Thought and Language*. Cambridge: MIT Press.

22. Hartmann, H. (1939/1958). *Ego Psychology and the Problem of Adaptation*. New York: International Universities Press.

23. Behrends, R. S. (1986). The integrated personality: Maximal utilization of information. *Journal of Humanistic Psychology, 26*, 27–59.

24. Seeman, J. (1959). Toward a concept of personality integration. *American Psychologist, 14*, 633–637.

25. Wexler, D. A. (1974). Self-actualization and cognitive processes. *Journal of Consulting and Clinical Psychology, 42*, 47–53.

26. Hunt, E. (1973). The memory we must have. In R. Shank & K. Colby (Eds.), *Computer Models of Thought and Language*. San Francisco: Freeman.

27. Zimring, F., Nauman, C. & Balcombe, J. (1970). Listening with the second ear: Selective attention and emotion. Paper presented at the annual meeting of the American Psychological Association, Miami, Florida.

28. Snyder, M. (1974). Self-monitoring of expressive behavior. *Journal of Personality and Social Psychology, 30*, 526–537.

29. McWilliams, N. (1984). The psychology of the altruist. *Psychoanalytic Psychology, 1*, 193–213.

30. McWilliams, 1984, pp. 208–209.

31. Felsman, J. K. & Vaillant, G. E. (1987). Resilient children as adults: A 40-year study. In E. J. Anthony & B. J. Cohler (Eds.), *The Invulnerable Child*. New York: Guilford.

32. Maslow, A. H. (1968). *Toward a Psychology of Being*. New York: Van Nostrand Reinhold.

INDEX

ABOUT THE AUTHOR

Laurence Miller, Ph.D., received his Doctorate in Psychology from the City University of New York. From 1982 to 1988, he was an Associate in Neuropsychology at Fair Oaks Hospital in Summit, New Jersey, and from 1988 to 1989 was Program Director of the Neurobehavioral Treatment Center at Fair Oaks Hospital in Delray Beach, Florida. Dr. Miller has also held a number of academic appointments and has lectured and written widely on topics relating to the brain, behavior, health, and society. His articles and columns have appeared in professional journals, as well as in such popular publications as *Omni* and *Psychology Today*, and he has been a guest on several radio programs. He is currently in private practice in Delray Beach, Florida.

Psychology Bestsellers from BALLANTINE

Before there was est, before there was assertiveness training, before anyone thought about whether or not they were OK, there was Dr. Eric Berne and the *Games People Play*.

16